CW00342294

The Book of
Staverton

An Ancient West Wiltshire Parish

Pete Lavis

HALSGROVE

First published in Great Britain in 2002

British Library Cataloguing-in-Publication Data
A CIP record for this title is available from the British Library

ISBN 1 84114 145 3

HALSGROVE

Halsgrove House
Lower Moor Way
Tiverton, Devon EX16 6SS
Tel: 01884 243242
Fax: 01884 243325
email: sales@halsgrove.com
website: http://www.halsgrove.com

Frontispiece photograph: *The Staverton Cloth Factory building which was purchased by Anglo-Swiss in 1897.*

Printed and bound in Great Britain by Bookcraft Ltd, Midsomer Norton.

CONTENTS

ACKNOWLEDGEMENTS

The author gratefully acknowledges the contributions made by many Staverton villagers, past and present, without whose help and interest this publication would not have been possible. Particular thanks to the following people and organisations who loaned photographs and other material, most of which has been used in the book:

John Arnold
Chris Cradock
Grace Holland
Betty Ludlow
Julia Meeres
Parker family
Peter Smith
Ambrose Stickney

Jo Beaven
Eileen and Eddie Gamble
Myra Smith
Vera Malyn
Nestlé UK Ltd
Trevor Porter
Jim Smith
Margaret Tucker

Laurie Bird
Roger Hammond
Malcolm Jacobs
Dot Marshman
Betty Osborne
Les Rackley
Staverton Club
Ann Wilmot

Janet Blake
Barry Hayward
Ray Lovell
Marian Matthews
Mick Osborne
Syd Ricketts
Staverton School
David Yates

Also, thanks to Stevie Broadwood for long hours on the computer keyboard inputting text for the book. Stephen Hobbs and staff at the Wiltshire County Records Office for their help, advice and assistance. My wife, Diane, and family for their support and encouragement. My daughter-in-law, Ursula, for technical support, help and guidance with the computer work. The villagers of Staverton for their help in verifying facts and information and contributing material, and the many people outside the parish who helped in a variety of ways and expressed their interest and good wishes in the compilation of this publication.

Feeding the swans from 'Bird's Wharf' on the Kennet and Avon Canal at Staverton.

INTRODUCTION

For such a tiny rural parish, the smallest in West Wiltshire, Staverton has a long and fascinating history starting from a time when prehistoric peoples left their pots and flint tools on village land later to be taken over and farmed by the Romans. The first established settlement in Staverton came around the ninth century when an Anglo-Saxon family exploited the rich pastures, woodland and river waters that surrounded their small enclosed farmstead. The water-power potential of the deep, fast-flowing River Avon was soon recognised and was later harnessed to drive village corn-mills and cloth factories right up to the late-nineteenth century, and its abundant stock of fish and eels was an important food source for many centuries.

Farming took up a major part of villagers' lives in the earlier centuries and the large open arable fields within the parish provided the food to sustain the villagers and the inhabitants of the manors of Trowbridge and Wyke. The village church and its priests dominated village life for centuries and Staverton's tiny stone religious building was the focal point of the community with the Church Vestry dictating the daily lives of parishioners until losing its historic power and influence in the Victorian era.

Staverton became heavily involved in the cloth industry from the fourteenth century and this later became the main source of employment for villagers until its decline at the end of the nineteenth century. The Industrial Revolution brought dramatic change and new opportunities for Staverton people from the late-eighteenth century, but also created many social and economic problems as the cloth-mills and farms became mechanised increasing unemployment, hardship and often despair for some village families. Those who took advantage of the technological advances that came with the Industrial Revolution were able to improve their social standing and some Staverton families made their fortunes from the new trade the canal and railway brought to the parish in the first half of the nineteenth century.

Formal education did not reach the village until the mid 1800s when the first parish school was founded, but from its basic beginnings the village school became an important community establishment turning generations of Staverton children into educated, responsible citizens many of whom later used the knowledge and skills they had been taught to take leading roles in community life looking after the interests of the parish and protecting its pleasant environment and idyllic rural way of life.

Nestlé also played an important part in Staverton's history, providing a secure and stable local industry for over 100 years, giving employment to generations of village families, supporting village institutions and organisations and making a valuable contribution to the local economy. The social life of villagers came to the fore in the early-twentieth century when the first recreation facility was provided and, over time, Staverton's sports teams earned a formidable reputation as keen competitors in the local leagues which they supported and often won.

Staverton, a tiny cluster of cottages and farms, a church, alehouse and mill, for over 900 years experienced very little outward growth until the late-twentieth century when the village began to expand southward as new housing appeared in the parish. This growth accelerated towards the end of the century and by the start of the new millennium Staverton and its population had doubled in size. Further planned expansion of the village over the next few decades will bring more new houses and roads, a considerable increase in population, and new community facilities and social amenities to support the influx of new residents. Staverton's unique style and culture, built up over 1,000 years, will inevitably disappear as the village grows and faces the many challenges and tremendous changes the technological age will bring in the twenty-first century.

This book is about village people, their social and domestic lives, their local crafts and industries, the trials and tribulations many suffered, the happier times they enjoyed, and the important part they played in shaping the village over the centuries, building up, caring for and supporting its institutions, and creating a community that is fiercely proud of its heritage and past achievements. I hope you enjoy reading *The Book of Staverton*; it has been a joy to write, and I thank the many villagers, past and present, who have contributed to this important local history work. A full list of acknowledgements will be found on the facing page.

Pete Lavis, 2002

Left: *The visible remains of medieval ridge-and-furrow ploughing in the field next to the Nestlé factory, 1985.*

Right: *Outline map of Wiltshire showing the belt of Oxford clay that runs through Staverton and forms the River Avon valley.*

Below: *The field called Blacklands where prehistoric, Iron-Age and Roman remains were unearthed in 2002.*

CHAPTER ONE

THE FOUNDATION OF THE VILLAGE & ITS FIRST INHABITANTS

The tiny village of Staverton in Wiltshire stands on a belt of Oxford clay that forms the River Avon valley. This expanse of blue-grey clay, which marks the edges of the river's flood plain, ends where the Avon leaves Staverton. The river cuts through a limestone belt as it meanders past Bradford-on-Avon westward to Avonmouth where it eventually empties into the Bristol Channel.

More than 150 million years ago Staverton was covered by the sea. Evidence of this came to light in 1966 when a large fossilized ammonite, a coiled prehistoric sea snail from the Mesozoic period, was unearthed during deep excavations to construct a new effluent-disposal plant at the Nestlé factory site in the village. As the sea receded and land settled, the River Avon found its course over the Oxford clay laying deposits of alluvium and river gravel across the wide bed. The river, much broader and faster-flowing in those days, transported millions of fragments of oolite sandstone, cornbrash and kellaways rock in its rushing waters and these can be found in the components of the river gravel. Animal fossils are often found in the gravel beds and occasionally the teeth of prehistoric mammals, such as the woolly rhinoceros, which must have died near the river banks when the gravel deposits were being laid down 40,000 years ago. The gravel beds, sometimes three-quarters of a mile from the present river course, lie about two metres below the surface and can be up to four metres thick in places. Along the length of the Avon in fields adjoining the river, past gravel workings have left a number of shallow pits and ponds. Gravel taken from these workings was

Victor Strugnell, age 15, holds the 150-million-year-old fossil ammonite unearthed at the Nestlé factory in 1966.

used in local building works in the eighteenth and nineteenth centuries and some of it almost certainly in constructions at the village mill, now Nestlé, and in other Staverton buildings and roads.

The River Avon valley was originally completely covered in trees, mainly oaks, and the section through Staverton formed part of the ancient Selwood Forest. Although it is difficult to say when Staverton first became inhabited it is possible that prehistoric nomadic people who ventured into Wiltshire used a shallow stretch of the river, somewhere near the present-day road bridge, as a crossing point. As ancient man gradually evolved from primitive hunter-gatherers to the first farmers, suitable places to settle down, build shelters and farm the land would have been desired. Staverton would have been an ideal spot with its plentiful supply of fresh running water, abundance of fish in the swiftly-flowing river, and a glut of game and wild animals in the surrounding woodlands.

Evidence that has recently come to light indicates that prehistoric, Iron-Age and Bronze-Age peoples were active within the village area although no traces of settlements from these periods have been unearthed within the parish boundaries. During archaeological excavations in January 2002, in a field known as Blacklands, evidence of prehistoric, Iron-Age, Roman and medieval activity was uncovered. A trench which was dug close to the B3105 revealed ditches, a post hole, prehistoric flint implements and fragments of Roman and medieval pottery. The two flint tools were particularly significant; a narrow tool shaped like a small knife, and a thumbnail scraper, both finds indicating that there had been prehistoric activity on the site. The outline of the ditches and the post hole were thought to have some agricultural connection and could have been parts of ancient field boundaries and fences. No evidence of ancient structures was found in the trench.

A second trench, near the centre of the field, revealed a two-metre-square layer of stones about a metre below the surface. The archaeological team were certain that it dated from the Roman period. Their conclusions were supported by the discovery of Roman pottery fragments and several large pieces of Roman roof tile. The flat layer of stones, lying within a wide ditch, contained parts of a stone gully running from north to south which could have been some sort of water conduit or drainage channel. Again, the excavators could not confirm any evidence of habitation and suggested the stone structure could have been the remains of a Roman corn dryer. The discovery of pieces of Roman roof tiles does, however, point to the possibility of a dwelling on or near the site although no firm evidence of one has yet been found to support this. Together with the finds of a variety of animal bones, the archaeologists came up with the theory that the artifacts could be the remnants of a Roman rubbish dump which was added to in the medieval period. What is significant is that these finds prove that there had been prehistoric, Roman and medieval activity in Staverton and that the lands around the village have been farmed and occupied for far longer than was originally thought. The excavated area sits on top of a low ridge which slopes down to the Avon on the north side and Small Brook to the south and would have been an ideal site for prehistoric and Roman settlers, particularly as it is the highest land point in Staverton with natural drainage to the south. Further archaeological excavations would be neccessary to establish whether there are buried foundations under Blacklands. At the time of writing the land has been designated for housing development and roads; construction work on these could reveal more ancient finds.

It is likely that the first permanent settlement in Staverton was established after Roman rule had effectively ended in Britain in the fifth century. The void left by their departure to Rome was quickly filled by an influx of Angles, Saxons and Jutes from present-day northern Europe. The Saxons soon became the dominant peoples and established themselves across the South West moving into what became Wessex. The Saxons often forced the native Romano-British to flee their villages and seek refuge in the hills or remote parts of Wales and Cornwall. By chasing away the British the aggressive Saxons were able to take over and occupy the small lowland farming communities, many of which had been deserted by their former inhabitants.

Remains of a Roman corn dryer unearthed on Blacklands in 2002.

There was a great demand for fresh areas of farmland from the rapidly increasing numbers of Saxon invaders and during this period the uninhabited and untouched areas of land around Staverton were taken over by Saxon families for settlement. To create the farmland needed to support an extended family the dense areas of woodland that covered Staverton were gradually cleared, and the plots of land obtained by felling the trees became the first 'fells' or fields. Staverton then became a permanent settlement; the Saxon family that commenced the land clearance would have constructed the first village farmstead, a wooden shack and outbuildings, near the banks of the river. The river was very important to this first settlement providing fresh water, plenty of fish and water power which would later be put to good use.

Despite the rapid settlement of Wessex by the Saxons in the sixth and seventh centuries they were still considered invaders by the isolated British tribes and many skirmishes took place between the new tenants and the native peoples. These first Saxon farmsteads were under constant threat of attack and strong wooden fences or palisades would have been erected to protect properties and animals, not only from marauding British tribes but also from the many wild beasts that inhabited the forests around the settlements. Staverton's first settlement was such a fortress and in the Domesday Book the village name appears as Stavretone, a word comprising the Old English word stavre meaning stave, post or stake, and ton or tone simply meaning a farm. Thus the name would indicate a farm with posts or a farm enclosed by a wooden fence of staves.

The early Saxon lords of Wessex were determined to hold on to their newly acquired territories and were quick to respond to attacks by native tribes and sometimes even their own hostile Saxon neighbours. Many local battles were fought between the Saxons and the British. In AD652, Cenwalh, King of the West Saxons, defeated a marauding British army in a skirmish just outside Bradford-on-Avon. Over the next two centuries the Saxons consolidated their hold on Wessex and their growing numbers began to spread out and enlarge their farms and landholdings. The next threat to the Saxons came from around AD865 onwards, with the Viking invasions. At one stage most of Wessex came under the control of the Norsemen when, after a series of defeats, King Alfred was forced to retreat to the marshes of Somerset where he reorganised his badly mauled forces. Whether the Saxon community at Staverton became embroiled in these conflicts is not known but it is likely that they would have been influenced to some extent by the fairly close battles, such as one at Edington in AD876 when Alfred, having raised a new army, routed the Danes and drove them back to Chippenham.

After the defeat of the Vikings, Wessex returned to uneasy peace and the Saxons continued to expand their landholdings. Fresh areas of woodland were cleared to create more farmland and the growing population began to turn the farmsteads into small hamlets. The Anglo-Saxon settlement at Staverton is indicated in the Steeple Ashton Charter of AD964 and the Bradford-on-Avon Charter of AD1001 in which the boundaries of the village along the Auene (Avon) and the Byssi (Biss) are clearly defined. Staverton, by this time, would have been closely allied to the larger Saxon settlement at Treubrig (Trowbridge) and would remain under its manorial influence until fairly recent times.

The steady growth of Staverton and Trowbridge during the seventh, eighth and ninth centuries necessitated the provision of a mill to grind the communities' corn. The deep, fast-flowing River Avon at Staverton was the ideal place to locate it. Staverton's first corn-mill was probably constructed in the ninth century on a natural bend in the river, roughly on the same site that now houses the Nestlé factory, and just upstream from a shallow ford that carried the track from the village across the meadows and on towards Bradford-on-Avon. This first corn-mill would have been a crude wooden structure with a thatched roof and just big enough to house the millstones and basic drive mechanism operated by a wooden water-wheel. The water-wheel would have been turned by a steady flow of water in a channel that ran off the river, past the mill, and back into the Avon further downstream near the ford. This was the first mill-stream and the flow of water down it was controlled by a dam of logs and a simple arrangement of wooden sluice gates. Later, stone weirs were constructed across the river making the control of water levels in the mill-stream much more effective.

By the tenth century the Anglo-Saxons had introduced a sophisticated administration and legal system, based on the manor, to govern the lands that they now occupied in Britain. The shires that had already been created were broken down into subdivisions called hundreds, each one having its own court to settle local disputes and obligations, like service to the lord of the manor and providing troops for the King's army. Staverton, at this time, was grouped with Trowbridge, Melksham, Hilperton, Chalfield, Trowle and Whaddon to form the Melksham hundred and came under the direct control of the manor in Trowbridge. Records show that a Saxon thegn called Brictric was 'holding' the lands at Staverton in 1042 as well as estates in Trowbridge, Trowle, Monkton Farleigh, Coulston and other areas of Wiltshire. When he died, his son, also named Brictric, inherited these estates and was 'holding' them at the time of the Norman Conquest in 1066. Staverton had grown into a small Anglo-Saxon hamlet with a few cottages, a corn-mill on the river, and a small area of farmland under cultivation.

William the Conqueror's invasion in 1066, and the defeat of Harold and his Saxon army at the Battle of Hastings, brought England under Norman rule. The Normans soon consolidated their hold over the country and, during the next few decades, William systematically transferred the ownership of the Saxon estates to the nobles and knights who had faithfully supported him during the Conquest. Many of the defeated Saxon chiefs were removed from their landholdings and replaced by the Norman nobility who took up residence in the former Saxon manors or hastily built motte-and-bailey castles, from where they took over the management of their newly acquired estates. To the people of Staverton this transition would have been gradual and relatively trouble free as they continued unhindered in their relentless toil of eeking a living from the land. By the mid 1080s William embarked on the massive task of recording all the land and properties he now ruled over in England and commissioned his officials to compile the famous Domesday Book which was started in 1086. Every hamlet, village and town in England would come under scrutiny and every detail of land area, property and population would be recorded and assessed for taxation purposes. Staverton was visited by William's Norman clerks in 1086 who noted every detail of the village and entered them in the Wiltshire section of

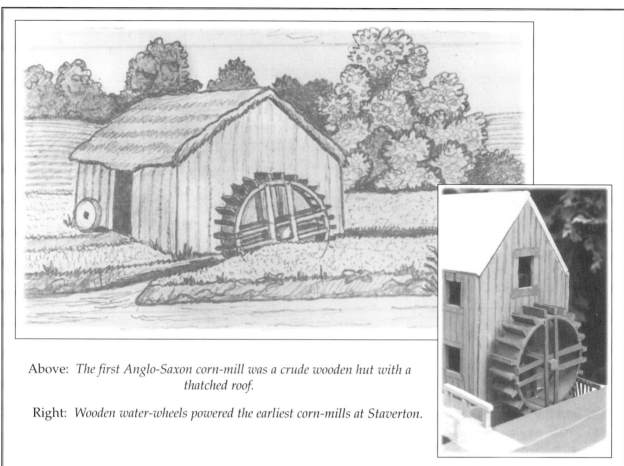

Above: *The first Anglo-Saxon corn-mill was a crude wooden hut with a thatched roof.*

Right: *Wooden water-wheels powered the earliest corn-mills at Staverton.*

An impression of how Staverton's first Anglo-Saxon farmstead might have looked in the ninth century.

the Domesday Book. This description of the village is the first detailed account we have of Staverton and gives a good insight into what the settlement was like in the eleventh century. The entry for Stavretone in the Domesday Book reads as follows:

Brictric holds STAVRETONE. His father held it before 1066. It paid tax for 5 hides. It has land for 3 ploughs. In Lordship there are 2 ploughs and 7 Serfs. There are 3 villagers and 2 cottagers with 1 plough. It has a mill that pays 20s., 20 acres of meadow, and 20 acres of pasture. The village is valued at 70s.

From this description we can work out that Staverton covered about 650 acres in the eleventh century, a slightly larger area than the present-day parish which was reduced in size towards the end of the nineteenth century. The village population comprised five families who lived in a cluster of wooden shacks on the high ground above the River Avon and close to the corn-mill. These villagers had a single plough with which to till the soil on their strips of arable land in the large open fields and this would have been shared by common agreement. The demesne lands in Staverton, farmed by the manor, enjoyed the use of two ploughs, and the seven serfs recorded as living in Staverton would be engaged solely in farming the lord's land. Most of the land around the village was arable and the crops and corn grown thereon would have fed the residents of the village and the inhabitants of the manor in Trowbridge. The 20 acres of meadowland and 20 acres of pasture, used for grazing animals and for providing winter fodder, were located near the River Biss and in Ladydown. The meadows on the north side of the Avon, in front of the Nestlé factory, did not belong to Staverton but formed part of the manor of Bradford-on-Avon. The parish boundaries in the eleventh century followed the south bank of the Avon to the River Biss, across to Ladydown and Islington, took in most of the Down and Hilperton Marsh and met again with the Avon roughly halfway between Staverton and Whaddon. The main feature of the village was the corn-mill which was sited on the south bank of the river near where the present-day Nestlé factory stands. It was the most valuable asset of the village in 1086 and was estimated to be worth 70 shillings for tax purposes.

A large stone weir on the River Avon controlled the flow of water down the mill-stream.

Just downstream from the mill was a ford which carried the rough track from the village across the meadows to Forewoods Common and Bradford Leigh. Evidence of the track passing through the river was discovered some years ago when the boatyard slipway was being dug out. Below the mud of the river bed were found large flat slabs of stone which must have formed part of the original paved ford, further evidence of which is indicated in a later spelling of the village's name, Staffordton, recorded in 1671. The present straight causeway across the meadows did not exist in the eleventh century but records indicate that there was a Saxon military road that ran from the Melksham road on the east side of Holt and down to the river crossing at Staverton. It continued to follow the river bank along the meadows before sweeping uphill through Bradford Woods to Forewoods Common and then onwards into Bradford-on-Avon. This military way would have been used to move the Saxon King's army rapidly from place to place to combat any threat from Wessex's enemies.

Farming was the villagers' only means of subsistence during the eleventh century and each inhabitant played his part in the cultivation of land. Anglo-Saxon agriculture was based on the open-field system and Staverton's two large common fields were divided into strips, each villager having an allotted number to plough and cultivate depending on his social status. These common fields were completely open areas of land with no dividing fences, hedges or walls, and were split into a north and south field by a track which ran from the river ford and along the headland towards Hilperton Marsh. The south field was bisected by a rough track, now School Lane, which branched off the main track and ran across the open field to enter Trowbridge somewhere near the Conigre.

At the time of Domesday, Staverton was surrounded on three sides by woods, this woodland lay just outside the boundaries of the parish and thus is not mentioned in the survey. The existence of woods can be established by studying nearby place names. Bradford Woods, more than twice their present size in 1086, enclosed the village on its north-west boundary and spanned an area from just outside Trowbridge to past Holt. Forewoods Common is derived from 'a clearing before the woods' whereas Bradford Leigh, further away, was 'a clearing in the

11

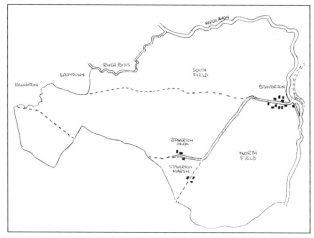

Top: *The paved ford was located just downstream from the present river bridge.*

Above: *Staverton Parish in the thirteenth century. Two large open fields lay to the north and south of a track that ran towards Staverton Wick and Hilperton.*

Below: *A map showing the Saxon military road that ran past the Staverton ford, along the river bank, and through Bradford Woods to Forewoods Common. Taken from the 1845 Bradford Tithe Map.*

woods'. Holt in the Anglo-Saxon language simply meant 'a wood' and evidence that this area was covered by trees can be found in the 1001 Bradford-on-Avon Charter which mentions a leapgate located close to the present-day Holt road. Leapgates were placed at the edges of woods low enough to allow the free access of deer but high enough to stop cattle and other domestic animals from straying into the forested areas. To the south of Staverton was an open marsh behind which was the Down, also covered in trees right up until fairly recent times. All woods and forests in those days were owned by the king and were subject to strict forest laws which protected the deer and game as they roamed freely through the vast tracts of woodland that surrounded the village. Many other leapgates were placed between the edges of these woods and the commons and their importance is indicated by frequent mention in local charters and land deeds.

Staverton's dwellings in the eleventh century were timber-framed huts, built with mud or wattle walls and thatched with straw or reeds. These one-roomed shacks, with earthen floors, were both family living accommodation and stabling for the cattle, pigs, goats and sheep. Chickens roosted in the rafters and an opening in the thatched roof acted as a chimney to remove the smoke from fire which was kindled for cooking and for warmth. Each dwelling had its own little garden plot and the vegetables grown in it normally ended up in the daily broth which constituted the family's main meal. This meagre diet was occasionally supplemented with home-made cheese, the odd piece of meat, oatcakes, wholemeal bread and milk. The milk came from the goats and ewes, the oxen being used mainly as beasts of burden to pull the carts and haul the heavy wooden ploughs in the fields. Meals were sometimes

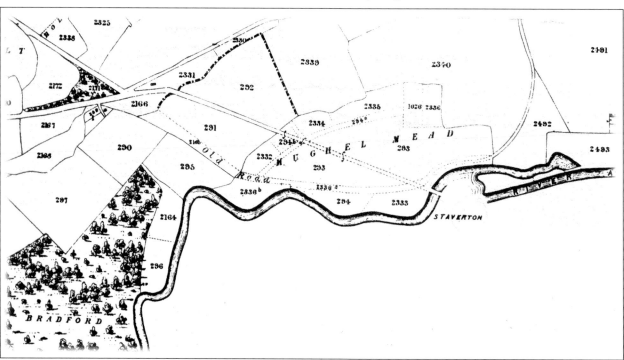

enhanced with fresh fish and eels from the river and honey, extracted from the beehives kept on every plot, was used to sweeten the food. Home-made ale, cider and mead were the main beverages and helped to swill down the very bland food during the meal. Coarse wool from the village flock was hand spun and woven into clothing and home-grown flax was fashioned into rough linen. Footwear was made from animal hides and leather attached to curved and shaped pieces of wood which were used to form the soles and heels. Rushlights, dipped in animal fat, provided a feeble, smoky light to illuminate the shacks in the evening and, combined with the thick fog of lingering smoke from the open fire, made the interior an unpleasant and unhealthy environment in which to live and sleep. Wax candles were used by the lord and his household in the manor house but, at the time, these were far too expensive for the ordinary villager to purchase and use. Most villages around the time of Domesday had their own priest although it is not certain that Staverton had a church in the eleventh century as none is recorded in the Domesday survey.

The arable land in the common fields was tilled with heavy wooden ploughs pulled by oxen. Teams varied from two to eight animals depending on the type of soil to be turned, and villagers held shares in a communal plough and ox team. The other two ploughs mentioned in the Domesday survey were owned by the lord of the manor and were used to till the demesne lands scattered amongst Staverton's open fields. Made entirely of wood, the Saxon plough was basically a long beam supporting a coultar, which cut the soil vertically, a share which cut horizontally, and a mouldboard which turned the soil over. The ploughing method used at the time of Domesday was called ridge and furrow, the object being to drain the soil and demarcate the ownership

of strips. Ox teams pulled the plough which was guided by the ploughman helped by a boy, usually his son, whose job was to lead and coax the animals. During ploughing the soil was thrown to the right, the team working clockwise around a strip to maintain the ridge. Difficulties were sometimes experienced in turning a long team at the end of a strip and to manoeuvre the plough around a narrow headland meant making a wide sweep forming a reverse 'S' typical of ridge-and-furrow fields. Evidence of Staverton's ridge-and-furrow ploughing can still be detected in some of the fields around the village and a good example remained right up until recent times on the land adjacent to the Nestlé factory. This was subsequently levelled and converted into the factory's main car park in 1987.

Staverton's corn-grinding mill, an important local industry in the eleventh century, was owned by the lord of the manor who insisted that all his tenants had their corn ground there, but later this monopoly was given up when the mill was leased to the millers although they were not allowed to charge for the service but could keep a portion of the grain, roughly a fifteenth, as payment. Millers invariably fiddled this quota and were often hauled before the Manor Courts where they were fined for their dishonesty. Many cases of this nature are recorded in local Manor Court proceedings and most villages began to look upon their millers as rogues and cheats. Staverton mill, at the time of Domesday, also traded as an eel fishery and would have paid some of its taxes in eels to the lord of the manor. Large quantities of eels were trapped in the wooden grills that protected the water-wheels from damage by floating debris and, in addition, special wicker basket eel traps were used in the mill-stream and log dams. Old records indicate that as much as 2 cwts of eels a day were being taken from Staverton's eel fishery. The mill appears to have provided a prolific and constant supply of these much favoured fish and records of the eel fishery at Staverton span many centuries after the Domesday survey.

Above: *Illustration of a medieval wooden plough and ox team from the fourteenth-century Luttrell Psalter.*

Right: *A drawing of how Staverton village may have looked in the eleventh century.*

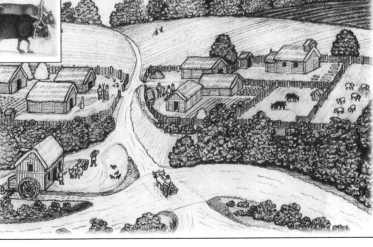

Above and right: *Staverton's first wooden bridge was replaced by a narrow stone packhorse bridge in the fourteenth century.*

Below: *The north side of the river bridge with its fourteenth-century arches and later raised parapet.*

CHAPTER TWO

THE LORDS OF THE MANOR

In 1086 the villagers of Staverton were paying their rents and dues to Brictric, the Saxon thegn of the manor. In 1095 he was removed and the lands were given to Edward D'eureux of Salisbury who was High Sheriff of Wiltshire. Edward's daughter Maud married Humphry de Bohun in 1110 and, as a wedding gift, her father gave her the Trowbridge estates, which included Staverton, and the handing down of these landholdings became known as 'the Honour of Trowbridge'. In 1125 Maud awarded the tithes of Staverton to Monkton Farleigh Priory, the Cluniac monastery of Mary Magdalene, which she had helped found some years earlier. Around the same time Humphry began converting the manor into Trowbridge Castle and his son, also named Humphry, married the daughter of Miles, Earl of Hereford and Constable of England. Their grandson, Henry, who later inherited the lands at Staverton, was created Earl of Hereford in 1200 and was one of the nobles who sided with the barons in their dispute with King John who immediately accused him of disloyalty. In revenge John subjected Henry to enquiry in the King's Court in 1212 when the authenticity of his title and the ownership of the lands he held at Trowbridge and Staverton were called into question.

King John held courts at Trowbridge in 1212 and 1215 at which time Henry was threatened with a writ against illegal ownership after William Longspee, the King's half-bother, laid claim to the estates that Henry held. William Longspee, the third Earl of Salisbury and later Sheriff of Wiltshire, had married the great-granddaughter of Edward of Salisbury's son Walter who, years previously, had been disinherited from his father's landholdings at Trowbridge and Staverton. King John supported his half-brother's claim to the estates and handed the disputed manor of Trowbridge with Staverton to William and his wife Ela, Countess of Salisbury, after the court case of 1215. Their holding of the lands, however, was very short-lived for when King John was forced to make peace with the barons, by signing the Magna Carta at Runnymead in 1215, he was obliged to restore the 'Honour of Trowbridge' to Henry de Bohun. Henry died in 1220 and two years later the Longspees resumed their court proceedings for ownership of the disputed estates which by 1229 had been allotted legally to Ela, Countess of Salisbury, who had held the lands briefly 14 years earlier. Throughout the remainder of the thirteenth century the manor and lands of Trowbridge and Staverton passed down through the Longspee Earls of Salisbury.

Throughout these ownership disputes Staverton remained a small farming community under the Trowbridge estates with the village mill grinding the corn and the fishery providing eels for local consumption. In 1236 Ela granted various lands and tithes to the Abbey of Lacock and included in one of the charters was the gift of the Staverton mill land to 'the Miller of Stavretona and his wife for life' indicating that the lot of the villagers was slowly improving and some of them had upgraded their social status to freemen. One of these freemen from Staverton was appointed to attend the Hundred Courts, usually held once a month at a designated spot in the area, and he helped administer the law and make decisions on the urgent affairs of the hundred. Towards

Above: *Eel traps being placed in the mill-stream of Staverton's twelfth-century corn-mill.*

Top left: *Effigy of William Longspee, lord of the manor in the thirteenth century, from his tomb in Salisbury Cathedral.*

the end of the thirteenth century the Staverton miller was selected to be one of the 12 jurors at the trial of the Abbas of Shaftesbury who had been charged in the King's Court with usurping the Crown's rights over certain matters pertaining to the manor of Bradford-on-Avon. Johannes de Staverton (John of Staverton) sat through the trial, held at Wilton, which ended with the prosecution being unable to prove the case and the proceedings were adjourned *sine die*. Records from 1295 show that John of Staverton was farming a mill in the village and paying 40 shillings for two messuages (dwellings and outbuildings) and some land. The eel fishing rights were being leased for nine shillings and there was a garden, the herbage from which yielded one pound and four shillings annually. John of Staverton is recorded again in 1303 as the miller of Staverton and the same garden mentioned eight years previously was now earning an additional three shillings and nine pence per annum for the fruits being grown there.

By the close of the thirteenth century the first stone houses began to appear in Staverton and were gradually replacing the crude wooden shacks that had been the villagers' dwellings almost from the settlement's foundations many centuries earlier. Wood, the normal building material used in the construction of the villagers' houses, was in short supply due to the ongoing clearance of the woodlands around Staverton, and the plentiful supply of local stone, some from nearby quarries, was an obvious substitute for the rapidly declining timber stock. This rough-hewn local stone was used to build rubble walls, rarely with any binding mortar, and straw, reeds and turf were still used for the thatching on the roofs. In later centuries stone tiles began to replace the thatch and towards the end of the nineteenth century, due mostly to the advent of the canals and railways, slate and clay tiles were being used for roofing. The new stone houses, however, did not initially improve much from the previous wooden shacks, remaining small, one-roomed dwellings

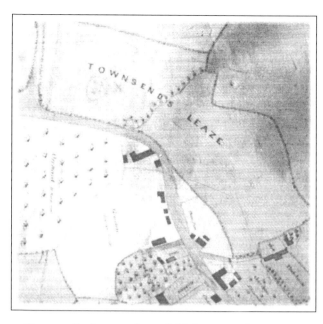

Townsend's Leaze, a large field that runs from School Lane to the Old Bear, is named after a fourteenth-century village farmer.

although some later added outside huts for storage or to house some of the families' domestic animals. The more wealthy villagers were able to build larger dwellings in stone, some having two or three distinct rooms for living accommodation, storage and animals. A cross-passage connecting front and rear doors separated the animals from the living area for the first time making living conditions a little more comfortable. Fires for cooking and heating were still in open hearths with the smoke and fumes escaping through the thatched roof or doorways making the interior very smoky and sooty. Unfortunately, these open fires, if not kept under strict control, could easily ignite the dry, highly flammable roofing material quickly burning the dwelling down which, according to old manorial records, happened quite frequently.

The village population was slowly growing and, to ensure that the ancient laws and customs of the estate were being maintained, the lord of the manor appointed a village tithingham, or Constable, in 1303. His main task was to ensure that the village tithes were paid and that the lord's lands and properties were protected. An inventory of the estate, made in 1311, showed that the population had doubled since Domesday and about a quarter of the manor's tenants were living in Staverton. The old Anglo-Saxon villein or freeman, sometimes referred to locally as a yardlander, farmed about 30 or 40 acres in the common fields, as he slowly improved his standing towards yeoman farmer and, of 40 tenants recorded in 1311, ten had achieved this status. One of these was 'William ate Townsend' who farmed land in the village in 1333 and whose legacy still lives on in the form of a field name, Townsend's Leaze, which is the large field that runs down from the railway

The first stone houses began to appear in Staverton in the late-thirteenth century.

embankment to the rear of the Old Bear. Staverton's tenants, now about ten families, farmed the two large common fields around the village and shared the meadowland and pasture on the banks of the River Biss. Each villager's ration of arable land, which was cultivated for crops such as corn, wheat, barley, oats, peas and beans, lay in long strips scattered through the common fields and use of this land was rigidly controlled.

By the fourteenth century Staverton had evolved into three separate small hamlets, the main settlement by the River Avon, a few dwellings at Staverton Marsh (near the present-day Marsh Road) and a tiny hamlet on land cleared later at Staverton Wick (now Wyke), the three communities being valued at 58 shillings in 1334. At the beginning of the fourteenth century the last in line of the Longspee Earls of Salisbury, a daughter Margarette, married Henry de Lacy, the Earl of Lincoln, and when he died in 1311 the lands at Staverton passed to Thomas Plantagenet, Earl of Lancaster, through his marriage to Alice de Lacy. Thomas died in 1321 and Staverton came into the possession of John de Warrenne, the Earl of Surrey, who 11 years later had his estates at Trowbridge and Staverton separated from the Melksham hundred to create a 'peculiar', the new arrangement being known as 'the Liberty of Trowbridge'. Being a peculiar meant that the churches in the Liberty were exempt from the jurisdiction of the Diocese and Bishops of Salisbury and this situation remained right through to the early-eighteenth century when the Diocese's authority was restored. The manor passed to John of Gaunt in 1347 after the death of the Earl of Surrey. John of Gaunt, the fourth son of King Edward III, was married to Blanche, the daughter of Henry Plantagenet, and already held other vast estates throughout England. His son, Henry, was later to become King of England after usurping the Crown on the death of Richard II.

By the mid-fourteenth century the living standards of Staverton villagers had marginally improved, they were slightly better off financially and many were able to improve on their new stone houses by adding to them or completely rebuilding them in a sturdier construction. This better standard of living was further enhanced, ironically, by the results of the Great Plague which broke out in 1348 and rapidly swept through the country killing 40 per cent of the population. It had reached Wiltshire by late 1348 and many deaths were recorded locally including some of the villagers of Staverton. Nearby Whaddon, quite a large community in the fourteenth century, was particularly badly affected with the majority of its residents being wiped out. Many of the dwellings were left empty and abandoned, the results of the plague being so severe that the village never regained its former status and became the tiny hamlet that exists today. Remains of these plague houses can sometimes be detected beneath the fields

around Whaddon and have often been exposed in recent times by modern ploughing methods. In some communities the numbers who died from the plague were so great that bodies were buried in mass graves away from the confines of the village and these fields where the mass burials took place were, for centuries, identified by the locals with such names as Badlands or Blackgrounds.

The devastation of the Great Plague and the sudden dramatic decline in the population changed the whole social structure of the country and worked to the advantage of the poorer classes. One major impact resulting from the deaths of many tenant farmers was the creation of vacant land and those who were lucky enough to survive the epidemic were able to take it over and increase their landholdings. The loss of labour to farm the demesne lands also forced the lord of the manor to lease out his previously unattainable farmlands and villagers were able to add further to their landholdings, many improving their social standing as a result. This acquisition of vacant land, however, was not always done legally and cases of villagers pinching adjoining strips of land was highlighted in a manorial record of 1358 when the Staverton tithingman reported that 'the Lord's park at Staverton had been broken and that a bound (edge of the demesne land) had been unlawfully ploughed up.'

The Staverton tithingman and the village miller are mentioned again in 1359 and the village eel fishery, the trade of which had been badly curtailed by the devastations of the Great Plague, was operating again in 1372 when it was leased for three shillings and four pence. The crippling effects of the Great Plague gradually eased through the latter years of the fourteenth century and the country began to move slowly into an era of new prosperity. By the end of the century the English cloth trade had expanded considerably and the fulling of cloth, up to this point carried out manually in the cottages, had become mechanised with the introduction of fulling stocks. The operation was thus transferred to the village corn-mills.

Fulling was the process by which the cloth was beaten in a trough of water to close up its weave and shrink the material into a kind of felt. Fuller's earth was added as a detergent to scour out the oil in the wool and prior to mechanisation this operation was carried out by skilled fullers who stamped barefoot on the cloth whilst soaking it in tubs of water. The invention of the fulling stocks eliminated this long and laborious manual task and took this essential part of the cloth finishing process out of the cottages and into the mills. Fulling stocks were pairs of heavy wooden hammers driven by the mill's water-wheel which, when rotating, raised and lowered them in sequence, by a simple method of cams on a wooden wheel, this action pounding the cloth at a consistent rate and for long periods of time. The introduction of

Above and inset: *Fulling stocks were large wooden hammers that pounded the cloth to close up the weave.*

Below: *The millstones in early mills were driven by a primitive peg-and-lantern-type gear.*

this mechanical method made the fulling much more effective and this resulted in a better overall quality of the finished cloth. Many of the village millers seized on this new potential for increasing their business and converted their corn-mills into fulling mills. Whaddon was recorded as having a fulling mill as early as 1303 and Staverton's corn-mill had been converted to full cloths by the end of the fourteenth century. The mill was enlarged and corn grinding and fulling was carried out side by side in the same

building on the banks of the Avon. The boom in the cloth trade also had an effect on the landowners and encouraged the manors to build up their flocks of sheep to the point where much of the land on the estates and commons was turned over to sheep grazing, often to the detriment of the smaller tenant farmers who subsequently lost the use of some of their valuable arable land.

One positive effect from the dramatic increase in the flocks of sheep now taking up much of the land around Staverton was the additional employment it created for local families. There was a need for more shepherds to tend the flocks, extra shearers were employed to remove the fleeces, and others found work washing, cleaning and carding the raw wool. Local spinners and weavers were kept busy by the increased demand for local broadcloth and this generated more work for the fulling-mill and those engaged on the dyeing and finishing of the cloth.

Staverton's first river bridge, built around the thirteenth century and constructed from wood, was sited by the ford and just downstream from the village mill. It was a very simple affair and just wide enough to allow the passage of an ox and cart. Its flimsy structure would have made it very vulnerable to the seasonal floods in the River Avon valley and, when these came, the bridge must often have been damaged or even swept away by the torrents of rushing water. As trade and travel slowly expanded a more reliable river bridge became essential and by the mid-fourteenth century Staverton's wooden

Left: *The south side of Staverton's river bridge with its nineteenth-century arches.*

structure was replaced by a stone bridge. This first stone bridge, like its predecessors, was fairly crude and located just upstream from the ford which remained in use when the water levels in the river permitted. Designed at the time to cater only for pedestrians, ox carts and packhorses, the bridge was very narrow, half the width of the present road bridge, and was built with no parapets on the edges of its carriageway. These were only added to the widened modern bridge in fairly recent times. Parapets on early stone bridges were deliberately avoided or built at a very low level so that they did not impede the wide loads being carried by pack-horses in the large wicker panniers strapped to their sides. A study of the north side of the present bridge reveals its fourteenth-century origins with its pointed arches and cutaways typical of bridge architecture during that period. The ribbing on the underside of the arches also confirms its era as this type of feature was common bridge-building practice in the thirteenth and fourteenth centuries. Close examination of the stonework on the north side of the bridge clearly indicates the original height of the parapets and the later extension that was added in the early-nineteenth century to raise the parapets to their present height. The distinct difference in the architectural style on the south side of the bridge, with its newer stonework and flattened arches, confirms that the bridge was enlarged to its present width in the early 1800s. For many centuries Staverton's river bridge has been the entrance to the village from the north and its difficult configuration, with its tight 90-degree bend in front of the factory, is a result of many changes in the siting and re-siting of mills and mill-streams in the past when horse-drawn traffic was the only consideration in the alteration of local roads.

John of Gaunt's son, Henry, became King Henry IV in 1399 and the estates at Staverton and Trowbridge became a royal manor as part of the Duchy of Lancaster. Being a royal manor it enjoyed greater privileges than ordinary manors with its judicial and ecclesiastical courts becoming more important, a situation that continued until the early-eighteenth century, when the ecclesiastical jurisdiction was finally returned to the Diocese of Salisbury. So Staverton, still a tiny village, began the fifteenth century under the control of the royal manor of Trowbridge and much had changed in its way of life over the last 100 years. Tenants' cottages, now more substantially built of stone, began to be divided into several separate rooms with closed fireplaces and chimneys. Villagers had been able to increase their landholdings and the servitude and restrictions of the previous centuries was gradually disappearing with the manorial interests of the demesne lands changing more towards the direct payment of rents.

In order for the village mill to carry out the fulling of cloths, improvements were made to the waterworks which included the construction of the first stone weir on the river. This became essential to control water levels and supply sufficient flows to power the increased workload of the mill. Staverton's eel fishery was still in use during the fifteenth century, apart from several short periods when the lease was not taken up, and together with the busy fulling-mill and corn-mill provided a considerable local industry for such a small village. The fishery was leased by William Besil, Robert Ashley and John Horton in 1414 and the mill came into the ownership of William Fisher in 1420. Between 1433 and 1438 it was recorded that 'the Fishery did not yield its accustomed rent because William Fisher's heir, his son, had not prosecuted his claim to it.' This lull in the operation of the fishery was only temporary and records confirm that it was being used again in 1451 and 1461 when the rent being paid on it was three shillings and four pence.

Weavers' cottages began to appear around the mill in the fourteenth century.

Right: *Cloth was first made in Staverton on a simple wooden loom.*

Below: *Staverton Wick (Wyke) had become a separate manor by the sixteenth century.*

CHAPTER THREE

WEAVERS & BROADCLOTH

Towards the end of the fifteenth century cloth was being produced in the village cottages for export to the Low Countries and Italy. It was a thick, undyed broadcloth which was fulled in the mill, hung out to dry on racks, and then packed up for transportation. Many of Staverton's villagers had become cottage weavers, labouring away on their hand looms producing lengths of English broadcloth that were handled by dealers in London who enjoyed a brisk trade with customers in Europe. The plentiful work encouraged a steady increase in the village population and, as the sixteenth century dawned, new cottages began to appear in Staverton. Tenant farmers were taking out leases on new land around the village that had become available due to further clearance of the local woodland. The large common fields around Staverton were still an important part of the agricultural framework although some of the land was starting to be enclosed, particularly by the yeoman farmers and the manor who wanted to better secure their landholdings.

Staverton remained under royal patronage in the sixteenth century and a property described as 'a parcel of the demesne land and pasture at Staverton, in the Lordship of Trowbridge', was, in 1504 leased for 40 years, by the Crown, to Thomas Lovell and William Erle. This was land at Wyke which had become a separate manor in its own right and which was leased again in 1535 by the Duchy to Richard Billett and Richard Erle for 60 years. The lease of this demesne land at Wyke Manor specified 'the site of a Manor House standing in half an acre' as well as various named pastures, crofts, closes and meadows, a rabbit warren, 16 acres in Staverton field and a common meadow called Thestfield.' Rabbit warrens, introduced by the Normans after the Conquest, were specially created mounds of earth built close to the manor house which provided a valuable source of meat for the lord and his household.

In 1536 Henry VIII granted the Royal Manor of Trowbridge and Staverton to his brother-in-law Edward Seymour, the Viscount Beauchamp, who later became Earl of Hertford and Duke of Somerset. He was, of course, the brother of Henry's third wife, Jane Seymour, and was later caught up in the royal

intrigues after Henry's death and was beheaded in 1552. Over the next seven years the estates at Staverton and Trowbridge reverted to the Crown until Edward's son, another Edward, was eventually restored to the Hertford title in 1559. The manor and estates remained with the Earls of Hertford until 1621 when they passed down to Edward's son, Francis, who later became Baron Seymour of Trowbridge. The Staverton tithes were leased to Christopher Dysmers in 1538, to Robert Woods of London 11 years later, and Thomas Ellis, a Trowbridge schoolmaster noted as one of the jurors in the murder case of Trowbridge clothier Edward Langford, was recorded as joint lessee of the demesne lands at Staverton in 1553. Staverton Wyke Manor was passed to Edward Baynton, chamberlain to Queen Jane Seymour, and a leasing agreement for the Wyke lands in 1552 describe them as being rented for various rates on different types of agricultural land. Pasture was being let at 3s.4d. an acre, meadow land at 6s.8d. an acre and arable land at 8d. an acre. The estate contained a common marsh, Staverton Marsh, located near the present-day marina development, where 'the men of Staverton and Wick intercommoned'. Staverton's stone bridge is described in 1540 by John Leland, the King's Antiquary, who must have crossed it during his travels through the area in the mid-sixteenth century. The bridge needed urgent repairs in 1562, some of the cost being met by the generosity of another Trowbridge clothier, Thomas Long, who had left the sum of £6.13s.4d. in his will, specifically for this purpose. Village houses continued to improve through the sixteenth and seventeenth centuries particularly those of the wealthier residents who had attained the social status equivalent to yeoman farmer. Their improved prosperity allowed them to build larger stone farmhouses, later adding extensions as the numbers of their servants increased. In these more substantial houses, upper floors and built-in fireplaces were constructed and glass gradually appeared in windows previously sealed by wooden shutters. Internal staircases replaced wooden ladders and better furniture such as wooden chests, cupboards and dressers began to replace the crude wooden shelves and boards that

Tentering racks for drying the cloth in a rack field near the Staverton mill in the late-nineteenth century.

had previously stored the household's meagre supply of crockery, cutlery and pots and pans.

Throughout the sixteenth century the Staverton eel fishery was still very much a going concern and, in 1552, was in the hands of Christopher Dauntsey. Staverton remained heavily involved in the local cloth trade, and the village fulling-mill, fulling cloths for the home and export markets, was purchased by a Calais wool merchant, Christopher Aleyn, in 1556. The authority of the manor was beginning to decline by the sixteenth century and Church Vestries gradually replaced the centuries-old role of the Manor Courts. Vestries, an elected body of Church officials, took over the responsibilities of looking after all parish matters and these included appointing annually the chapel wardens, waywardens and the village tithingman, the latter being mentioned in 1572 as serving the parish of Staverton. They also took on the responsibility of looking after the poor and, after the Poor Law Act of 1572, appointed a village overseer of the poor to administer the new legislation. The Great Poor Law Act of 1601 went further and resulted in the chapel warden and two 'substantial' villagers administering the funds they were obliged to raise from local taxes to pay for poor relief.

The village mill was leased to Walter Steyvans of Holt for 21 years in 1574 and he subsequently rented it out to John Grant of Bradford-on-Avon. Details of the agreement state that there was 'a house, a grist mill, two mill hams with racks on them, and other lands.' It appears from this account that during this time the mill was still grinding corn, had a pair of fulling hammers, and tentering racks to dry the cloth. John Grant set about finishing his cloths in the Staverton mill and must have been quite expert at it because on one occasion he was paid £10 for 'a particularly fine specimen of cloth' by a merchant venturer named William Shepperd. Robert, John Grant's son, also followed his father into the cloth trade and when he married Bridget Hulbert, daughter of a Slaughterford clothier, his father agreed to secure certain copyhold lands to him and build him a house as a wedding present. He also agreed to full and dress all Robert's cloths in his Staverton mill but, due to a family dispute involving Robert's stepmother, he failed to secure the lands or build the house as promised. Robert eventually had to build his own house 'fit for his habitation and trade of clothing' but the cost of doing this as well as supporting a wife and four children left him penniless and unable to continue his business. The situation became so desperate that Robert was forced to take his father to court to seek compensation 'for breach of promise'.

A list of Staverton taxpayers from 1576 included the names of other members of the Grant family, George Graunte and William Graunte, who together with Lewes Smythe, Phylype Waytye and Anthony Pyckerynge were the principal village families in the late-sixteenth century and all probably engaged in the cloth-making trade. The English cloth-making business at the time was strictly controlled by guilds who ensured that all cloth workers, especially the weavers, completed an apprenticeship before taking up the trade. Some village cloth workers, however, practised their trade illegally and in 1612 a Daniel Chevers of Staverton was fined for working as an unqualified weaver because he had not served his time as an apprentice. The manor of Staverton Wyke came into the hands of Sir Henry Vinor in 1591 and the following year he leased the demesne lands of the manor to William Tipper and Robert Dawe. Sir Henry, a descendant of Henry Vinour, the Sheriff of Wiltshire in 1488, married Mary, daughter of Robert Long of Whaddon, and they are recorded as living in the manor house in 1616 which by now had been built into a fine stone mansion with elaborate carved oak panels internally and intricate stonework externally, a section of which displayed the Vinor coat of arms. The manor burnt down in 1625 and, although rebuilt in the Jacobean style, the strain of the disaster was too much for Sir Henry who died the following year leaving the house and estate to his son Richard, the last remaining Vinor heir. During the Civil War Richard sided with the King and was one of the Staverton ratepayers who was forced to support the Parliamentary garrison at Chalfield in 1645 by handing over eight oxen, valued at £10 in cash; the entry being recorded in the garrison accounts as 'sequestration money from a delinquent'. When Richard died 'without issue' in 1647 the manor and estate descended to Susanna Lewis and Mary Bythesea as part of the manor of Chapmanslade and Godwell.

The seventeenth century dawned with much uncertainty in the woollen industry, the problems being compounded by James I's insistence that the dyeing and finishing of the English broadcloth should be carried out at home instead of in the Low Countries and Germany. To ensure that his royal prerogative was enforced he suspended the merchant venturers in 1614, causing a great deal of hostility within the trade and from the dealers abroad. The merchant venturers were the backbone of the cloth exporting trade and, without them being able to operate effectively, the industry virtually halted. This politically motivated situation had a devastating effect on the local cloth industry, hit the weavers and fullers severely, and by 1616 half the looms in the area were idle. The King was forced to reinstate the merchant venturers in 1617 but, by that time, the damage had been done and the English broadcloth trade would never fully recover. Further problems worsened an already bad situation when the Thirty Years War broke out in Europe in 1618. The crisis became so acute that many clothiers had abandoned their trade by the 1620s. The effect of this serious decline in the cloth trade on the local population was added to by corn shortages and a series of bad harvests forcing many villagers to seek poor relief. The situation deteriorated in the late 1620s when the price of wheat almost doubled. As well as contending with local food riots, the loss of land and woodland due to enclosures meant that many poor village families were evicted from their homes.

Interior of a weaver's cottage showing the large wooden hand loom.

However, things did slowly begin to improve over the next few decades as the cloth industry gradually recovered, aided by the introduction of the medley, a lighter cloth made from dyed Spanish wool. This was firmly established in England by the 1640s. The new cloth, made from wool which had to be dyed and mixed before spinning, had virtually taken over the traditional broadcloth industry by the time the English Civil War broke out in the mid-seventeenth century. Local cloth makers, concerned about the threat to their businesses, began introducing coloured broadcloth to try and compete with the new medleys and by the end of the 1600s the long-established white broadcloth trade was nearly extinct. Staverton's mill was affected by the depression in the cloth trade in the early years of the century but slowly responded to the changes and played its part in helping the local cloth industry back to a new prosperity. The demand for the new cloth began to bring more business to the fulling-mill and provided badly needed work for the village cottage weavers. Weaving families began to move into the area and new cottages started springing up on small plots of common land, a technically illegal practice as it infringed the historic common rights. These new cottagers were unable to get legal rights to freehold. Many weavers' cottages began encroaching on the edges of the large common fields around Staverton and the problem became so serious by 1660 that five of these new Staverton cottagers were

brought before the Manor Court in Trowbridge and charged with not obtaining freehold for their hastily erected homes. They were ordered by the Court to pull their illegal cottages down but no records exist to confirm that these orders were ever enforced. It seems unlikely that they were as subsequent cases mentioned the same cottages over and over again.

The Civil War, fought between Crown and Parliament, dragged the whole country into conflict in the mid-seventeenth century and Staverton, like most other small communities throughout England, although not the site of any major Civil War battles, was affected by the presence of various occupying forces and later, in 1645, found itself on the fringes of some local skirmishes. Wiltshire, with its agricultural wealth and abundance of cloth-making communities, was of great importance to both sides in the Civil War and its geographical location made it a vital route for the competing armies as they chased each other across the width and breadth of the English countryside. At the start of the war most people in West Wiltshire generally supported the Parliamentary cause but after the Battle of Roundway Hill, just outside Devizes, were forced to submit to Royalist control. However, elements of the Parliamentary forces garrisoned Calne, Chippenham and Malmesbury during mid 1644 and nearby Chalfield Manor was also garrisoned for Parliament in August 1644 by Colonel Devereux with his 200 soldiers and their 100 horses. Surrounding towns and villages, including Staverton, came under his control and were forced to support this occupying force by means of a weekly tax levied on each community under Chalfield's area of jurisdiction. Most of these villages, already severely impoverished by the economic decline in the early half of the century, found it extremely difficult to meet the demands of the Chalfield garrison and defaulters were ruthlessly pursued by bands of occupying soldiers and made to hand over goods, animals and personal possessions if they were unable to pay their share of the taxes. Many villagers were on poor relief due to the loss of local employment. An insight into the seriousness of the poverty at the time is indicated by accounts of one of these enforced tax collections, carried out in late 1644, when only £56 in cash could be raised, the balance of the levy demanded being made up from seized goods. The villages around Chalfield were also forced to provide rations to support the garrison and accounts from the period list a whole range of produce donated by these communities who experienced great difficulties in providing enough to feed their own families.

23

In the two years that Chalfield was occupied large quantities of beef, mutton, bacon, beans, malt, beer, fish, wheat, bread, butter, spices, turkey, chickens, eggs and cheese were requisitioned by the Parliamentary soldiers to feed the garrison troops. Hay and oats also had to be provided for the unit's 100 horses. In 1645 William Tarrant, the collector for Chalfield garrison, recorded in his accounts that Staverton taxpayers were forced to provide sheep, cattle, malt and several large amounts of money. Besides the eight oxen taken from Richard Vinor of Wyke Manor, Mrs Yerbury had to supply a flock of sheep, valued at £18, and villagers were forced to contribute 16 bushels of malt worth 2s.6d. a bushel. The accounts record that Mrs Yerbury, labelled a delinquent because of her loyalties to the Crown, also had to hand over £8 in cash, and overall Staverton contributed £86 in goods and money to the Chalfield garrison in 1645 alone. Some villagers, unable to pay the demanded levies in cash or produce, were forced to provide free labour to the garrison repairing and strengthening the defences and collecting in the harvest. Troops from both sides passed through the area regularly and often stayed in local villages overnight demanding free quarters, and stabling for their horses, in many cases the poor cottager and his family being turned out of their beds for the night. When soldiers were billeted in the villages the residents were often subjected to their rowdy behaviour along with pilfering, intimidation and violence, looting, damage to their properties and the occasional case of rape. Villagers' animals, clothing and personal possessions were often stolen by the less disciplined troops and vital crops in their fields were damaged or sometimes completely ruined.

As the war progressed into early 1645 Royalist forces occupying areas to the south of Trowbridge began attacking the Parliamentary garrisons at Calne, Chippenham and Malmesbury and, by February, had gradually overrun them. Despite this, Sir Hardress Waller's Roundhead brigade managed to occupy Trowbridge in March and he began making plans to attack the Royalist garrison at Devizes. Hearing of the threat, the Royalist commander at Devizes, Sir James Long, decided to withdraw his cavalry to the safety of Bath and began retreating through Melksham and on to Bradford-on-Avon and the Somerset border. The Trowbridge Roundhead brigade, alerted of Long's movements by scouts, hurriedly deployed northward cutting off the retreating Royalist cavalry between Melksham and Bradford-on-Avon. A battle ensued near Holt with Waller's troops scattering the surprised Royalists and chasing them through the lanes and tracks towards the south-east of Trowbridge taking 300 prisoners and capturing Sir James Long, the cavalry's commander. Staverton, close to this action, became caught up in some of these skirmishes and bewildered villagers may well have witnessed the fleeing Cavaliers at full gallop racing through the village hotly pursued by Roundhead forces.

Several weeks later the Parliamentary garrison at Chalfield was briefly besieged by Goring's Royalists but managed to hold out. The manor remained in Parliamentary hands until relinquished at the end of the war in September 1646. The only remaining events of the Civil War to affect Staverton came on 17 September 1645 when Cromwell encamped with 500 troops in Trowbridge whilst making plans to attack the Royalist garrison at Devizes. It was subsequently captured by his Parliamentary forces a week later.

Following the death of the last Vinor heir the Minshull inheritance was split and in 1667 the tithes of Staverton Wyke were passed to Mary, wife of Thomas Bythesea. Details of the Wyke estate at that time describe 'a 50 acre common field at Hilperton Marsh which was shared by the tenants of Staverton and Hilperton', and part of the Down had become enclosed leaving only 25 acres of common. The tithes were being paid to the rector of Trowbridge in 1671, amounting to £1.13s.4d. with Staverton fulling-mill paying 9s. annually. These tithes were said to be paid 'by ancient composition and custom, the greater tithes of the demesne lands not being paid to the Rector but the lesser tithes being commuted for a rent charge.' By the same custom 'the herbage of the churchyard of Ye Chappell of Staffordton' belonged to the rector who was also allotted 14 acres of the Down land 'to the west of the track to Staffordton' for 'the grazing of 18 oxen and a bull'.

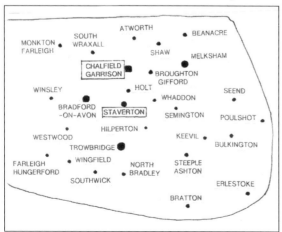

Above: Map of the skirmish in 1645 when Waller's forces captured Long's Royalists. Oliver Cromwell (left) and a 1645 leaflet proclaiming Waller's local victory.

Left: The area including Staverton that came under the jurisdiction of the Chalfield Parliamentary garrison in 1644.

CHAPTER FOUR

THE GROWTH OF THE CLOTH INDUSTRY IN THE EIGHTEENTH CENTURY

By the end of the seventeenth century Staverton was beginning to grow and weavers' cottages had sprung up near the fulling-mill although the village area had not yet expanded further than the present-day Square. Land enclosure was taking up large amounts of the common land around the village and the fulling-mill was becoming a major source of employment for the local cottage weavers. At this point the village comprised about 30 properties and the population had increased to over 100 inhabitants, more than half of them involved in the cloth trade and the rest in the cultivation of the farmland around Staverton. Farming methods had improved considerably since the days of the wooden plough and strips in common fields, and many new crops were being introduced such as clover, ryegrass, samfoin, cabbages, kale, rape and turnips. Marl and lime was used as fertilizer. The increase in the amount of enclosures had a detrimental effect on small farmers while allowing the bigger landowners to increase their acreages.

Throughout the eighteenth century most Staverton families relied on the cloth industry and the land for their livelihoods. The cottage weaver, and his whole family, would work year round employed in the cloth-making process. The wives and children spent their time washing and carding raw wool and spinning the yarn which was then used by the weaver to produce lengths of cloth on a hand loom usually located on the upper floor of the cottage. Many village cottages had been converted for weaving, their large upper-storey windows giving a good degree of natural light essential to the intricate weaving process. Some of these weavers' cottages can still be seen around the village although most have now been demolished or altered beyond recognition. Six or eight spinners were needed to keep a busy loom supplied with yarn and every member of the family would be engaged in the work, particularly during peak times when locally-made cloth was in great demand. Some village families would complete the whole cloth-making process by dyeing and fulling the material inside the cottage or in an outhouse or workshop attached to it. Others left the finishing work to the village fulling-mill, the whole operation being organised and controlled by local clothiers who, during the boom years of the West-of-England cloth industry, had become some of the wealthier men in the district.

For three or four weeks of the year village families helped to gather in the harvest; the more skilled job of cutting and scything the grass and cereal crops was carried out by specialist reapers brought in by the farmer, with the binding, lifting, carrying and stacking performed by the villagers. Whole families were also employed in the gleaning and picking of root crops such as potatoes, turnips, swedes, beans, peas and cabbages. The vegetables left over in the field were eagerly collected up by the younger children and taken back to the cottage to supplement the families' food stocks. Any remaining time in the busy year of the villager was spent cultivating the small garden plot and fattening up the odd animal, a

The rank of weavers' cottages known locally as 'Coalash' that used to stand opposite the Bear.

By the end of the eighteenth century, Staverton's mill (right) had grown to a considerable size and carding machines (below) had been introduced.

Right: *A spinning-wheel.*

Below: *Spinning-jennies began to appear in the Staverton area, c.1775.*

sheep or pig, which was usually slaughtered around Christmas time and not only provided the festive meal but kept the family in meat throughout the winter months.

With the increase in trade and travel throughout the eighteenth century the river was used extensively to transport goods and, although it was difficult for boats to negotiate upstream on the River Avon due to the many weirs supplying the mills, cargo and passengers from Staverton were regularly ferried downstream towards Bath and Bristol. Travel over land in the early-eighteenth century was very difficult, the tracks and lanes being in a very poor state, thus most transport of heavy goods was performed by pack-horses. Each packhorse was fitted with wicker panniers which could carry up to $2^1/_2$ cwt and whole trains of laden beasts, sometimes up to 50 in a long line, would carry locally-produced goods and cloth across country from town to town. Cattle, sheep and pigs which were to be sold for meat were driven 'on the hoof' to market by drovers who used well-trodden tracks and lanes. Many of these old drovers' routes can still be identified in the countryside around the area such as the sunken tracks and green lanes around Whaddon, Steeple Ashton and Bradford-on-Avon. During the eighteenth century it was rare for villagers to leave the small community of Staverton but, on the occasions when they did visit a neighbouring village or town for fairs and market days, they would use the intricate network of footpaths that connected the different settlements. A number of these long-established footways still survive around Staverton but the use of many rapidly declined following the improvement of main pedestrian routes and local roads during the nineteenth and twentieth centuries. Wealthy landowners, farmers and mill owners could afford to keep horses and would ride from place to place using the system of bridleways that connected towns and villages; those bridleways that survive at the time of writing are still legally protected, today being used solely for leisure pursuits.

Most of the villagers' domestic requirements could be catered for by the wide range of local or cottage industries and anything that could not be obtained locally was usually purchased during the weekly visit to the fairs and markets in Trowbridge and Bradford-on-Avon. Pedlars, tinkers and pack-men were regular visitors to the village trading a whole range of merchandise from pots and pans to material, ribbons and pins. Many of these travelling salesmen were viewed with suspicion by villagers because of the suspect source and quality of their

Henry Purnell kept a pig and chickens on his garden plot behind the Coalash cottages, a common practice amongst villagers in the eighteenth and nineteenth centuries.

wares and the reputation they had acquired over the years for stealing, trespassing and sleeping rough. Rumours, most unfounded, were rife that tinkers and the like were child stealers and villagers were quick to round up their younger offspring and keep them locked indoors when these sorts of characters were known to be in the area. On numerous occasions tinkers and pedlars were attacked and driven out of Staverton by irate residents and the Parish Constable who feared their presence in the village.

In 1716 the Wyke tithes were converted to John Lewis by the Bytheseas but whether this was absolute or in settlement has not been determined and this is the last time the Wyke tithes are recorded. John Bythesea died in 1747 and Wyke House descended to Thomas Bythesea on his marriage to Elizabeth Lewis in 1758. The Bythesea family remained in possession of Wyke House right up until the early-nineteenth century and often worshipped at St Paul's Church where records of Bythesea marriages and baptisms can be found in the church registers. The Trowbridge and Staverton tithes remained with the Seymour family until 1750 when, on the death of Algernon, the seventh Duke of Somerset, they were split between his immediate family and his three half-sisters. By the 1770s the manor had lost its historic influence and in 1779 was passed to the Duke of Rutland who, two years later, put the estates up for sale. The remaining lands were split into lots and sold off between 1781 and 1791 after which the ancient demesne lands passed into the private ownership of local farmers and landowners. A map of the manor estates drawn for the Duke of Rutland in 1780 shows that the principal village landowners were James Rudman with 168 acres, including the lands at Smallbrook, Stephen Smith with 100 acres, and Isaac Smith with 64 acres which included Blacklands and the Bear Ale House and garden. Prince Sutton was farming 20 acres at the bottom of School Lane and James Shrapnell was in possession of the Staverton mill and its adjoining lands.

The land sale document of 1785 refers to lands and houses in Staverton, 'part of the Manor of Trowbridge', being sold at auction which was held at the George Inn on 28 September. Fields called Upper and Lower Hilly Grounds, about 12 acres by the River Biss, went under the hammer together with Little Bishop's Mead and Upper Worls, a further 8 acres in Hilperton Marsh. Two houses in Cottles Barton, at the bottom of School Lane, plus other houses and lands within the village totalling 11 acres, and the Bear Ale House, were also included in the sale of the demesne lands.

Staverton mill was leased by the Houlton family in the early 1700s and they later obtained the freehold. The mill continued to full cloths and grind corn through the early years of the 1700s but due to another depression in the woollen trade the gap between the wealthy clothiers and the ordinary cloth workers began to grow even wider as local mill owners, desperate to retain their profit margins, began keeping the weavers' wages down. The standard of living for cloth workers had deteriorated so significantly by 1726 that local riots broke out in protest at the low wage rates and the mill owners were accused of cheating by making the warps longer and thus devaluing the weavers' work. If these troubles were not bad enough, in 1730 a serious smallpox epidemic swept the area and over the next ten years devastated the population, claiming many lives locally. In 1753, before the community had time to recover, a second epidemic broke out and the situation became so bad that a special house was set up in Hilperton Marsh to examine and isolate the sick and prevent them spreading the very infectious disease through the narrow and confined streets of Trowbridge.

In 1729 Staverton mill was being used by Richard Papps, described as 'the Maltster of Staverton', who had taken on a young apprentice called Samuel Clifft and, by the description of his trade, was brewing beer, or preparing the barley for it, alongside the other functions of the mill. Thomas Clark appears to have been using the mill in the 1740s and, again, it was put up for sale in 1756 when it was described as having 'two grist mills and four fulling stocks' and was purchased by John Hackett. He insured the property in 1764 as 'a Grist and Fulling mill' and had recently added a dyehouse. Tenants between 1764 and 1770 were a partnership of John Harper and John Hillier and the mill came up for sale yet again in 1776 when it was purchased by James Shrapnell 'a Miller and Mealman'. His ownership of the mill turned out to be short-lived and he was declared bankrupt two years later. The sale document of 1778 describes the property as having 'a Miller's house, a Grist mill with a pair of French millstones and a Fulling mill with 6 pairs of stocks.' It was obvious that over the previous 50 years the mill had grown to a considerable size and by 1780 was being powered by four water-wheels, had three pairs of millstones, five pairs of fulling stocks and a bolting-mill. The bolting-mill comprised a series of vibrating troughs covered with muslin-type cloths of varying mesh sizes and was used in the separation of flour and bran. Between 1780 and 1785 Staverton mill was described as having 'two grist mills and four tucking stools (fulling stocks)' and was being operated by a Mr Goodeve. From 1792, a firm called Hart & Co. from Bradford-on-Avon were running the mill which was said to be providing plenty of work for local weaving families and attracting more into the area. Village cottages were converted into weaving shops, and houses in neighbouring villages were put up for sale 'with rooms large enough to take spinning machines'. The West-of-England cloth trade was reaching a peak and village weavers and other craftsmen associated with the industry were being provided with plenty of work by the local mills. However, the era of full employment generated by all the manual operations needed to produce a length of cloth was gradually being threatened by mechanisation as forward-thinking clothiers looked for ways to improve their businesses and reduce their labour costs.

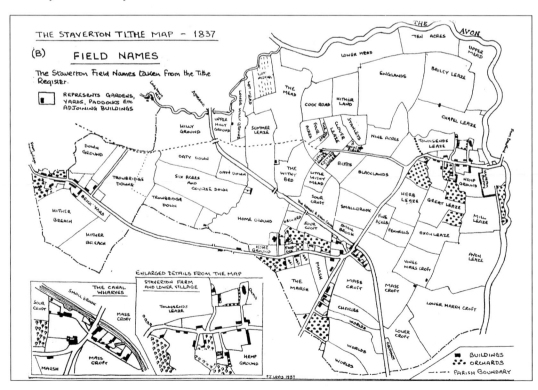

Left: *Field names on the Staverton Tithe Map of 1837.*

Around 1775 spinning-jennies began to appear in the area and the first carding machines had been introduced before the close of the century. Carding was the process used in the manufacture of broadcloths and involved opening up the fibres of the raw wool prior to spinning. Initially done by hand using teasles inserted into a wooden frame called a hand card, this manual operation later changed to using nails or wires inserted into strips of leather fixed to wooden handles. The carding machine contained rows of teasles on a series of rotating cylinders and gradually replaced the manual process, effectively making the hand-card operation redundant. Towards the end of the eighteenth century the mechanisation of the woollen cloth industry had started to take away many of the old hand-operated processes, much to the dismay of the cloth workers who were now facing the prospect of becoming redundant. The realisation that their livelihoods were under serious threat had notable repercussions on the Staverton mill in the early years of the nineteenth century.

The Church Vestry, elected annually by the village ratepayers, remained responsible for the poor of the parish when their duties further increased with the passing of the Poor Law in 1722. This law introduced the setting up of workhouses, and the Vestry had the unenviable task of deciding when to send destitute villagers and their families to these infamous institutions, one of which was located in nearby Semington. Vestry officials also became responsible for appointing the village waywarden to look after the parish's paths and tracks, a post which became much more important after 1770 when the turnpike road system came to Staverton. The Turnpike Act of 1768 had introduced a toll-road from Trowbridge to Hilperton Marsh via the Down and several years later the road extended through the village to the river bridge. This necessitated the construction of a toll-house and gate at the top of the hill by the church gates. In the meantime, toll-roads had branched out from Bradford-on-Avon to Holt and by the end of the century had linked up to the village via roads from Forewoods Common and a road from the river bridge to the toll-gate in Holt. These new roads had to be kept under repair by the parish and part of the maintenance work to keep them in good order required the widening and repair of the river bridge in 1792. Staverton's toll-gate was a tall structure, painted white, and stretched across the road at the top of the hill. The turnpike cottage was a small square building on the east side of the road, it had a tiny office at the front and housed the village toll keeper and his family. Anything entering or leaving the village at that point had to pay a fee and the various toll charges were painted on a wooden board which was fixed to the side of the cottage. A scale of charges covered the different types of horse-drawn transport, for the droving of animals and for carts laden and unladen that wished to pass the turnpike.

The toll fees charged on the turnpike roads in the area at the end of the 1700s were as follows:

Any horse or beast drawing a carriage 3d.
Any horse or beast drawing a wagon, wain or cart 4d.
Any horse or beast not drawing – laden or unladen 1d.
Droves of oxen, sheep or cattle 10d. a score.

Toll-gates and turnpike roads remained in force until the mid 1800s when the responsibility for maintaining the roads was placed upon the county through the Highways Act of 1835. Up until the end of the eighteenth century roads and rivers were the only means by which to travel through the land; by the late 1700s other methods of transport were being invented and were soon to come to Staverton when in 1790 the famous engineer John Rennie surveyed the proposed route through the village for the forthcoming Kennet and Avon Canal. At the turn of the century Staverton would witness the biggest construction project in its history as hundreds of navigators descended on the village to build bridges, locks and wharfs and dig out the channel that would become the revolutionary new water highway linking Bristol with London.

Staverton's tithingman was responsible for dealing with stray animals and any found on the roads or properties around the parish were captured and shut into the village pound until their owners came forward to claim them. The pound was a small stonewalled enclosure between the Old Bear and Staverton farm buildings with a lockable wooden gate. Owners who came to retrieve their animals had to pay a fine and, in extreme cases of public nuisance, the captured beasts could be confiscated. By the close of the eighteenth century Staverton had grown into a busy cloth-making village with most of the cottages converted for home weaving. The village population had doubled since 1700 and the mill had become the main source of employment for local families.

Staverton's toll-house in the late-nineteenth century.

Above: *St Paul's Church stands on a high bank overlooking the River Avon.*

Left: *St Paul's Edwardian church gateway.*

Staverton's earlier Chapel of Ease which dated back to the fourteenth century.

CHAPTER FIVE

CHURCH & CHAPEL

St Paul's Church stands on a high bank overlooking the River Avon on the northern boundary of the parish and to some extent is hidden from view by the houses that crown the hill leading down to the river bridge. Visitors to the area only discover the existence of the church here by finding the quaint Edwardian gateway that is sandwiched between two of the older village cottages. The narrow path that leads down from this gateway and runs between the tall hedges of the cottage gardens brings the tiny church of St Paul's, with its pleasant churchyard, into view. The present church, almost completely rebuilt in 1826, is constructed of ashlar with a Welsh slate roof and replaced an earlier and much smaller Chapel of Ease that occupied the same site. The foundation of the very first church in Staverton is not known but there was almost certainly a religious building on this site from the thirteenth century. Staverton, from Anglo-Saxon times, formed part of the manor of Trowbridge and remained very much under the town's ecclesiastical control right up to the early-nineteenth century. At the time of the Norman Conquest in 1066 Staverton was a tiny Anglo-Saxon hamlet with a small population of farmers and a corn-mill on the banks of the river. A Saxon thegn, Brictric, held the estates for King Edward and it is assumed that he controlled these landholdings from the manor house in Trowbridge. The Domesday survey of 1086 describes 'Stavretone' in some detail but makes no mention of a church in the village although it does not necessarily mean that one did not exist at the time. We know from recent research that the Norman clerks who compiled the Domesday entries did not always record a settlement's religious buildings, a classic example of one of their omissions being that they also made no mention of a Saxon church in Bradford-on-Avon, built in the early-eighth century and definitely in existence in 1086, but not recorded in Bradford's Domesday entry.

But, as no documentary or architectural evidence exists from that time, it is assumed that the village

St Paul's Elizabethan silver chalice, hallmarked 1577.

did not have a church in 1086. At the end of the eleventh century Staverton came into the possession of Edward of Salisbury who subsequently passed the lands down to his daughter Maud, wife of Humphry de Bohun, the builder of Trowbridge Castle. In 1125 Maud appropriated the tithes of Staverton to Monkton Farleigh Priory, the Cluniac monastery of St Mary Magdalene, which she had helped found a few years earlier. It is probable that when this association was formed arrangements were made for the Farleigh monks to provide a religious service for the villagers of Staverton. The monks would travel to the hamlet and conduct services for the community, probably in the open air, and on the same high bank that now houses the present church. As Staverton's population grew over the next few centuries a religious building was provided, a crude wooden structure with a thatched roof, sited on the same spot that had acted as a meeting-place for the earlier gatherings. This first chapel was a very primitive affair with an earthen floor, no seats, and very few decorations apart from simple mural paintings on the walls depicting such Bible scenes as The Last Judgement. A mass bell, in a small thatched bell cote, would summon locals to church and as they were mostly illiterate at that time few could understand the services which were always conducted in Latin during the twelfth to fourteenth centuries. Trowbridge and Staverton, originally part of the Melksham hundred, became a peculiar in 1322 and this arrangement became known as the 'Honour of Trowbridge'. Being a peculiar meant that the churches in the honour were exempt from the jurisdiction of Salisbury Diocese and this unusual situation remained right up to the early-eighteenth century. The main Parish Church for the villagers of Staverton would have been St James' in Trowbridge but because it was difficult and inconvenient for local people to get to the town in those days the existing religious building in the village would have been a Chapel of Ease. The rector of Trowbridge became the patron of the living and St James' curates were sent to the Staverton chapel to conduct the worship and look after the souls of the villagers.

By the fifteenth century a more substantial church building was provided, this time constructed in stone but still retaining thatch on its roof and a short bell tower. The first documentary evidence of a church at Staverton comes in 1535 when the *Valor Ecclesiasticus* refers to the 'Capella de Staverton' (Chapel of Staverton) and notes that one of the curates from St James' Church was made perpetual curate of Staverton. During this time the nation's religious establishment was in great turmoil with the 1534 Act of Supremacy abolishing the Pope's power in England, this subsequently leading to the Dissolution of the Catholic Monasteries between 1536 and 1539.

The result of these upheavals led to the foundation of the Anglican Church and despite later attempts by successive monarchs at papal reunion England's religious doctrine was never to return to the authority of Rome. The effects these dramatic changes had on the villagers of Staverton must have been quite profound as worshippers suddenly found themselves faced with the introduction of the first English prayer book, witnessed the confiscation of their church valuables and were subjected to compulsory attendance at all church services. Those who failed to comply with the new law were punished by the Church Courts and were either fined or forced to make confessions before the priest and chapelwardens. Church Vestries, which had gradually taken over the role of the old Manor Courts, were now responsible for all parish matters including the appointment of chapelwardens, waywardens, the tithingman and the village overseer of the poor, a post created after the Poor Law Act of 1572.

By the end of the sixteenth century St Paul's Chapel of Ease had been upgraded with enlarged windows and stone tiles to replace the thatch on its roof and bell cote. It was a tiny building, only about a third of the size of the present construction, but sufficient enough at that time to cater for the small village population who were summoned to attend services by the peeling of the mass bell. The chapel had slowly recovered from the traumatic results of Henry VIII's purge on the Catholic Church and some of its valuables had been replaced, including the acquisition of a solid-silver Elizabethan chalice made for St Paul's in 1577. St Paul's still possesses this rare and priceless item of church plate but because of its great antiquity and value it is now kept safely locked away in the vaults of a local bank and is only taken out and used on very special church occasions. The cup used to dispense the wine during communion services in the church today is a silver-plated replica of the 400-year-old Elizabethan chalice; it was presented to St Paul's by Julia Blease in 1932.

Religious events again took a dramatic turn during the first half of the seventeenth century with village worshippers becoming alarmed by the controversial reforms being introduced by William Laud, the then Archbishop of Canterbury, changes many perceived as an attempt to restore Catholicism. Puritism also began to take a hold locally forcing some Anglican ministers to be removed much to the dismay of dedicated churchgoers, these actions stimulating the growth of Nonconformity amongst local people. The Puritans, with their much stricter religious doctrine, frowned on the playing of games on Sundays, had altars, murals, stained glass and musical instruments removed from churches and banned church festivals such as the popular church ales. John Pelling is recorded as being the curate at St Paul's in the 1620s and a few years later, Richard Randail, an Oxford graduate and Trowbridge schoolmaster, was conducting services in Staverton's tiny Chapel of Ease. Here the wealthier village families now had their own pews at the front while the poorer members of the congregation would stand during the worship or, if lucky, find a space on the one or two hard wooden benches provided at the back of the nave. Public penance was still an occasional feature at church services, the parish armour and weapons were kept in the building and the Royal Arms, introduced by Henry VIII, were hung above the chancel arch as a visual reminder that the monarch was still the supreme head of the Anglican Church.

The English Civil War, which broke out in 1642, was to further disrupt the country's religious way of life and, after the Parliamentary victory over the Royalists, led to many more Anglican vicars and curates being replaced by Puritan ministers. The rigid beliefs of the new order led to the Book of Common Prayer being banned, all church trappings being removed or destroyed, and the display of the Royal Arms prohibited. Many Anglican worshippers were strongly opposed to the loss of their prayer book and the banning of church festivals which, since the dramatic upheavals of 1534, had become an accepted and very important part of the Anglican religious doctrine. Village people became more and more disillusioned with the new puritanical regime and many began boycotting this strict and, to them, alien religion in protest. During the 1650s St Paul's was almost abandoned and the new Church authorities made proposals to unite the ailing Staverton Benefice with Holt and Great Chalfield. The plan never materialised, however, and after the Restoration of the Monarchy in 1660 the proposal for the merger was finally withdrawn. Anticipating the damage the new Puritan authorities could do to their beloved village church, supporters of St Paul's managed to hide some of its property away in friendly hands before it could be confiscated under Cromwell's new religious order.

Some of these items later became the subject of a court case which took place at Devizes Quarter

Sessions in 1658 and concerned the illegal disposal of St Paul's valuables. An account of the proceedings recorded:

James Bartlett of Devizes disposes that one Bayley of Stafferton came to him and told him that he was Churchwarden (of St Paul's) and that for a long time they had had no prayers in their church because they were annexed to another place. The pulpit cloth was in one man's hands, the communion table cloth in another's, the silver bowl in another's and the bell was to be sold. He desired the examinant to buy the bell promising that if it should be called into question he would buy a new bell, and in July last year (1657) the bell was brought to the informant's house who paid the said Bayley £5.3s. for it.

It is obvious from this account that the Staverton Church officials feared that St Paul's would never reopen and had made arrangements to sell off some of its valuables. The Puritan Church authorities, trying to recover these missing items, had made enquiries and some of the receivers of these goods had panicked and informed on the sellers for fear of reprisals. After the Puritans were ousted from power, most of these church items were returned from safe-keeping and St Paul's was able to reopen and continue providing a place of worship for villagers. The Bayley mentioned in the court case appears to be William Bayley (Bailey) of Staverton who ran a draper's business in Bradford-on-Avon and lived in a dwelling called The Mansion House which stood near the gates of St Paul's Church in the seventeenth century. The Bayley family enjoyed a good standard of living, ran a successful textile business, were able to issue their own tokens in 1668 and lived in a substantial house in the village, all of this indicating that they must have been one of the wealthiest Staverton families during this period.

St Paul's Royal Arms, painted in 1801, has badly eroded in recent times.

The Restoration of the Monarchy in 1660 led to a complete reversal of the religious policies enforced during Cromwell's brief reign, the Anglican doctrine was quickly restored and the disliked Puritan ministers thrown out. The altar, removed under the Puritans, was reinstated at the east end of St Paul's, the Book of Common Prayer was revived and the Royal Arms, banned by Cromwell, re-hung above the chancel arch. For ordinary villagers, however, the damage had been done and many worshippers had already moved away from the re-established church and joined other Nonconformist groups that had emerged in the area.

Surviving registers of marriages, births and burials at St Paul's Church date from 1673, about the same period that Robert Hyatt was noted as being curate at Staverton where 'prayers and sermons are said once a fortnight in the evenings and the sacrament at Easter, Christmas and Whitsun.' William Wayte and Thomas Bendall were chapelwardens in 1680 when St Paul's was described as having 'no fund or estate appropriated to it' and John Grant was carrying out the chapelwardens' duties with Thomas Bayley in 1694.

Tombs and headstones were starting to appear in the churchyard, poor boxes were placed inside the chapel and St Paul's Vestry began paying rewards for the destruction of vermin, at the time considered to be a great hazard to public health. Churchwardens' accounts right up to the middle of the nineteenth century carry many entries of fees being paid to Staverton villagers for handing in dead vermin such as sparrows, hedgehogs and foxes. Payments varied from a farthing for each sparrow, one shilling for a fox and residents received four pence for hedgehogs, the most numerous of creatures killed and handed in. Thomas Barnard is noted as chapelwarden in 1697 and the 'Stafferton Chappell' is mentioned again in a Terrier of 1704 and a Presentment of 1717 which described the state of the building and reported that the chancel door was 'much out of repair'.

Staverton's church life continued to evolve as the eighteenth century dawned and St Paul's began introducing musicians and singers to accompany the church services. The social standing of villagers was evident from the seating arrangements in the chapel. This social pecking order is confirmed by an entry in an old St Paul's register which records that in 1722 'a seat built by Jonathon Dalmer, William Grant and Thomas Lawrenor, at their own charge, and for (use) of each family to sit in' was 'ye second double seat in the north side of the Chappell'. The front pews were being occupied by the Bythesea family of Wyke House, the Bayleys, the Grants and the Smith families who all appear to be the wealthiest and most prominent villagers at that time. Interior walls of the chapel were whitewashed and boards displaying the Ten Commandments were hung on the walls on each side of the chancel arch. Memorials were now being allowed inside the chapel, for those who could afford them and a fine marble tablet commemorating the Smith family, dated around the mid 1700s, is preserved on the south wall of the present church building. The Parish Clerk, elected annually by the Easter Vestry, and in those days an important and prominent Church official, occupied his own personal pew in front of the congregation and one of his duties during the services was to read aloud each line of the hymn before it was sung by the congregation, most of whom were unable to read. This eighteenth-century church custom was known as 'lining out'.

Since the religious upheavals of the mid-seventeenth century, however, many villagers had become Dissenters and although persecuted by the State for many years and later restrained, began to be reluctantly accepted when the Toleration Act of 1689 went some way towards recognising them by insisting that their activities were licensed. These groups initially met in village houses and certificates had to be obtained to make their meetings legal. A Nonconformist meeting-house is recorded in Staverton in 1791 when Peter Collier applied for permission to use his house as a chapel. The application was supported by other Staverton Dissenters such as William Lindzey, William Axford and William Hudd. At around the same time, William Hibbard's cottage was being used as a meeting-place for Nonconformists and his licence application was signed by Joseph Dean, William Axford, William and Joseph Lindzey and Job White. Two decades later James Bull, a Wesleyan Methodist, was granted a licence to use his dwelling for 'Chapel' worship, his request being backed up by William Dalmour, Samuel and John Marks, James Ricketts, Thomas Richards, Stephen Gay, George Rison and James Pullin. Relationships between church people and Nonconformists in Staverton appeared to be quite amiable during this time and indications of this can be seen from a church record of 1820 when Wesleyan James Bull was quite happy to mend the pathway leading down to St Paul's. Many Nonconformists, in fact, worshipped in both church and chapel and most had no choice but to use St Paul's for their weddings, baptisms and burials, as the religious ceremonies of Dissenter groups were not officially recognised by the State. St Paul's records contain many entries of Nonconformists' babies being baptised in the church in the eighteenth and nineteenth centuries including the children of Thomas and Jude Rawlings, Robert and Elizabeth Dean, Isaac and Mary Smith and John and Susannah Milsom. Marriages of Staverton Nonconformists also had to take place in St Paul's and entries in the eighteenth-century registers record the names of Staverton couples of many religious persuasions who had to make their vows at the only officially recognised wedding ceremonies conducted by an Anglican minister.

The Church Vestry, who were responsible for the poor of the parish, had their duties further increased in 1722 with the introduction of workhouses. Vestry officials also became responsible for appointing the village waywarden to look after the parish's roads and paths, a post which became much more important after 1770 when the turnpike came to Staverton. Charles Hodgkin is recorded as curate at St Paul's in the 1780s when evening prayers were said every alternate Sunday and a Mr Reece was carrying out this duty in the 1790s when an afternoon sermon was instituted provided that 'sufficient monies can be collected to defray the Curate's expenses'. Chapelwardens' accounts continued to report on the poor state of the building and repair work was constantly being carried out. Nathaniel Bissey, chapelwarden in 1798, complained that the church roof was 'much out of repair' and the exterior stonework badly needed re-pointing. The money for these repairs was normally raised from the church rate and in 1800 the new chapelwarden, Thomas Bissey, recorded that 13 guineas had been collected for that year.

The nineteenth century was a period of enormous social change for the religious life of Staverton and its villagers, bringing with it a new church, the first village school, the growth of Methodism, a Staverton Parish in its own right and a new vicarage to house its first resident preachers. At the start of the century, villagers were worshipping in a very old Chapel of Ease which was tiny and in a very bad state of repair. It was served by curates from Trowbridge who were generally unfamiliar with village people and their everyday problems, services were not always regular, sermons were too long, pews were only available to the wealthier families and the building was cold and damp. The despair of these unsatisfactory conditions turned many ordinary families towards the alternative Methodism, which had grown in popularity through the previous century and, although conducted in village houses, the services were considered simpler and brighter. Others turned away from religion altogether in the early years of the nineteenth century and less than half of the villagers attended any sort of religious worship.

Above: The front cover of St Paul's Baptism Register which dates from 1673.

Due to the plentiful work being provided by the local cloth industry, there was a dramatic growth of the village population in the early 1800s and enormous strain was being put on the tiny village chapel which began to struggle to accommodate those who wished to attend services on a regular basis. The major cause of great discontent though, was the declining standard of living, increase in the death rate, poverty and destitution especially amongst the immigrant cloth-working families who invariably blamed the Church for the situation and, as some perceived it, their 'abandonment by God'. This had the effect of driving more people away from the Church, especially in the difficult years of the mid 1800s and attendances gradually declined towards the end of the century. Nevertheless, St Paul's continued to be a going concern for those who stuck to their faith and a number of dedicated and committed Staverton families ensured that the village church was kept alive throughout the trials and tribulations of the nineteenth century.

James Beaven became the chapelwarden in 1804 when the Vestry accounts still recorded payments for the capture of vermin, two new doors were fitted to the chapel porch by Samuel Bryant in 1808 and a new Bible was purchased in 1810 for £4.8s., a considerable sum of money in those days and the equivalent of almost two months' wages for a village labourer. Further repairs were carried out the following year by John Deverell, a local builder who added to his £9 bill the sum of 16s.2d. to provide 'beer for the men' who had helped with the work. John Brown was appointed Parish Clerk by the Vestry in 1815, with an annual salary of two guineas, and John Crabbe had taken over as Staverton's curate. The previous year the famous vicar and poet George Crabbe had arrived in Trowbridge as rector of St James's and he occasionally officiated at St Paul's during his 18-year incumbency. George Crabbe became a champion of the poor in his earlier days as a minister and wrote many poems on the plight of the poverty-stricken farm labourers and hand-loom weavers who invariably ended up in the appalling parish workhouses of the nineteenth century. One of his poems describes the conditions in these institutions and part of it read as follows:

Theirs in yon house that holds the Parish poor,
whose walls of mud scarse hear the broken
door;
There, where the putrid vapours flagging play, and
the dull wheel hums doleful through the
day;
There children dwell who know no parents'
care, Parents who know no children's love,
dwell there!
Heartbroken matrons on their joyless bed,
Forsaken wives, and mothers never wed;
Here, on a matted flock, with dust o'erspread,

the drooping wench reclines his languid head;
For him no hand the cordial cup applies, or wipes
the tear that stagnates in his eye.

George Crabbe died in 1832 and is to be remembered locally not only for his literary works but also his colourful sermons at St Paul's, some fragments of which can be found in the church records archived in the County Records Office.

Constant repairs were being made to the chapel in the early years of the nineteenth century with the windows needing attention in 1819 and the Vestry reporting that James Bull had been paid five shillings for 'mending the road (path) to the church' in 1820. Edward Cooper, Staverton cloth-mill owner, became chapelwarden in 1821 and immediately began making plans to rebuild and enlarge the tiny village chapel which had been the community's place of worship, in various forms, since the thirteenth century. Cooper's Mill, then in its heyday, was providing plenty of work for local people and many weaving families and other cloth-trade workers had moved into the village at the turn of the century. This influx of new potential worshippers had put a strain on the tiny chapel of St Paul's and difficulties were being experienced in coping with the larger congregations now attending the services. Another factor which had accelerated the rebuilding programme was the growth of Methodism in the village which had increased so much by the early-nineteenth century that it warranted the building and opening of a new Wesleyan chapel in 1824.

The Chapel of Ease was replaced by the present church building in 1826. A picture of this stone chapel, painted in 1806 by Wiltshire artist John Buckler, shows what the building looked like and gives a good indication of its size and style. It was constructed from local stone, roofed with stone tiles, and contained a small stone-tiled bell cote at the west end of its roof. The tiny nave was rectangular in shape and led into an almost square chancel at the east end. A small wooden door was located in the south wall of the chancel and long narrow slit windows gave limited natural light to the interior on the north and south sides. The larger east window was arch-shaped and divided into two lights by a central column which rose into an elaborate design of carved stonework at the top. This stonework

The Smith family marble tablet inside the church.

consisted of a circular four-petal-shaped window below the arch point and two small triangular-shaped apertures which filled the gaps on each side where the two main window openings became bottle-shaped at their tops. The window appeared to contain plain glass and was crowned by a thick arch-shaped stone moulding; its style would date it to the fifteenth century. A pitched-roof porch, which seemed large in comparison to the size of the rest of the building, was located at the south-west corner of the chapel and was entered through an arch-shaped stone doorway which was closed by a stable-type wooden door. Small narrow slit windows were inserted centrally into the east and west walls of the porch and narrow buttresses ran off each side at the bottom half of the front wall. Located centrally in the south wall of the nave was a small square window, again divided into two by a central column and terminating in a simple carved stone design at the top where the window openings formed rounded arches. Small circular apertures, two above each window, completed the design in the stone areas created each side at the top of each arch. The design of the building indicates that a similar window was positioned centrally in the north wall of the nave and that the porch was a later addition. Although the west end of the building cannot be seen on the painting, it is probable that a window of similar size and style to the east window was situated here.

George Crabbe, the famous vicar and poet who preached at St Paul's in the early-nineteenth century.

The east and west ends of the building were supported by small tile-capped buttresses and the bell cote at the west end of the roof contained one small bell, the rope of which hung down against the west wall of the interior. No records are found to indicate what the interior of the chapel was like but a conjectural plan formulated from studies of the painting can give a good idea of how it was arranged. The floor area of the nave was approximately 432 square feet and could only have accommodated about 12 rows of pews. This would indicate that the seating capacity of the building was about 60, which seems to be confirmed by statements taken from records made during the rebuilding of the present church. To allow access from the porch into the central aisle the south-west third of the nave could not be used for seating and probably housed the font which was situated close to the back wall. Buckler also illustrated the font in 1806 and close examination of the drawing would indicate that it is the same font which was retained and installed in the present church. Assuming that a pulpit was located against the east wall of the nave, this would leave only enough space for four rows of pews on the south side. The remainder of the seating would have been situated in the north side of the main building and a small space to the left of the inner porch doors could have accommodated a further few seats. The chancel took up approximately 154 square feet of floor space and was larger than the existing chancel. Apart from the Holy Table at the east end we do not know how the chancel was furnished but, as no vestry attachment existed, it must have contained a large wooden chest to keep the chapel registers, church plate, bread and wine, candles, vestments, books and other church essentials.

A village rate of 6d. in the pound was collected in 1825 to help provide funds for the rebuilding of St Paul's, a grant was obtained from the Society for Promoting the Enlargement and Building of Churches, and Edward Cooper provided the rest from his own pocket. Sufficient funds were available by 1826 and the complete rebuilding of St Paul's commenced. The old Chapel of Ease was virtually demolished and the new building erected was more than double the original size. Local stone was used in the reconstruction and very little of the old chapel was retained apart from various pieces of stonework which can still be seen in the present church. To record the building of the new St Paul's, a notice was displayed in the church and can now be seen on the west wall of the porch. It reads:

This Chapel was rebuilt and enlarged in the year 1826 by which means 120 additional sittings have been obtained in consequence of a grant from the Society for Promoting the Enlargement and Building of Churches and Chapels. 100 of that number are declared free and unappropriated for ever and are in addition to 60 previously provided.

The rebuilt church, at this point, consisted of nave and chancel only, the porch and vestry being finally added over 35 years later.

New gates were installed at the entrance to the churchyard in 1829. Walter Marriott became St Paul's curate in 1832 and by 1835 the seating capacity in the church had been increased to 220 with the addition of tiered pews in the south-west corner. In 1839 Staverton became a separate parish in the gift of the rector of Trowbridge and would now, for the first time in history, have its own resident vicar, the first one being the Revd J.R. Prityman. He only remained for two years and once again St Paul's was looked after by curates; A. Douglas in 1841, J. Langhorne in 1842, C.S. Row in 1843 and L.W. Hinton from 1844 to 1847. The living was endowed for £100 in 1844, a large sum of money in those days, but the first incumbents had to live in Trowbridge until Staverton vicarage could be provided. George Garret was elected Parish Clerk in 1845 and Benjamin Cooper, James Howell and Walter Newth were churchwardens between 1846 and 1849. In 1848 St Paul's once again had its own vicar when the Revd M.S. Berry became the incumbent and he was followed by the Revd Richard Vigors in 1859.

Staverton's first Church of England school was opened in the village in 1850 and occupied part of the warehouse on the canal wharf. The building, attached to Wharf Cottage, was owned by the Kennet & Avon Canal Co., and leased to St Paul's churchwarden Walter Newth who became one of the founder managers of the new school. Samuel Hooper, John Cooper, William Webber and Frederick Blake were recorded as churchwardens between 1850 and 1857 and around this period George Garrett, the Parish Clerk, was given an increase in his salary to four guineas provided he agreed to 'keep the church and church walk clean, toll the bell and provide evergreens at the Christmas and Easter festivals'. The Revd Philip Maddock became Staverton's vicar in 1860 and his arrival coincided with the addition of the porch and vestry at St Paul's and the building of the village vicarage in which he became the first occupant. The need for a village vicarage had become quite pressing by the late 1850s and an appeal was launched to provide Staverton Parish with a parsonage house. An acre of land had been secured between the railway and the canal and subscriptions were sought to finance the building costs which were estimated at £1,150. The appeal stated that the parish now had nearly 700 inhabitants and that there was the possibility of great increase 'in consequence of the Staverton Woollen Factory being about to be worked by a public company.' The village cloth factory had been closed for 18 years and reports that the Government had acquired it in the late 1850s were subsequently denied. However, negotiations had been taking place with various interested parties on the purchase of the mill site and it was on the strength of this that the exaggerated statement of 'a great increase' had been made. This, of course, did not materialise although a new business called the West of England Woollen Manufacturing Company did set up operations in the mill in 1864. Donations for the new vicarage were given by local landowners and village people, £100 was obtained from Queen Anne's Bounty, and a considerable sum from the incumbent, the Revd Philip Maddock, and many local clergy. Materials and services were supplied by local tradesmen and businesses including the donation of 5,000 bricks

from Trowbridge Brick Company, and the building was completed and occupied by early 1861.

Church services were enhanced in 1861 when an harmonium was purchased and placed 'in the gallery' as a gift to the parish. The fund-raising activities to provide the instrument were organised by Miss Blake who managed to collect over £45 towards the cost. However, the financial burden on St Paul's was ever increasing and by 1870 the situation had become so acute that collection boxes were placed by the church door to help generate more funds. Initially, the response was favourable, 12 shillings being collected on the first two Sundays, and by 1873 over £12 was being received annually in voluntary contributions.

With Trowbridge beginning to expand northwards from the mid-nineteenth century a new ecclesiastical area was needed in order to look after the influx of potential new worshippers. Staverton had to give up some of its ancient parish area when the new Trowbridge Parish of St Thomas was created in 1870. From the very earliest times the ecclesiastical parish had comprised the village of Staverton and the hamlet of Staverton Wick, now Wyke. The parish boundaries extended to Victoria Road, a large part of the Down and Islington, and stretched across the Lower Wyke farmlands as far as Ladydown. Marsh Road and the land that is now occupied by Queen's and Princess Gardens formed the south-east section of the parish and the northern and western parish boundaries formed a long line along the Avon and the Biss. The formation of St Thomas' Parish meant that Staverton would lose some of its Victoria Road and Down areas and this invariably led to a reduction in the number of churchgoers on the outskirts of the parish, who in the past would have travelled to St Paul's to worship.

George Garrett, Parish Clerk for 29 years and noted as 'a most exemplary christian' in the church registers, died in 1874 and was replaced by John Purnell as clerk and sexton in 1875. William Blake and George Woods were the churchwardens in the 1870s and Florence Hannum played the harmonium during church services in the 1880s for which she was paid an annual fee of £2. St Paul's Church choir is noted at this time although there may have been one in existence many years before this, probably from when musicians and singers were introduced in the eighteenth century. The Revd Philip Maddock retired in 1888 after 28 years as St Paul's minister and the Revd Theodore Cavell became the new village vicar the following year. Educated at St Bee's College, he had been incumbent at parishes in Ipswich, London, Yorkshire and Derbyshire and had left St Paul's in Poole to become Staverton's vicar. He was a relative of the famous nurse Edith Cavell who was shot by the Germans in the First World War for assisting the escape of British and French POWs from Belgium.

Above: *The present St Paul's Church.*

Inset: *Notice in the church porch
commemorating the rebuilding of St Paul's in 1826.*

Left: *Revd Philip
Bainbridge Maddock,
first resident village
vicar 1860 to 1888.*

Left: *St Paul's
stained-glass east
window installed
by the Hargreaves
family in 1890.*

Right:
*Walter Newth,
chapelwarden in the
1850s and founder
manager of the first
village school.*

The stained-glass east window in St Paul's was installed in 1890 by the Hargreaves family, owners of the Staverton cloth-mill from 1870 to 1891. The window was in remembrance of Mary Elizabeth, the eldest daughter of James and Elizabeth Hargreaves, who died on 19 March 1887, aged 30. It features the four evangelists with a central light of Our Lord raising Jairus' daughter from the dead, and above it a representation of the Ascension into Heaven. The Revd Theodore Cavell died in 1897 and Stuart Ridley became Staverton's vicar in 1898. He claimed to be a direct descendant of Bishop Ridley, the Bishop of London in Queen Mary's reign, who was burned at the stake in 1555 for his opposition to Mary's Catholicism.

Throughout the nineteenth century, Staverton's religious life had undergone considerable changes and now faced the twentieth century with a new church building but ever-decreasing congregations due to the dramatic reduction in the parish population, mainly caused by the decline and eventual closure of the village cloth factory. The century started on an optimistic note with a steady growth in the population of the village. The increase in the number of families attending church services prompted the rebuilding and

enlargement of St Paul's. The drift to Methodism had been contained and services had been enhanced with the introduction of organ music and the choir. However, this peak in the fortunes of village church life was soon to be eroded as Staverton's social problems worsened, resulting in many people turning their backs on religion. Although the village had its own resident vicars from the 1850s onwards the decline continued, not helped by the loss of part of the parish in 1870, and by the end of the century St Paul's was struggling financially and faced the prospect of a considerable reduction in support. One glimmer of hope at the close of the century came from the take-over of the cloth-mill site by a condensed-milk company with the anticipation locally that this new business would create more jobs and encourage people to remain or move back into the village.

At the beginning of the twentieth century Samuel Bird and William Clark were the churchwardens, Maria Purnell was the organist and Herbert Purnell had been appointed to the position of Parish Clerk. St Paul's tiny churchyard was reaching capacity by 1901 and fears were expressed that it might have to be closed to burials unless more land could be obtained to extend it. The urgent need to find funds for a larger graveyard and the ever-increasing costs of running the church presented a severe financial crisis in 1903 and rummage sales and requests for donations were organised to help raise badly needed extra money to clear the church's debts.

In 1905 the Revd Albert Isherwood came to Staverton as the new village vicar. He had previously been incumbent at Worton and Marston and was a prominent Freemason serving as their provincial Grand Chaplain. One of his first tasks as the new vicar was to bring the churchyard plans to a successful conclusion. The extra land needed, to the north of the church, was obtained and a village collection raised nearly £50 to help pay for the cost of the work and provide fencing for the new ground. A number of villagers volunteered their services to carry out the work and erect the iron fencing, completing the job by 1906. The total

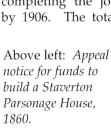

Above left: *Appeal notice for funds to build a Staverton Parsonage House, 1860.*

Rear view of Staverton's vicarage built in 1861.

cost of the alterations had come to £80 and Dr Wordsworth, the Lord Bishop of Salisbury, attended the opening ceremony and conducted the service of consecration. A new organ was purchased in 1908 to replace the old harmonium and gas lighting was installed in the church in 1910 replacing candles, used for centuries to illuminate the interior.

Frank Couzens, George Jacklin and Samuel Bird were churchwardens during the years of the First World War, Edward Drayton was the sexton with a salary of £7 per annum and the organist, now Mrs Maria Endru, had her fees increased to £5 per year. The hostilities that broke out in Europe in 1914 brought great anxiety to village families as many Staverton husbands, fathers and brothers were sent off to fight in the trenches of northern France and Belgium. By the end of the war four years later, seven men from the parish had made the supreme sacrifice and their names were recorded for posterity on the church's brass eagle lectern which, from that moment on, became the village war memorial.

Sunday School outings, organised by Amelia Rogers and her helpers, Milly and Lilly Bird, continued in the 1920s and George Wiltshire and William Vezey took it in turns as church organ blowers. Victor Blake and Donald Rogers were churchwardens in 1922 with Bert Foreman taking over from the latter the following year. Vestry minutes from 1924 indicate that the church finances had improved and go on to praise the efforts of Fred Purnell and his wife for 'keeping the church and churchyard in such an excellent condition'. Proposals were made in 1925 to replace the weather vane ('the present one is nearly 60 years old') and to repair the bell which had recently become 'out of order'.

The brass altar cross was presented to St Paul's in 1926 by Mr and Mrs Donald Rogers who dedicated it to the memory of Howard Purnell, a chorister of the church, and the first village man to lose his life in the First World War. Donald Rogers was the manager of the Nestlé and Anglo-Swiss Milk factory in the village, formerly the Staverton cloth-mill, where Howard Purnell had worked as a tin shop fitter before being enlisted for active service at the start of the war. Church heating became a much debated subject over the next few years and proposals were made to provide gas radiators in the aisles as the old heating system was considered to be beyond repair. This scheme, however, did not materialise and the problem was temporarily resolved by the provision of a replacement boiler for the old hot-air system. Mabel Vezey played the organ in the 1920s and '30s, the fees being increased to £8.10s. in 1930, and the organ blowers, Lewis and Jack Purnell, received one shilling for every Sunday they 'performed'. Victor

Revd Theodore Cavell, Staverton's vicar from 1889 to 1897.

'Bucky' Hale also took a turn at organ blowing although on occasion the music became very 'jumpy' when he was in one of his 'funny moods'. In 1932 a unique anniversary was commemorated at St Paul's when James Osborne was congratulated and presented with an award by Revd Isherwood for completing 50 years' service as a member of the church choir. Also that year, the growing concerns about the security of St Paul's priceless Elizabethan silver chalice, which had always been kept in the Vestry, resulted in the Church Council deciding that it should be deposited for safe-keeping in the vaults of a local bank. A replica was brought into use in 1932, purchased from a generous gift to St Paul's by Julia Blease who, four years later, also provided the carved oak communion rails that were installed beneath the chancel arch. In 1937 the Revd Albert Isherwood passed away and the village mourned the sad loss of one of its longest-serving incumbents. During his 31 years as Staverton's vicar he had become very involved in the life of the community, had presided over the enlargement of the churchyard, major repairs to the church building and the renovation of Staverton School, a village institution in which he took a great interest and to which he was a frequent visitor. Many older villagers have happy memories of the annual church fêtes on the vicarage lawns, hosted by the vicar and his family, and the weekly Bible classes run by Mrs Isherwood and helpers.

Victor Blake and Frank Couzens, the new churchwardens in 1938, welcomed the Revd Francis Maunder as the new village vicar. His arrival coincided with the installation of electric lighting in the church in replacement of the old gas lighting system. The new vicar, like his predecessor, also showed a very keen interest in village life, supported the school in many activities including swimming, helped to run the local Scout troop, took on the role of Parish Clerk in 1940 and was the village's Air Raid Warden in the early years of the Second World War. In 1941 Ethel Blease and Harry Bird were elected churchwardens and both continued in office right through the war years. As with the First World War, many parish men were called up to serve in the Armed Forces and, by the end of the war, the names of three more Staverton men had been added to the village war memorial in the church.

Albert Matthews succeeded Mr Fred Purnell as verger in 1947 and Ernest Tasker became the second churchwarden on the death of Harry Bird in 1949. In the early 1950s John Blake, William Legg and Ethel Blease carried out the churchwardens' duties at a time when the Church Council was becoming concerned about the untidiness of the graveyard and the

Left: *Revd Stuart Ridley, St Paul's vicar, 1898 to 1905.*

poor condition of some of the graves. A churchyard committee was set up and discussions took place to decide on what actions were needed, these including a proposal to level any unkempt graves. Many plots had been neglected and become overgrown and known relatives of the deceased were contacted to ask for their support in improving the situation.

St Mary Magdalene's Church in Hilperton Marsh, built at the behest of the Clark family of Wyke House in 1899, was merged with St Paul's in 1954 to form the Staverton Churches and in future both would be looked after by a joint PCC and the vicar of Staverton. At St Paul's, Vera Malyn was appointed assistant verger in 1956 and the following year her daughter Valerie took over as organist on the retirement of Maria Endru who had provided the music at church services for over 50 years. Ceiling-level gas heaters were installed in 1957 to replace the outdated hot-air heating system which, in recent years, had become very inefficient and too costly to run. Repairs to the roof and bell tower were carried out in 1960 and Vera Malyn took over the role of verger on the death of her father, Albert Matthews, who had been St Paul's verger and sexton for the past 13 years. Later that year the church organ was moved from its position in the south-east corner of the nave and re-sited on the other side of the aisle in the north-west corner. In the early 1960s Vera Malyn also took on the role of church organist, and the church registers of 1964 recorded the burial of Albert Bath 'a faithful servant of God' and past sexton and organ blower at St Paul's. The very physical job of organ blower was finally phased out in 1969 when an American pipe-organ with electric blower replaced the old manual organ, and the security of church valuables was greatly improved when a modern Chubb safe was purchased in 1970 and installed in the vestry. The parish came to the end of an era in 1970 with the death of Revd Maunder because, as events turned out, he was to be the last resident village vicar of Staverton. The future of St Paul's was again under discussion and in 1971 proposals were made to merge Staverton's churches with Holt. However, after long and sometimes emotional debate, it was finally decided that Staverton's churches would join with Hilperton and from now on St Michael's rectors would look after the needs of the parish and conduct the services in St Paul's and

St Mary's. The Revd Peter Matthews was rector of Hilperton at the time and welcomed the two Staverton churches as they joined with St Michael's and St Mary's, Whaddon, to form the much larger benefice created by the merger. Not long after the merger the empty Staverton vicarage was sold and some years later was converted into a care home for the elderly under the name The Old Vicarage.

Further alterations took place to St Paul's in 1972 when the front pew on each side of the nave was removed, the altar table enlarged and a memorial plaque to 'Frank' Maunder was placed on the south wall of the nave. John Blake and Wilfred Stone were churchwardens in the early 1970s, and in 1974 a pneumatic pipe-organ was purchased for £60 and replaced the old American organ in the north-west corner of the nave. The ceiling was repainted in 1975 and the following year the tiered pews in the south-west corner were removed and replaced with the two pews taken from the front of the church three years earlier. Major repairs were also carried out to the exterior of the building with the roof being over-hauled, some defective timbers being renewed and the old iron guttering being removed and replaced with square-section plastic piping. The churchwarden's position was filled by Phylis Blease in the late 1970s and in 1980 a proposal was made by the new Hilperton rector, the Revd Philip Bell, to remove the church gates which in recent years had become unstable and unsafe due to cracked stonework on the pillars. The proposal was rejected by the Parish Council and the Local Authority, the latter subsequently placing a preservation order on the structure to ensure that it was maintained. Later that year the Parish Council arranged for repairs to be carried out to the damaged gateway by stonemasons sent up from the nearby Nestlé factory. Peter Woodman became the new churchwarden and immediately embarked on a major programme of refurbishment to the interior of the church. The building was completely rewired and new lighting installed, at the cost of over £800, and the old outhouse on the north-west corner of the church, used in the past to store fuel for the boiler, was demolished. The following year the interior walls were stripped back to the bare plaster, re-coated with polyskin, repainted with Limo-wash, and essential repairs were carried out to the interior stonework. Floors were treated with preservative and some areas of the exterior stonework were repaired and re-pointed.

Congregations had steadily fallen and financial support had dwindled by the 1980s and this situation had run St Paul's into another crisis by 1984.

A public meeting was called in September to discuss the future of the church and indications at the time were that if more support was not forthcoming, St Paul's would be in danger of closing. Many villagers at the meeting agreed to help and extra funds were promised with some pledging regular

Left: *Donald Rogers, the Nestlé factory manager, was also St Paul's churchwarden in the 1920s.*

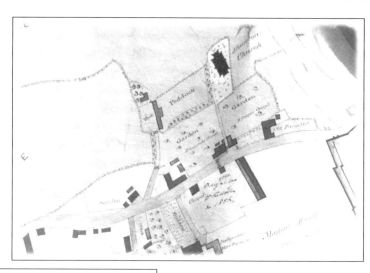

Above: *The size of Staverton's churchyard before its enlargement in 1906.*

Above: *Church interior in 1909. The Royal Arms can be seen hanging above the chancel arch.*

Above: *Revd Bobby Magill, present benefice vicar, presenting church organist Vera Malyn with a gift on her retirement in 2001.*

St Paul's in the early 1900s showing the boiler-house chimney protruding above the tower.

donations by covenant. The crisis has been temporarily averted but Staverton people were left in no doubt that their continued support would be vital to secure the long-term future of their village church.

Janet Blake became churchwarden when Peter Woodman and family moved away from the area and the benefice staffing was strengthened by the arrival of Deaconess Kay Holloway. The parish lay preacher, Hugh Hoskins, who had conducted many services at St Paul's, was ordained into priesthood in 1985 at a special service held in St Michael's, Hilperton, and presided over by the Rt Revd John Neale, Bishop of Ramsbury. His ordination turned out to be a very timely event, he was put temporarily in charge of the benefice whilst a replacement was sought for the retiring Philip Bell, who had been Staverton and Hilperton's vicar for the past seven years.

In 1986, Richard Hicks, previously with the Swanborough Team Ministry, became the benefice vicar and, later that year, further external work was carried out at St Paul's by a Manpower Services Team sponsored by Nestlé. The churchyard fence and church gates were repaired and painted, the churchyard was tidied up, some old graves renovated, and the lamp standard on the pathway cleaned and re-painted. Nestlé also supplied a mason to re-point the exterior stonework of the building and repairs were made to the vestry doorway. Pete Lavis took over as churchwarden in 1987 and made arrangements for the church interior to be redecorated. A section of flooring in the south-west corner of the nave was repaired and a bookcase constructed from the front pew by the font. The ceiling of the nave was cleaned and re-painted, the chancel walls and ceiling redecorated, and the main entrance doors stripped, treated and varnished. Hugh Hoskins left the benefice in 1987 to take up a ministry in Calne and Christina Nunn came to the parish as deacon to succeed Kay Holloway. The south-east window of the nave, damaged by storms in the spring, was repaired in July 1988 and the fine old copper beech tree in the north-west corner of the churchyard was pruned and treated by tree surgeons after some of its branches had become unstable. Ex-schoolteacher Sue Wilkins took over the role of deacon in 1990 and the following year the large west window in St Paul's, which had deteriorated badly in recent years, was almost completely replaced by Baker's, a firm of church glaziers from Weston-super-Mare, after sustaining more damage from severe storms the previous winter. A great deal of repair and redecorating work had been carried out on the church over the last 20 years and all the hard work and dedicated effort that had been put in by everybody during that period was rewarded with a very satisfactory report from the church surveyors. The report, arising from the 1991 quinquennial inspection of the building, indicated that the fabric of St Paul's was generally in a sound condition and no major faults were immediately evident. Some minor problems were listed in the report which recommended repairs to the vestry door, attention to missing slates and sections of guttering on the roof, and treatment of the floor and woodwork against insect infestation. In response to the report a brand new exterior door was fitted to the vestry and all other tasks were completed in 1992.

In December that year the outdated gas heating system failed and was subsequently condemned by the Gas Board. Temporary heating was brought into the church and investigations were carried out in early 1993, principally by St Paul's treasurer Ray Wickings, to find a suitable modern replacement system. A fund-raising appeal was launched to raise over £2,000 and by the end of the year sufficient money had been donated for the purchase and installation of six electric quartz halogen heaters which were suspended just below the ceiling on each side of the nave.

The total cost of providing this new heating system had come to just over £2,400, most of this amount being given in generous donations from St Paul's supporters both inside and outside the parish. The new heaters placed an added strain on the church's long-established electrical system and in April 1995 St Paul's had to be rewired with a split-phase system and new fuse boxes to eliminate the risk of newly installed electrical equipment overloading, the work costing an additional £480. By 1995 the old church organ, provided in 1974, had begun to deteriorate quite badly. Keys were sticking, some notes had gone dumb and it had become very difficult to play properly. The PCC launched another fund-raising appeal in the middle of the year to replace this old instrument with one that had been offered to St Paul's free, although transportation and reassembly costs would have to be met. The appeal ran through into the summer of 1996 when, again, thanks to the generosity of many local people, the fund-raising target was reached. The new organ, offered to St Paul's by Vivien Galloway of Poole, Dorset, was finally installed at the back of the nave in August 1996 by Osmunds of Taunton and the remaining pews in the tower base were removed to accommodate the new instrument's electrical control boxes. A special service to bless and dedicate the new organ was held in St Paul's on 27 October 1996. The service was conducted by the Bishop of Ramsbury, the Rt Revd Peter Vaughan, and a packed congregation, including special guest Vivien Galloway, were treated to a rousing organ recital by Alan Harwood, Director of Music at Salisbury Cathedral. St Paul's new organ had been hand built by Miss Galloway's late father in 1953 and was used in a Poole boarding school until 1993 after which it became redundant and had to be found a new home. It is a two-manual pipe-organ with pedals, four ranks of pipes supplying the stops for the keyboards and a rank of 16-foot wooden pipes to create a bourelon

Above: *The parish war memorial.*

Right: *Vicarage fête in 1915 with Miss Bird on the left and Miss Blake on the right.*

Top right: *Revd Francis Maunder, St Paul's vicar from 1938 to 1970.*

Right: *Revd Albert Isherwood, Staverton's vicar for 32 years, 1905 to 1937.*

Left: *James Osborne being congratulated by Revd Isherwood in 1932 for his 50 years in the church choir.*

Above: *St Mary's Church, Hilperton Marsh, joined with St Paul's in 1954 to form 'The Staverton Churches'.*

Right: *Revd Philip Bell, benefice vicar from 1978 to 1986.*

Left: *Revd Peter Matthews was benefice vicar in 1971.*

Right: *Mary Blake presents flowers to Mrs Isherwood at the church fête in 1915.*

Left: *Revd Richard Hicks, benefice vicar from 1986 to 1997.*

pedal stop. To coincide with the new organ a framed remembrance scroll, beautifully inscribed by Anne Gimson, was placed on the south wall of the nave and commemorated the past loved ones of the many people who had subscribed to the organ appeal fund. The scroll was also dedicated to the late Alice Purnell, a lifelong worshipper at St Paul's, in whose honour a large sum of money had been given towards the appeal for the new heaters several years earlier.

Richard Hicks retired in October 1997 and, with wife Irene, moved north to set up a retirement home in Brampton, Cumbria. During his 11 years as the benefice vicar he had chaired the governing body of Staverton School and was one of the leading campaigners in securing a new primary school for the village. He had been the driving force behind initiatives to raise finance for extensions to St Michael's Church and improvements to St Paul's which was now equipped with a new organ and heating system. His wife, Irene, had also been very pro-active in the benefice, was a regular helper at Staverton School and an active member of St Paul's and St Mary's PCC.

The new vicar, the Revd Bobby Magill, arrived in the benefice in May 1998 and, with wife Claire and children Ian, Flora and Annie, set up home in the recently modernised Hilperton Rectory. His previous post had been as assistant curate at West Moors near Wimborne, Dorset, and he was installed as priest in charge of the Staverton and Hilperton benefice at a special service held in St Michael's on 12 May, the service being conducted by the Bishop of Salisbury. Revd Magill was soon active among his new 'flock' taking a keen interest in both village schools, becoming Chair of Governors at Staverton School in 1999, promoting the ministry amongst the children of both communities as well as looking after the religious and spiritual welfare of all the residents of the benefice. He was instrumental in activating the next phase of improvements at St Paul's which resulted in funds being raised to completely carpet the nave and vestry and to install exterior lighting along the churchyard path. These two projects were completed by December 1998, at a cost of £1,350, making St Paul's a much brighter, safer and more welcoming church for village worshippers to attend.

Other additions to the church as the new millennium approached were a new frontal for the pulpit reading board, made and presented by Lesley Warne, the purchase of a new lectionary and the provision of a new notice-board on the wall outside the church gates, the cost of purchasing the latter being met by an anonymous, and very generous, local benefactor. The new vicar also introduced a weekly news sheet which detailed the services being held in each benefice church and listing events taking place that week as well as other useful items of church information.

As Staverton moved into the new millennium, St Paul's continued to struggle financially and numbers of villagers attending the services further declined. To try and raise badly needed funds for the church and to generate more interest and support, concerts, dinner evenings and an annual Christmas fayre were organised by the PCC, the latter becoming a very successful and well supported yearly event, raising nearly £1,000 in 2001. Annual musical evenings with performances by Stonar School orchestra and choir and the Ros Pendry Ensemble were held in the church and a very successful Organ-fest was held in 2001 with recitals by four guest organists. Julia Meeres' superb Christmas dinner evenings at Brookfield raised money in 1999 to purchase a new set of hymn-books for St Paul's. The new form of Common Worship was introduced in millennium year with revised and simpler service books, and family worship replaced the old-style evensong one Sunday each month.

The quinquennial inspection of St Paul's in 2001 resulted in a reasonably good report and, again, no structural faults were discovered. Recommendations were made to replace the guttering which had eroded and caused some water seepage the previous year, repairs were needed to the vestry chimney, and some areas of plasterwork on the internal walls needed attention. Plans were drawn up in 2002 by a St Paul's fabric committee, headed by church treasurer Jo Beaven, to raise funds to rectify these minor faults.

St Paul's had undergone a number of modifications over the last few years and was now reasonably well equipped to take the church and its worshippers into the twenty-first century. Much was being done to generate more interest and an effort was being made to halt the decline in support of Staverton's historic church which had provided a place of worship for generations of villagers since the thirteenth century. St Paul's will continue to serve the community and due to the loving care and dedication bestowed

Top: *Revd Isherwood opening the church fête in 1915.*

Above: *Kath Purnell, Methodist Chapel Sunday School teacher from 1945 to 1985.*

on it by many people over the years should remain a welcoming and important village institution well into the new century. However, if this situation is to continue, the villagers of Staverton must make a commitment now to ensure that their church is cared for in the years ahead and by doing this St Paul's long-term future will be assured.

STAVERTON'S METHODIST CHAPEL

Wesleyan Methodism began to take hold locally in the mid-eighteenth century and its founder, John Wesley, was known to have preached in Trowbridge in 1754 and again in 1780. Adam Clarke, a great preacher of Methodism, also came to Trowbridge and eventually married a local girl. By the turn of the eighteenth century the new faith had spread into the villages and many Staverton Nonconformists, who had been using their cottages as meeting-houses, adopted the religion and eventually acquired their own religious building in the village. Staverton's Methodist Chapel, a small square building built of ashlar with a Welsh slate roof, was constructed in 1824 and, at the time, was designed to seat 100 if its raised west-end gallery was used. It was very well supported during the remainder of the nineteenth century although weddings, christenings and burials still had to take place in the Anglican church of St Paul's across the road. Baptisms were allowed after 1867 and 59 were recorded to have taken place in Staverton's chapel between 1872 and 1983.

The building was badly in need of repair by 1884 and £65 was required to pay for the work. A local cloth worker, Samuel Chapman, was entrusted with the fund-raising and appeared to have had a little trouble completing the task aided by a donation of one sovereign from the Revd Guy Mark Pearse. The chapel continued to flourish in the first half of the twentieth century with a well supported Sunday School, run by chapel trustee and Sunday School superintendent Frederick James Usher, Bible classes and social activities including outings and entries in local carnivals and parades. Mr Usher died in 1945 and a specially designed pulpit was installed in the chapel in his memory in 1949. New trustees were appointed in 1948 and these included Mr and Mrs Fielding, Walt Ludlow, Kath and Norah Purnell and Wyn Matthews. Walter Ludlow became the chapel secretary, Bill Fielding carried out the duties of

chapel steward between 1945 and 1977, and Kath Purnell assisted by Betty Ludlow ran the chapel Sunday School until its closure.

A new organ was purchased in 1948 for £10 and organists in the mid 1900s were Norah Newbury, Jean Fielding and Betty Ludlow. Major repairs to the roof were carried out in 1979 at a cost of £1,775 when the chapel's principal preacher was the Revd John Murray. By the 1980s the Revd Noel Shepherd had taken over, but support for the chapel, and particularly the Sunday School, had considerably declined. The Sunday School finished in 1984 and the decision was reluctantly taken by the few remaining trustees to close the chapel the following year, the last service being conducted by the Revd Roy Wareing on 7 July 1985. Now redundant, the chapel was put up for sale and was purchased by Nestlé who later used it as a store for their factory archives. Staverton's Wesleyan Chapel had served the community for over 160 years but lack of support in the latter half of the twentieth century led to its demise and Methodism, which had enjoyed a considerable following in the previous century, finally came to an end in the village.

Top: *Staverton's Wesleyan Methodist Chapel built in 1824.*

Above: *The small gallery at the west end of the Methodist Chapel.*

Above left: *The Methodist Chapel sign indicating times of service.*

Left: *Chapel Sunday School, early 1900s.*

Below: *The Methodist Chapel Bible-study group, 1916.*

Below left: *Organists Betty Ludlow* (left), *Wyn Matthews* (centre) *and chapel steward Walter Ludlow outside the chapel in the 1950s.*

Staverton Methodist Chapel Tableaux 'Slings and Arrows', c.1920. Left to right, back row: Kate Purnell, Dora Lane, Dorothy Fralley, Grace Purnell, Lil Purnell, Frances Purnell, Florence Fralley, Elsie Lansdown, Meryan Watson, Gert Holloway, Gladys Stevens; front: *Ken Fryer, Lawrence Watson, Albert Purnell, Win Purnell, May Holloway, Gladys Fralley, Arthur Fralley* (lying down), *Vera Watson, Bill Purnell.*

CHAPTER SIX

VILLAGE EDUCATION & SCHOOLS

Many generations of Staverton children received no formal education until the middle of the nineteenth century when the first village school was founded. Prior to this, the only education available to working-class village youngsters was that being taught in the Sunday School by the local vicar and his helpers, and this, of course, was totally religion based. Most children received some form of basic education at home from their parents, who were themselves mainly uneducated. Families at this time were large and often very poor, as soon as children were deemed old enough, sometimes as young as six years old, they were sent out to work in order to help supplement the family income. Sons and daughters of the local gentry generally fared much better and were usually sent to private schools for their education; alternatively a governess was employed to teach the children at home. The cost of private school fees or a home tutor's salary was way beyond the financial means of most ordinary families. The children of the poorer families found employment in the weaving and cloth-making industries while many of the young girls in the village were put into service as maids and kitchen helpers in the large houses of the wealthier local families. From 1833, the year of the first Factory Act, the young children at work in the factory and weavers' cottages were subjected to annual scrutiny by government inspectors to ensure that they were not being exploited by the clothiers and mill owners. An account of such an inspection at Staverton mill in 1833 stated that the factory children 'were fit and healthy, well clothed and respectable' indicating a dramatic improvement from the scandalous abuse of child labour in the previous centuries.

In the early-nineteenth century there were growing concerns in Parliament and amongst Church leaders about the state of the nation's illiteracy, these highlighted the need to provide adequate schooling for the country's children and, in 1811, the Church of England set up the National Society for Promoting the Education of the Poor, this leading to the first elementary schools being founded. These first schools were provided using grants from the National Schools Society and had to be financially supported from the local parish rates, the generosity of the local clergy, and donations from wealthy businessmen and landowners. Parents who wanted their children to attend the newly opened schools also had to pay a small weekly fee of several pence per child. Initially, the new schools had no trained teachers and were usually run by the local vicar and his wife who enlisted the help of several of the educated ladies of the village. Few qualified teachers were available to run the schools until formal teacher training was introduced in the 1830s. By 1833 grants were being made annually by the National Schools Society and in 1839 diocesan inspectors were sent into each school to ensure that religious education formed the main part of the curriculum. From the 1840s onwards schools were subjected to two inspections per year, one by the Church authorities and the other by government inspectors whose task it was to ensure that the Education Act was being implemented and that standards were being maintained.

The first school in Staverton was founded in 1850 in a building adjacent to Wharf Cottage leased from the Kennet & Avon Canal Co. by Walter Newth who became one of the school managers. The building, now gone, was a converted canal warehouse, the outer wall of which followed the line of the present pavement alongside the cottage and up to the canal footbridge. The only trace left of this building is a stone window frame which can still be detected in the bridge abutment at the rear of Wharf Cottage. At first, the school had no permanent teacher and was run by the village vicar, Revd Prityman, and a group of voluntary helpers. The inspector's report of 1857 stated that the school had 50 pupils on the books but suffered from the fact that it only had a temporary mistress who was aided by two pupil teachers. Staverton's school managers responded quickly to these criticisms and Emily Hooper was engaged as the school's first permanent headmistress.

In those early days the schooling was of a very basic nature conducted in a small single-roomed building with rows of wooden benches in the middle and a few desks around the inside facing the walls.

The monitorial system, introduced by the National Schools Society, was the principal means of teaching and meant that some of the older pupils, usually the ten- and-eleven-year-olds, gave instructions to younger children under the scrutiny of the headmistress. Tuition revolved around the three Rs, reading, writing and arithmetic, with the addition of needlework for the girls, and was based on the standards system. The Bible was used for most of the teaching and pupils were taught to recite passages from it, learn the words of hymns and prayers and be fully conversant with the Catechism. Rewards were given for attendance and good work, and punishments dished out freely for lateness, bad behaviour and idleness which usually involved a child losing a mark, being shut in a closet, publicly washed if dirty and untidy, and standing in a corner wearing a fool's cap, the forerunner of the dunce's cap.

The problems caused by using untrained pupil teachers to instruct other children were soon recognised and, after 1846, the teachers had to pass an annual examination set by the school inspectors. In 1862 a new Education Act revised the standards system and children were examined annually by the inspectors with pupils being tested in standards one to six. School grants were given depending on the results of these examinations. A pupil over six could earn a grant of 4s. for attendance and 8s. for passing the tests, but lost 2s.8d. for every failure in reading, writing and arithmetic. Pupils under six years of age were exempt from examinations and earned a grant of 6s.6d. for the school if their attendance was good. The Revd Philip Maddock became the village vicar in 1860 and, with his wife, became very involved in the running of the school. By 1863 attendance at the school varied from between 46 and 76 and the headmistress, Emily Hooper, was being assisted by one of the older girls, Jane Hale. Schooling at this time was not compulsory and children did not attend for a number of reasons; the older girls were kept at home to help mothers with household chores and to look after their younger brothers and sisters, whilst the boys would help their fathers in the garden and on the land. Parents often removed their children from school before they were ten years old as they were useful wage earners and helped to supplement the meagre family income. Absences were particularly rife in the autumn when children were kept out of school to help out with the annual gleaning. Gleaning was the labour-intensive task of gathering in the harvest and the children were sent out into the fields to help pick vegetables, potatoes and fruit, and assist with bringing in the cereal crops. Heavy rain and snow decimated attendance at the school as few children had suitable footwear or coats to wear in severe storms. Many girls, and some boys, were taken out of school to be sent into service as maids, kitchen helpers and stable lads in the local large houses with 12 girls leaving Staverton School in 1863

Staverton's first school was situated on the canal wharf, 1850.

to go into service; one of these returned the following day for 'being too small to carry out the duties required'. Other children left to take up work in mills and workshops and, in addition to the 12 going into service, three more girls left the school that year to become apprentices at dressmaking.

Constant family migrations, as fathers looked for work, were also responsible for varying school numbers and in 1863 19 pupils moved away from the parish with their parents, many going to local towns where they hoped to find work in the woollen mills. Family hardships also took a toll and three pupils were sent to the union workhouse in Semington for relief when their mother died and their father was unable to look after them. Local events also affected the school attendance figures; annual fairs in neighbouring towns and villages kept many children from turning up for school as they were lured instead by the excitement of spending the day with family and friends. Although children were constantly leaving the school their places were soon filled and, when several ten- and-eleven-year-olds were admitted to the school in 1863, the headmistress expressed alarm that 'they could not even read or write the alphabet'.

The village vicar, Revd Maddock, visited the school almost daily taking the children in scripture lessons and hymn singing, while his wife attended several times a week to instruct the girls in needlework and to present the weekly rewards for good attendance. The pupils were taken to the church every Ascension Day and on several other festival days during the year. In the 1860s only one week of holiday was allowed in the summer and the school day started at half past nine in the morning and finished at four o'clock in the afternoon, one-and-a-half hours were allowed for lunch.

Four children were taken out of the school in 1864 to go into service, including the pupil teacher Jane Hale, several more moved away from the village with their families, one boy was dismissed for bad behaviour and one taken away by his worried mother who feared he might fall into the canal and drown. Attendances were badly affected for three days in March due to severe flooding around the village but once this subsided the numbers turning up for school dramatically increased to nearly 100 on some days. The inspector's report of 1864 was critical of the school's toilet arrangements, there being only one, and commented that 'this is very objectional arrangement' and 'no further grants would be made to the school unless separate offices with distinct entrances were provided for the two sexes.'

The inspector's report for 1865 was also critical, this time of overcrowding, and ordered that the school must be enlarged or attendance reduced to the required limit. Attendances varied wildly with only nine turning up on one day in January due to heavy snowfalls, and as many as 96 on one day in May. Numbers dropped dramatically again in October and November 1865 when a measles epidemic swept through the parish and as many as 42 pupils were away with the illness at one stage. The annual summer break was increased to two weeks in 1865, to three weeks in 1867, and pupils were now allowed to take a week's holiday at Christmas.

In 1867 the government inspectors were unhappy about the lack of space in the school and complained bitterly that 'the numbers exceed Article 51/A of the Education Code, on scholastic and sanitary grounds.' This stated 'that each child should be entitled to 80 cubic feet of space.' The school managers were again ordered to increase the space available or reduce pupil numbers and the report concluded that no grant would be given for five pupils who had failed their examinations. Now forced to act, the managers had the school enlarged in August 1868, to the satisfaction of the inspectors who reported that the establishment was 'satisfactorily conducted and the accommodation was now sufficient.'

Headmistress Emily Hooper was now being assisted by two pupil monitors, Mary Hale and Ellen Hudd, and the school witnessed a revolution in child health care in September of that year when all the pupils were vaccinated against smallpox by Dr Taylor. New inspection methods were introduced from 1871 when grants could be awarded for extra subjects such as geography and history, and pupils could earn an additional 3s. grant for passing tests in these new categories. Some confusion, however, was noted in the annual inspection for that year, the report concluding that 'arithmetic is very weak in the lower standards, the mistress not realising that long division was required in Standard 2.'

Ellen Hudd, who had been acting as one of the pupil teachers over the last three years, left the school in June and her place was taken by another of the older girls, Emma Chapman. Walter Newth, the original founder of the village school, and one of its longest-standing managers, died in November 1874 and all of the pupils were taken to St Paul's Church for his funeral service. He had been foremost in nursing the school through its early stages, financing much of it at his own expense, and had been a very familiar figure to staff and pupils through his frequent visits. After the trials and tribulations of the first 25 years the school was beginning to settle into a well-run and orderly establishment, this being evident from the inspector's report of 1875 which noted that 'the school is going on well and the managers may feel satisfied with the work that is being done.'

The examining methods were changed again that year, the awarding of annual grants being based on class achievements rather than individual results. Revd Maddock and his wife continued to attend the school regularly and every May invited the pupils to a treat in the vicarage where each was given a drink and a sticky bun. Pupil monitor Emma Chapman continued to assist Miss Hooper and passed the required examination which allowed her to retain her position. The inspector's report of 1876 noted that more desks were needed and the following year complained that reading and arithmetic was weak in all standards. Emily Hooper, the headmistress, resigned in 1878 after more than 20 years of faithful service and was replaced by Elizabeth Leaver who took over the 65 pupils now on the roll and appointed a new pupil monitor, Annie Dallimore, in September. As in past decades, attendance was still a problem for many pupils with the annual gleaning still taking place in the autumn. Boys were leaving school under age to take up jobs and there was the annual exodus of families moving away from the parish, some emigrating to Australia, New Zealand and America. Numbers attending were greatly reduced again in October 1878 when a measles and whooping cough epidemic swept through the village affecting many of the pupils, the attendance situation being further compounded when 12 children were forced to leave the school when it was discovered that they came from the parish of Hilperton and should not have been admitted in the first place.

Military activities had always been a great

attraction to young boys through the ages and the Staverton lads were no exception, most of them staying away from school on 13 December because they had spotted soldiers exercising in the neighbourhood, and spent the day following their movements. The African wars were being fought at the time and the local regiments were being mobilised and sent abroad to support the British Army's campaign in South Africa. These absentees received punishments on their return and one boy was threatened with expulsion by Revd Maddock because it wasn't the first time he had absconded from school. School fees were increased in 1879 and parents were now expected to pay 2d. per week for their oldest child and 1d. a week each for the rest of their children who attended school. Annual rewards were given to pupils every July by Mrs Perkins-Clark and all the children were invited to Wyke House for a treat which consisted of quite a lavish tea party and games on the lawn. Ventilation in the school was criticised in the inspector's report of 1879 which noted that 'the smoky, dark interior made reading very difficult.'

The old school building on the canal had become totally inadequate and pressures from the inspectors forced the managers to resolve the situation with the provision of better accommodation. A new schoolhouse would have to be found and plans were made in 1880 to provide one. Grants were obtained from the National Schools Society, a piece of land purchased from Dr Samuel Keddle, the largest village landowner in the nineteenth century, and builders engaged to construct the new building. The new school would be erected on a narrow strip of land between the railway and the lane which ran from the main road and across the fields to Ladydown, this rough track becoming School Lane after 1880. Work on the purpose-built, two-roomed schoolhouse, constructed by George Smith, was commenced in May 1880 and Mrs Perkins-Clark, the Lady of Wyke House, was invited to lay the foundation stone. Meanwhile, schooling continued in the cramped, unsuitable warehouse building on the canal and Annie Dallimore took on the role of pupil teacher when Emma Chapman left in April.

Poorer families found it difficult to meet the demands of the new fees, introduced the previous year, and their children were occasionally barred from lessons because they hadn't brought their pence. New writing slates were purchased in the summer of 1880 and Mrs Perkins-Clark again presented the annual rewards for attendance and needlework, and hosted the yearly treat for pupils at Wyke House.

Staverton's new school opened on 18 October 1880 and, at last, the infants could be segregated from the older pupils and taught in the smaller of the two rooms. Pupils and staff soon settled into their new accommodation, Rebecca Purnell was appointed a pupil monitor and, at the year's end, another measles epidemic affected half the pupils attending the school. Heavy snowfalls closed the school for several weeks in January 1881 and, due to the long period the pupils were away, extra schooling was arranged for three Saturdays in February. School attendance had now become compulsory and eduction officers regularly checked the registers and sent warnings to parents whose children consistently failed to turn up. The first school group photograph was taken in July and, later in the year, concerns were expressed for the pupils' health when a smallpox epidemic broke out in the village causing a number of deaths amongst some older residents. Annie Dallimore failed her annual examination and the inspectors warned the managers that if she failed again the school grant would be reduced.

The curriculum was changed again in 1882 when a standard seven was introduced and in future the level of grant would depend on the pupil's rating of 'fair, good or excellent'. The constant exodus of pupils continued with Rebecca Purnell leaving in February to be replaced by Ethel Stinchcombe on a trial basis. Elizabeth Leaver, the school's headmistress since 1878, was taken ill in April and the managers were told by her doctor that she needed a long period of rest and relaxation. Unable to return until July, her position was covered alternately by Miss H. Leaver and Miss Trim, and the unqualified Annie Dallimore, who had been under notice to leave since March, finally departed in September to be replaced by new pupil monitor Kate Taylor.

Although attendance was now compulsory, many of the older pupils still stayed away in the autumn to help with the annual gleaning and some children were still refused admittance because their parents were unable to pay the weekly fees. Elizabeth Leaver's continued illness and long periods of absence meant her eventual replacement and Laura Barnes took over as the new mistress in March 1883. She quickly asserted her authority by 'severely punishing' 13 boys for skipping school to follow a steam tractor all the way from Staverton to Mr Candy's farm at Bradford Leigh. The pupils' annual treat in July included a barge trip down the canal, as well as the usual tea party laid on by the Clarks at Wyke House. By the end of the year pupil teachers Kate Taylor and Ethel Stinchcombe had left the school and Florence Hannum had been appointed a pupil monitor to help teach the infants. The Revd Maddock gave the pupils a rare treat in January 1884 when he presented a magic lantern show in the schoolroom. The year's annual illness season came in July when attendances were again decimated, this time by a chicken-pox epidemic. Local fairs, markets and other social events were still great attractions for local children, the managers eventually recognising this fact by giving the school a day off in August so that pupils could attend the Trowbridge Flower Show.

Another school milestone was passed in 1886

Left: *The new village school opened in 1880.*

Below: *Staverton pupils in front of the school, 1917.*

Left: *Maria Purnell, Staverton School infants teacher, at the turn of the twentieth century.*

Above: *Alphabet needlework made by pupil Florence Barnett in the 1890s.*

when the older pupils, who up until this point had been using slates and chalk, commenced writing in books. Slates and sand trays were still retained for the younger groups. Compulsory attendance had increased the pupil numbers over the last few years and by 1887 the infants' class was overcrowded with 37 children occupying the small room in the school, a space intended to cater for 22. The inspector's report of that year commented 'the number in this room must be reduced or the annual grant may be endangered under Section 96/A of the Education Code.'

Revd Maddock, the village vicar and a great champion of the school for 29 years, died in 1889 and the Revd Henry Theodore Cavell became the new village preacher. Florence Hannum, who had been appointed assistant mistress only the previous year, left the school in June and Maria Purnell, who had recently qualified as a pupil teacher, took her place. Whooping cough swept through the school in early 1890 and had reached epidemic proportions by February with many pupils being affected by this very distressing and, in some cases, life-threatening illness. This epidemic had subsided sufficiently by the summer for the pupils to enjoy another barge trip to Dundas, organised by Major and Mrs Clark, and to attend the wedding of the vicar's daughter, Katherine Cavell, who had often helped out with teaching at the school. School fees were abolished in 1891 and the less wealthy parents now had no excuses to keep their children from being educated. Teaching amenities were improved in 1891 with the purchase of 56 new desks, the mistress reporting that all pupils now had a desk space. An extra day's holiday was given in July so that pupils could visit a circus in Trowbridge and in September many of Staverton's schoolchildren attended a Sunday School tea party which was laid on in the newly opened St Mary's Church Hall in Horse Lane, Hilperton Marsh.

School numbers dropped dramatically in 1892 when many families were forced to move away from the village to seek employment after the closure of Staverton's cloth factory at the end of 1891. The factory had been a major employer in the village and

local cloth workers and weaving families, who suddenly found themselves unemployed, had little choice but to move out of the neighbourhood to seek new work. The annual inspection of that year did not go too well either with the examiners reporting that the children were backward in arithmetic; grammar was only fair and geography knowledge 'not sufficient to receive a grant'.

To add to the problems another whooping-cough epidemic swept through the school in November seriously disrupting the already pressurised teaching schedule. School leaving age was raised to 11 in 1893 but due to the mass exodus from the village the previous year this did not significantly increase the numbers of pupils on the registers which were recorded as only 48. The doom and gloom of the previous two years was somewhat lifted in July when pupils were given two days extra holiday to mark the occasion of the royal marriage of the future King George V, the festivities including a huge tea party in Trowbridge for local schoolchildren. Laura Barnes continued to make her mark as headmistress, ably assisted by Maria Purnell, who taught the infants, and a good report on religious knowledge was received from the annual diocesan inspection. Several new children started in 1894 increasing the pupil numbers to 54 and prompting the inspectors to report that 'the classroom is not big enough and may have to be enlarged'. Their report also complained that 'the playground was muddy and one seat in the boy's office was found to be dirty'.

Maria Purnell, the infants' teacher for the previous eight years, left the school in January 1896 to take up a similar position at St Thomas' School and Lily Purnell was appointed to replace her as a pupil teacher. The annual diocesan report, normally good, was critical this time saying that 'the infants did poorly and that improvements in teaching are needed before better results can be achieved.'

Reading, writing and arithmetic, plus needlework for girls and drawing for older boys, became obligatory subjects under the teaching regulations introduced at the end of 1896 and object lessons were being taught in the lower standards. The year 1897 turned out to be a memorable one for the school in a number of ways starting with the sad news that Major Clark, of Wyke House, who with his wife had taken a great interest in the school and had hosted the annual treats for years, died in February. The inspector's

School pupils with Governess Barnes (black dress) *and teachers Amelia Hayes* (left) *and Maria Purnell* (right), *early 1900s.*

Left: *Staverton School pupils, 1915.*

report was critical of the teaching stating that 'an older teacher must be got for the infants as the probationer is not capable of teaching them.'

School managers, worried by the recent poor performances and concerned about the falling standards, especially in the infants' class, persuaded Maria Purnell, who had left 18 months previously, to return to Staverton as the infants' teacher. The village vicar, Revd Theodore Cavell, who regularly taught scripture at the school, was taken ill in May and sadly died whilst convalescing at Weymouth in June. He was buried at St Paul's on 28 June and the whole school, shocked by the sudden loss of one of their regular helpers, attended the funeral service. Just a week before this tragic event the pupils had been given three days extra holiday to join in the Jubilee celebrations of Queen Victoria's 60 years on the throne, and another casual holiday was given in July for children to attend the Hilperton Methodist Band of Hope annual treat.

Lily Purnell, who had found her two years as pupil teacher very difficult, left the school in February 1898 although a marked improvement had been noted since the re-engagement of Maria Purnell, this being reflected in the annual inspector's report, which stated that 'the infants are in good order and have made good progress although care must be taken to prevent overcrowding in their small room.'

Revd Stuart Ridley became the new village vicar in 1898 and, as had been the case with his predecessors, he visited the school regularly to take the pupils in religious instruction. The school leaving age was increased to 12 in 1899 and the 60 pupils now on the registers were being given four weeks' holiday in the summer months. Good progress continued with the infants who were being 'creditably taught' although overcrowding had again become an issue with the inspectors complaining that 'the room must be enlarged and provided with a cloakroom and blinds.' On 28 June 1899 pupils were given a day's holiday for Queen Victoria's Diamond Jubilee

celebrations but the usual autumn day off to attend the circus in Trowbridge was no longer given although many pupils still absented themselves on that day to go and watch the show.

Local education authorities were set up in 1900 and the school received its first grant of £10 from them, half to increase the teachers' salaries and half to provide the much needed cloakroom which was constructed in May. The Board of Education grant was increased to £14 in 1901, some of it again to increase the teachers' salaries, the rest to purchase new books, and Mabel Gibbs was appointed a pupil monitor to assist in the infants' class. Everybody was given a special day's holiday on 30 April to celebrate the victory in Africa and the whole village flocked into Trowbridge to welcome back the Wilts Regiment Volunteers who had fought so heroically in the Boer Wars. Peace was finally declared in June 1902 and this was celebrated with another day's holiday. Earlier that year Florence Pollard had become a pupil monitor and the inspector's report again noted that the infants were making good progress although reading, geography and arithmetic needed attention in the middle standards. The diocesan inspection complained that the hymn singing was poor but religious knowledge was generally good, and an aid grant of £15 was awarded by the Education Board to maintain salaries of the teachers who now had 65 pupils to look after. Good reports were received in 1903, the government official noting 'an improvement over the previous year with history and geography satisfactory, drawing good, and the infants well advanced.'

A new departure from past annual treats came in July 1903 when the older pupils were taken by train on a day-trip to Weymouth, and interest in nature was stimulated in September when the Revd Ridley, a great collector, displayed his large collection of coral and shells in the classrooms to help expand the pupils' knowledge of natural history.

From 1904 pupils were expected to stay at school until they were 14 but this ruling had not yet been made compulsory. However, any pupils wishing to leave before this age, to take up work, had to sit an exam for a Labour Certificate, and two Staverton pupils passed the test in March. Slates, which had been the school's primary writing medium since its foundation in 1850, were finally dispensed with in October when the infants were given exercise books and encouraged to write with lead pencils. By now, local authorities were becoming more involved with the control of education and the health of pupils and by 1904 had started sending doctors into schools to

Left: Staverton School concert, Christmas, 1918. Left to right, back row: Mabel Vezey, Olive Wiltshire, Alice Purnell, Christopher Fryer, Annie Pearce; seated: Doris Hallett, Edith Purnell, Violet Hayward; front: Jessica Purnell, Florence Taylor.

Right: *Staverton School play, 1922. Left to right, back row: Arthur Matthews, Louis Purnell, Stan Milsom, Bill Purnell, Jack Purnell, Bert Matthews; third row: May Angell, Kath Wells, Louisa Taylor, Dorothy Goodson, Violet Escott, Emily Milsom, Jack Beaven; second row: William Escott, ?, Gertie Brown, Rene Milsom, Eric Price, Vic Taylor; front: Dorothy Matthews, Dora Phelps, Zena Watson, Daisy Hayward, Violet Brown.*

Above: *Staverton schoolteachers Amelia Hayes (right) and Maria Purnell, c.1916.*

Right: *Staverton School performing a maypole dance on the lawns of Wyke House, c.1916.*

examine the children. Dr Ewing visited Staverton School in November, for the first time, in what turned out to be the forerunner of the school's annual medical inspection. Laura Barnes and Maria Purnell, the two mistresses, received great praise in the annual inspection of 1905, the report going on to say that 'the children are in good order, the teachers have worked zealously and carefully and the infants are well advanced.'

The Local Education Board made money available for several improvements in the school including the complete replacement of the woodblock floor in the main classroom. Parliament passed the Provision of School Meals Act in 1906 which allowed local authorities to provide a meals service, although at this stage it was not compulsory and it was some years in the future before Staverton School was able to serve dinners to pupils. The Revd Albert Isherwood became the new village vicar at the start of the year and a supply teacher, Maud Sartain, was taken on temporarily in July to work on alternate weeks with the infants. Further government legislation in 1907 made school medical examinations compulsory and introduced the free-place system which allowed some pupils to attend local secondary schools. Florence Pollard, the pupil monitor, left the school in May and Miss Sartain was appointed full time to increase the teaching staff at

Doris Hallett in the school concert, 1922.

the school. The year came to an end with several cases of diphtheria reported amongst pupils, and a few of the older children gained their Labour Certificates and left to start jobs.

The introduction of compulsory medicals in 1907 prompted a bout of feverish activity by the Local Education Board and the school received two doctor's visits in 1909, the examinations including the weighing and measuring of each pupil. Scales for this exercise were sent around from school to school in those days, Staverton usually sharing with Holt and Broughton Gifford schools. Maud Sartain, one of the infants' teachers, who had been at the school for three years, left at the end of March and was immediately replaced by Amelia Hayes in early April. The recent emphasis on improving primary education, since the formation of LEAs, led to more ideas, one being the provision of books on loan from the County Library from which Staverton received its first delivery of 60 in May 1910. After a period of time, these would be exchanged for books on loan to other local schools. Good reports were received from the annual inspections in 1910 which enthused that 'the school was doing well and the infants excellent', but complaints were also made about the bad state of the playground which was 'full of potholes which were constantly filled with water'.

Staverton School, infants' class, 1940, with teacher Miss Pullen. Left to right, back row: ?, *Margaret Selman, Bert Gay,* ?, *Ann Stevens,* ?, *Peter Woodman, Ron Thickett,* ?, *Maureen Rose;* centre: ?, ?; front: *Heather Smith, Norma Brown, Barbara Bridger,* ?, *Myra Hughes,* ?, *George Gay, Mary Hallett,* ?, ?, *George Buckland, Neil Hallett.*

Many school days were lost in early 1912, initially due to very severe storms which completely flooded Marsh Road preventing many Hilperton Marsh pupils getting to the village, and most of February was lost when a serious outbreak of mumps incapacitated 32 of the children and doctors ordered that school be closed for a month. Music was a subject now being regularly taught in the school and this was greatly enhanced with the gift of a piano from Lord Fitzmaurice, of Bradford-on-Avon, in January 1914. The new instrument was an enormous benefit to Miss Hayes, herself a skilled musician who competed annually in the Wiltshire Music Festival, and who could now teach the older pupils how to play the piano and also give a musical accompaniment to the children's singing. New desks arrived for the infants' class in October but the inspector's report for that year was very critical of the building saying 'although the newly asphalted playground was good, the interior was very untidy and better toilet facilities were needed.' At the time the school only had bucket toilets in a primitive wash-house which had a rainwater tank and large boiler overhead fuelled from a grating beneath it. There were three bucket toilets for the girls and three for the boys which were emptied and cleaned daily. Drinking water was obtained from a tap on the outside wall which had a battered enamel mug chained to it and more often than not was frozen up in the winter. The bigger of the two classrooms was divided by a flimsy red curtain with the 12- to 14-year-olds in one half and the 6- to 12-year-olds in the other. Each contained a blackboard and long desks with no backs and ink wells set into them which had to be shared one between two. The Ten Commandments and 'My Duty to God', were framed on the wall and each end of the room displayed a picture of the monarch, King Edward VII, and the teachers sat at desks on raised platforms, one in each half of the divided room.

The classrooms were heated by big coke-fuelled tortoise stoves which were so temperamental that the teachers had to constantly battle to keep them working. Pupils were taught to read from sheets of words draped over a stand and the infants used sand trays and a rounded stick to practise their writing before receiving slates and slate pencils in the early 1900s. The pupils were summoned to school by the ringing of a bell which was housed in a bell cote on the roof and operated by a long piece of rope. The small playground had a large acacia tree in one corner. The schoolmistress in the early 1900s was known to everyone as Governess Barnes, her daily attire was a tight tweed bodice, long skirt with large buttons and fancy braiding, and she walked to school from her home in Trowbridge. Maria Purnell, the infants' teacher, was the organist at St Paul's and coached the church choir. She also taught the pupils how to maypole dance, something they would perform at village fêtes and other events in neighbouring towns.

Left: *School concert, 1922. Left to right, back row: Edith Escott, Edith Purnell, Louisa Taylor, Dorothy Goodson; front: Doris Hallett, Kath Wells.*

Below: *Some of the evacuee children who were sent to Staverton during the Second World War.*

The school medical services were further improved in 1915 when nurses began to visit and examine the pupils. Nurse Webb attended in October of that year and Nurse Nixon on three occasions in 1916. Wartime conditions had not affected schooling very much up until this point but began to have an influence in the middle of the year when the school was closed for three weeks so that all children could help with the haymaking to support the war effort. The pupils' euphoria at getting additional time off was, however, very short-lived as the Education Board remedied the loss of valuable schooling time by reducing the annual summer break to three weeks. The following year, besides helping with the harvest and haymaking, pupils were also given a day off in October to go blackberrying for the soldiers fighting in the trenches. Earlier in the year a severe measles epidemic, which affected a large number of the 87 pupils between May and June, caused another four weeks of school closure. Staverton pupils and teachers were able to witness an historic event on 9 November 1917 when they joined thousands of local people in welcoming the King and Queen on a wartime visit to Trowbridge.

Amelia Hayes, the infants' teacher for the past eight years, left the school in November and was replaced in March 1918 by Gladys Barnes, a supplementary teacher. Blackberry picking took place

Staverton School pupils, 1949.
Left to right, back row: *Jean Watkinson, Ruth Morris, Marian Osborne, Jill Stevens, Maureen Walton, Maureen Newbury, Jean Bailey;* third row: *Marian Rawlings, Valerie Morgan, Brian Scrine, Adrian Durham, Michael Osborne, Malcolm Fido, John Woodman, Ray Hinton, Mike Tucker, Marian Newbury Janet Buckland;* second row: *Ray Lovell, Jenny Bailey, Gillian Maunder, Cynthia Morgan, Marilyn Thickett, Marion Jacobs, Margaret Curtis, Maureen Jacobs, Richard Matthews;* front: *Tommy Brown, Wendy Newbury, Sheila Hinton, Sandra Bailey, Marilyn Escott, Wendy Gay, Valerie Malyn, Norma Rawlings, David Newbury.*

Left: *School play, 1949.* Left to right, back row: *Pauline Thickett, Janet Rose, Rosemary Cleary, June Rawlings, Jill Stevens, Glenda Hallett, Maureen Newbury;* front: *Ruth Morris, Marian Osborne.*

Below: *Don Burch* (left) *and Pete Lavis looking at the exhibits in the school's centenary history exhibition, 1980.*

School concert, 1945. Pictured are: *Gerald Parsons, Norma Brown, Marilyn Thickett, Ann Stevens, Barbara Bridger, Janet Rose, Ron Thickett, Pauline Thickett, Grace Bridger, Doug Smith, Alan Osborne, David Bath, Maureen Rose, Margaret Selman, Shirley Tadd, Neil Hallett, John Bridger, Michael Tucker, Rose Cleary, Rita Newbury, Geraldine Morgan, Bob Beaven, Pauline Escott, Peter Woodman, Brian Bailey, Mike Escott, Marian Osborne, Myra Hughes, Christine Morgan, Marian Jacobs, Glenda Hallett, Heather Smith, Maureen Jacobs, Mary Hallett, Ray Hinton, John Woodman.*

again in that year, this time on two separate days in September and October. School medical services expanded further with an annual dental inspection and more frequent visits from the school nurse. This extra attention, however, did not prevent the annual bout of illness which came in November. The school was closed for two weeks and 35 children were put in their sick beds suffering from influenza. By the end of the war, the school leaving age of 14, first proposed in 1914, was made compulsory. In the 14-year period prior to the enforcement of this legislation, 40 per cent of all Staverton pupils left education before attaining this age. Peace was declared in 1918 and an extra week of holiday was given in October to celebrate the victory. A community tea party was enjoyed by villagers and every school pupil was presented with a commemorative medal. With the war over, the school returned to a normal routine, 75 children were being taught there at the beginning of 1920. Laura Barnes, the headmistress since 1883, retired in March after 37 years of faithful and dedicated service and Elizabeth Thomas took over as temporary head for two months until Elizabeth Mills, the new replacement, commenced her duties at the end of May. Miss Dix had been appointed to look after standards one and three in March, and school manager Donald Rogers, also manager of the Nestlé factory, was invited to present the annual awards. An extra prize of a watch, chain and badge of honour was introduced in April, presented by Donald Rogers, to be awarded to the pupil who was 'most respectful, honourable and upright'; the first proud winner was young Stanley Bath. New plans for physical training in schools were being introduced by 1922 and, in March, Miss Walmesley, the local PT organiser, visited the school to discuss the current fitness methods with the teachers.

Pupils numbered 66 in 1922 but this figure began to drop steadily over the next few years. Miss Dix left in September, after only a short stay, and Miss Underwood was engaged to replace her. Fairly good reports were received from both LEA and diocesan inspectors in 1923, the former stating that 'discipline was much improved' and the latter adding that it was a 'well conducted school with a very good tone'. Free scholarship places were introduced in the Education Act of 1907 and local authorities began to build secondary schools in the early 1900s. Staverton pupils benefited from this new arrangement with one student being awarded a free place at Bradford-on-Avon Secondary School in July 1924.

The emphasis on sports in schools had been growing steadily over the previous few years and in May 1926, for the first time, Staverton had several competitors in the area sports. The next year 17 pupils took part and the school was closed for a day in June so that everybody could go and support the County Sports. A number of pupils gained free scholarships to the Trowbridge High Schools in 1927

and nine Staverton girls attended the newly formed domestic science course, held for four weeks at the Hilperton Institute. Earlier that year the health authorities arranged for several of the Staverton pupils to receive free cod-liver oil, Nurse Gibbs attended regularly and Dr Semple carried out two medical inspections.

The school bell, which was used to announce the daily start and finish times, broke in February and teachers had to use a whistle until it was eventually repaired in July. School numbers continued to fall and by 1929 the registers contained only 48 names. Dental and medical inspections were carried out in the reading rooms and the troublesome stove, used to heat the infants' class, was replaced with a new one in 1930. Pupil numbers dropped lower and lower and by the end of 1931 there were only 32 children being taught at the school. It was this year that the older pupils were automatically sent to secondary school in Trowbridge, nine left in July, two to attend the Boys' High School, and the rest to Adcroft Senior School. Elizabeth Mills, the headmistress, was taken ill in June and Doris Marriott, a supply head, came to take charge of the school in her absence. Four weeks later Miss Mills, who had recently undergone a serious operation, died in Salisbury Hospital and the whole community mourned the sad loss of the lady who had taught the village children since 1920. Mrs Marriott was appointed permanent headmistress in 1932 and, in June, new dual desks replaced the long desks which had been in use for many years. From 1933 Dr Jean Murray started visiting the school to carry out medical examinations and concerns were raised about the safety of the coke stove in the main classroom which, it was later realised, was in danger of gassing all the pupils. The defective heater was repaired over the Christmas period and 1934 was able to start in a much more pleasant atmosphere. The inspector's report for that year was complimentary and commented that:

...very good work has been done in this junior school since it came under the direction of a new head in June 1931. The infants' class is a happy one and the children are receiving careful and effective training. There has been a marked improvement in the whole school with good progress being made in P.E., games and music.

Despite the good reports, however, numbers of pupils attending the school were still dropping and reached their lowest level in 1935 when there were only 30 names on the registers. Silver Jubilee celebrations for King George V took place in May with pupils attending a tea party and receiving souvenir medals from Phylis Blease and the Revd Isherwood. Nurse Gibbs examined the pupils' hair on eight occasions during the year and happily reported that

Left: *Staverton School soccer team, 1978. Left to right, back row: Jonathon Francis, Mike Lavis, Stuart Mercer, Andrew Sims, Dave Clark, Gareth Francis, Matthew Noble, Ian King; front: Jonathan Evans, Paul Vowles, John Clark, Ian Coates, Mark Jones.*

Right: *Staverton School netball team, 1978. Left to right, back row: Julie Suggett, Jenny Palmer, Karen Smith, Andrea King, Claire Davis, Ruth Garby; front: Vanessa Austin, Georgina Hodgson, Tracey Blake, Isabel Langley.*

Staverton School support staff, 1970s. Left to right, back row: Eileen Gamble, Gillian Horobin, Miss King; front: Pauline Hodgson, Jacky Stanley, Sylvia Brown.

Staverton School staff, 1970s. Left to right, back row: Mavis Smith, Valerie Sims, Sue Woodman (secretary); front: Doris Hallett (caretaker), Alice Moody (head), Elaine Darlington.

Right: School group, 1982, with Eileen Gamble (left) *and headmistress Alice Moody* (right).

Left: Miss Sims' class in their Victorian costumes to celebrate the school's centenary, 1980.

Right: Miss Smith's class, 1980.

Below: Mrs Moody's class, 1980.

Right: *The Staverton School team who won the Wilts. Youth Drama Festival held at Wharf Theatre, Devizes, in July 1985.* Left to right, back: *Caroline Pittard, David Collins;* centre: *Sarah White;* front: *Jonathon Stuart, Mark Sheppard.*

heads were clean. Teeth were also being examined carefully and 26 of the 30 pupils had to receive dental treatment in March 1936. The Horlicks Malted Milk Co. presented the school with a gas ring in July and this was duly fixed up in the main classroom to dispense hot drinks to the pupils. In September 1937 Revd Isherwood died; he had been Staverton's vicar for 31 years and was a great supporter of the school. His daughter presented the school with a framed portrait of him which was hung in the main classroom.

There were two more three-week closures in November 1937 and March 1938, the first due to a chicken-pox epidemic, and the second a measles infection affecting 18 of the 30 pupils. The whole school was also given a one-day holiday to attend the Bath and West Wilts. Show. As a result of a medical inspection in May that year, seven pupils were being given free Horlicks to boost their strength. Gladys Barnes, the infants' teacher for 20 years, sadly passed away in July 1938 and after the five-week summer holidays Miss Pullen took over the vacant position.

In early 1939, with the Second World War imminent, an air-raid shelter was hastily constructed in the field behind the school, all children were fitted with gas masks and in May there were practice evacuations. Headmistress Doris Marriott left in September to take up a similar post at Steeple Ashton School and Mrs Downing took over as the new head at Staverton. The war was now raging and the threat of air attack on Britain's major cities was great. Staverton took in its quota of evacuees in June 1940 and saw 38 children arrive under the charge of Miss Bastin. Due to the lack of space in the school, 28 of the evacuees had to be taught in the reading rooms just over the road.

In November the pupils were taken to the cinema in Trowbridge to see *Pinocchio* and, due to the wartime continuation of summertime and muslin on the classroom windows, the school start time was delayed until 9.45a.m. Food production was now vital to the war effort and the school received a directive in early 1941 that any waste ground around the building must be cultivated. Further outbreaks of whooping cough took a hold on the children in January and the school had to be closed for four weeks. Immunisation against diphtheria was administered to all pupils, once at the end of the year and again in January 1942. The school had to be closed for a short period in February as wartime shortages meant that there was not enough fuel for heating. The annual trip to the cinema took place in March, this time to see the film *Fantasia*. Food production requirements took priority in September when the school was shut for three weeks so that pupils could help with potato picking. Miss Beames took over as the infants' teacher in March 1943 when Miss Pullen left to take up a position at Marshfield School. Potato harvesting took place again in October forcing a two-week school closure, and an outbreak of impetigo in

November kept a number of children away from their lessons. *Snow White* was the cinema treat for pupils in July 1944 and an extra half day's holiday was granted in August to reward everyone for helping to exceed the target for the 'Salute the Soldier' fund-raising effort.

School facilities were vastly improved at the start of 1945 when electric lighting was installed. The new energy source had been brought into Staverton in 1938 but the installations had been delayed by the war. Prior to 1945 the school relied on gas lighting and before 1880, the year the Victorian schoolhouse was built, candles and oil lamps provided the only source of illumination. The war in Europe ended in May 1945, the nation rejoiced at the victory, the school was given two days off to celebrate VE Day and pupils were taken to the cinema in Trowbridge to watch the film *Henry V* being screened. The following year the village set up a memorial fund and many social events were organised to raise money, including a fête at Wyke House in August. The number of children attending the school dropped after the war; by 1947 there were 48 on the registers. Princess Elizabeth's wedding was celebrated with an extra day's holiday on 20 November 1947 and the following June the pupils were taken on their first school pantomime trip to Bath. The Nestlé factory in the village had been heavily involved in the Australian Food Parcels Scheme at the end of the war and on 5 March 1948 received a visit from the Duchess of Gloucester, who was a patron of the scheme. All the pupils from the village school were taken down to the factory to welcome the royal visitor who stopped and chatted to some of them as she toured the plant. April started with a mumps epidemic which affected half of the pupils but had cleared sufficiently by the end of the month to allow them to visit Tucker's Farm in Holt to watch the cows being milked and other farm tasks. Miss Beames, the infants' teacher for six years, was married in April to become Mrs Yandall, and the new school nurse, Mrs Radnedge, became a familiar figure as she visited regularly for health inspections right up until the late 1960s.

The 1945 Education Act paved the way for school meals and free milk, the first meals being served at Staverton in 1950 from a newly installed kitchen on the railway side of the main classroom. Other major changes came as a result of the Act and the school was taken over by the LEA in 1950. It became a Voluntary Controlled School meaning that the LEA would now meet all its running costs. Continuing world tension and the UK's involvement in the Korean War led to increased military activity in the area in 1951 and the school was closed for two weeks in October due to Army manoeuvres nearby. George VI died in 1952, Elizabeth II came to the throne, and her coronation in 1953 was celebrated with a day's holiday, a children's tea party, sports events and a commemorative mug for each pupil.

VE celebrations on the school playground, 1995.

The next few years of the school's history were fairly uneventful apart from frequent requests from the school managers to have proper flushing toilets installed in the building. Mr and Mrs Charlie Lovell became the school caretakers in 1955 and another measles epidemic affected most of the children in 1957. The older pupils were taken on an educational trip to watch the *Wiltshire Times* being printed in 1958. Mrs Downing, headmistress for 20 years, retired in December 1959 and Alice Moody filled the position in April 1960. Classroom heating was improved in 1960 with the fitting of a new gas convector heater, an electric water heater was installed over the sinks in the large room, and the long awaited flushing toilets finally arrived in September.

School numbers had dropped to their lowest level on record in 1961 with only 24 pupils being registered, but increased slightly to 29 when the new pupils arrived after the summer holidays. The first competitive sports matches took place in 1962 when a school team played a rounders match against Hilperton School, and in June five of the older pupils took part in the annual Primary Schools' Choir Service at Salisbury Cathedral. Increasing traffic volumes through the village in the 1960s began to cause concern about the children's safety and in January 1963 Walt Ludlow was appointed as the first school lollipop man to help pupils across the busy and very hazardous B3105. Badly needed repairs and refurbishments took place in 1964 with the kitchen being modernised, the toilets redecorated, and heaters installed in the outside toilet blocks to help prevent the annual freeze-ups. Further work was carried out during the summer holidays with the classrooms and lobbies being redecorated, the main classroom floor repaired, the ceiling lowered, and the infants' room floor renewed. A two-acre field at the rear of the school building was purchased from the Blease family and converted into a long awaited school sports field which was ready for use by 1965. Quite a number of new children had been admitted over the past two years and pupil numbers had increased to 38 by 1965; 16 of these were infants and, due to the smallness of their classroom, overcrowding again became a serious issue. The problem was further compounded the following year when pupil numbers jumped to 50 and teachers reported that the infants' class was 'too crowded for comfort'. Urgent requests for more accommodation were finally heeded by the LEA in 1967 when a Pratten classroom was delivered and erected within two weeks in January. There were now 61 pupils in the school and the subsequent overcrowding was eased when the infants moved into the new portable. Heating in the new Pratten failed to work initially and Mrs Yandall had to come to the rescue by providing a temporary electric heater from her home. She retired in mid 1967 after 24 years as the infant teacher and staff, past and present pupils, managers and parents assembled to present retirement gifts and bid a fond farewell to a much-loved and respected figure who had done so much for the eduction of village children in the post-war years. Mavis Smith took over the infants' class in September, Mrs Ashton arrived as a temporary teacher the following May, and teaching was greatly enhanced in September 1968 with the acquisition of a new radio and a 19-inch TV set. Despite the extra space gained from the new Pratten, overcrowding was still a problem and it was decided that no more rising-fives could be admitted following the summer holidays. Teaching strength was increased in early 1969 when Mrs Darlington arrived to give her services for one day a week and cycling proficiency tests, introduced in 1967, resulted in eight pupils receiving their certificates. The school soccer team had their first competitive encounter when they visited Hilperton School at the end of the year and, although putting up a spirited fight, eventually came out the losers. This disappointment was reversed in February 1970 when a school team won the Area Road Safety Shield in the finals held at Holt.

Revd Frank Maunder, Staverton's vicar and regular helper at the school, died in May. He was to be the last resident village incumbent. Swimming lessons for pupils were aided by the opening of a new pool in Bradford-on-Avon, the school making its first visit in September, and free school milk was phased out that year under Margaret Thatcher's review of education spending. By 1972, road safety had become a real concern. Pupils travelling to and from the school from the Hilperton Marsh area had for years 'taken their lives in their hands' when daily negotiating the dangerous stretch of road over the blind canal bridge. This hazardous situation was greatly relieved in early 1973 when a new pedestrian footbridge was constructed on the north side of the narrow road bridge. A small pottery kiln was purchased in January and in March parents were invited into the school for the first time to help the pupils with their reading. Valerie Sims took over from Mrs Ashton in April 1973 and after the summer holidays Mrs Bailey joined the teaching staff.

In the mid 1970s school football and netball teams, coached and run by several parents, began playing regular matches against other primary

Above: *Staverton School pupils and staff, 1980.*

Left: *Staverton School 'orchestra', 1990s.*

Above: *School visit to RNAS Yeovilton, 1972.* Staff and parents pictured include: *Sue Woodman, Marian Matthews, June Gale, Eileen Gamble, Elaine Darlington, Alice Moody.*

Above: *Staverton School pupils enjoying a trip on the canal with Wessex Narrowboats, 1990s.*

Right: *School class on a residential trip, early 1980s, with teacher Hilary Shaddock.*

schools in the area, the 1977 soccer team having a particularly successful season winning nearly all of the 20 matches they played. An influx of new starters after the 1973 summer holidays pushed pupil numbers to 100, the highest they had ever been, and this lead to grave concerns about the impossible conditions and total lack of proper facilities in the tiny school.

In 1974 it was realised that not only were conditions cramped, but also the buildings were deteriorating badly and many urgent repairs were needed, the roof was leaking, the floor rotten in places and the walls were full of damp. The school's first PTA was formed in February under the chairmanship of parent Arthur Akerman and, after many protests by parents about the lack of funds and resources being allocated to the school, an action group was formed to put pressure on the LEA. It was to be another 20 years, however, before the problems were finally resolved

The old school's bell tower takes pride of place on the forecourt of the new school.

with the provision of a bigger school, the decision to replace the old building being accelerated by the advent of several large housing developments within the school catchment area which had generated a considerable increase in the numbers of children who had to be educated in the parish. Meanwhile, staff and pupils struggled on in the old school which, by 1980, had 70 children on the registers. Despite the difficult conditions, a threat of closure in the late 1970s was vigorously opposed by governors and the PTA, chaired respectively by Janet Blake and Eddie Tovey, who were backed up by parents, staff and head teacher Alice Moody who put up a tremendous fight and eventually persuaded the LEA to keep a school in the village.

The old Victorian school's centenary was celebrated in 1980 with a series of events on the school field

and a history exhibition in the large classroom. The following July Alice Moody retired after 21 years as head teacher and Chris Cradock was appointed as her replacement in September 1981. Pupil numbers varied in the 1980s but gradually increased to almost 100 by the start of the 1990s. A number of teachers were employed at the school throughout this period and these included Jenny Elvin, Monica Ridgeway, Keri Williams, Ros Marshall, Hilary Shaddock, Meryan Tober, Jane Billa-Vercella and Heidi Ferguson. Doris Hallett was school caretaker and cleaner for many years, Karen Lovell took over the school crossing patrol from Sylvia Brown and Pauline Hodgson and Eileen Gamble supervised the midday meals, the latter replacing Pam James as school secretary and taking on the role of clerk to the governors. During the 1980s a new cloakroom was added to the rear of the school building and a small car park was laid between the infants' mobile and the top of School Lane, the work being carried out and financed by Nestlé. Since the 1970s Staverton's Victorian schoolhouse had been unable to meet modern educational requirements, and cater for the growing numbers of pupils. The long campaign fought by staff, governors and the Parish Council to acquire a new school for Staverton finally paid off when, in 1993, the LEA accepted that the old school was no longer suitable and agreed to finance the provision of a new educational establishment.

The construction of Staverton's brand-new primary school, costing £1.2 million, commenced in early 1995 and was completed a year later. Built on the old school's sports field, Staverton's new eight-classroom school opened in April 1996 and at last the children could be taught in a comfortable,

Staverton School pupils and staff, 1990.

Left: *Staverton's new primary school, opened in 1996.*

Right: *Construction work on the new village school, 1995.*

spacious and modern environment, something their predecessors never had the opportunity to experience. Constructed to the latest design by Wallis Western, the new school has large classrooms off a wide central corridor, a spacious hall, kitchen, staff room, toilet blocks at each end, offices and project rooms. There are also large hard-surface play areas front and back, a small nature reserve in one corner of the play area and landscaped grounds with a large car park. A new sports field has been provided across the road at the bottom of School Lane. The state-of-the-art facility was designed to meet the educational needs of the community in the first decades of the twenty-first century. When the old Victorian school finally closed, its bell tower was removed and placed on the forecourt of the new school as a lasting memorial to a long-standing Staverton institution that had provided a place of education for parish children for over 100 years.

A couple of years before the move to the new school, Phil Allen was appointed deputy head teacher, Jeanne Bergin took over the infants' class and Mandy Raikes-May became the school's administration officer when LMS was introduced in the late 1970s. Chris Cradock retired in 1997, Elizabeth Bannister became the new head in January 1998 and by the year 2000 there were 239 pupils in the new

The new school sports field at the bottom of School Lane.

school being taught by Phil Allen, Jeanne Bergin, Jill Vincent, David Waldron, Sheila Claridge, Leslie Talbot, Louise Wilford, Caroline Barlow, John Farrell and Marie Veale. The increase in pupil numbers at the start of the new millennium meant the school had almost reached its capacity and a ninth classroom was added to the rear of the building in 2001 to help cope with an anticipated further growth. Eddie and Eileen Gamble, two of the school's longest-serving governors and helpers, retired in 1998 and Mervyn Saunders took over from Revd Richard Hicks as chair of governors for 18 months before the new benefice vicar Revd Bobby Magill assumed the role assisted by the governors' long-standing vice chairman Keith Purnell.

The school population had grown considerably since 1996, the building was being used increasingly as a community amenity outside of school hours and was equipped with the latest technology in learning aids including banks of computers, access to the internet, and the school's own website. Staverton's schoolchildren, whose predecessors had for a century and a half been taught in a tiny, overcrowded Victorian building, at last had a superb modern facility, with a skilled and dedicated team of teachers, support staff and governors, in which to advance their education.

Staverton School soccer team, 1995.

Left: *Staverton School staff, 1997.* Left to right, standing: *Phil Allen (deputy head), Jeanne Bergin, Louise Wilford, Jill Vincent, Karen Lovell (ESA);* seated: *Chris Cradock (head).*

Above: *A gig-mill, the main cause of the shearmen's riots.*

Left: *Cloth making had become mechanised by the early-nineteenth century.*

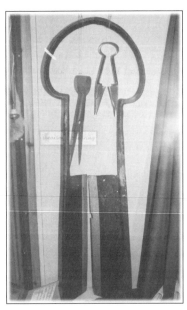

Right: *The mill manager's house was attacked by the rioting shearmen in 1802.*

Above: *The large iron shears used by the shearmen.*

Right: *A shearman dressing a piece of cloth.*

CHAPTER SEVEN

THE STAVERTON SUPERFINE WOOLLEN MANUFACTORY

As mechanisation increased within the woollen-cloth trade, clothiers became aware of the potential for successful business and began seeking areas with good water supplies beside which to build their new machine-worked cloth-mills. Staverton, an ideal site located on the banks of the fast-flowing Avon, had a long history of successful mills and in 1800 a Bradford-on-Avon clothier, John Jones, bought the village mill and made plans to convert it into a brand new woollen-cloth factory. The old mill was pulled down and the unique, up-to-date stone building that was erected in its place would later establish Staverton as one of the major cloth manufacturing centres in the West of England.

John Jones' new Staverton mill was quite an impressive sight, it was the largest mill in the district, covering a reputed 28,800 square feet and was called the Staverton Superfine Woollen Manufactory. The imposing six-storey main building was adorned with a central bell tower, built squarely over an enlarged mill-stream and was flanked by ranges of two-storey outbuildings. Power to drive the mill came from the waters which flowed through three large flumes below the building and operated the water-wheels. A contemporary description of the mill boasted that 'its power is estimated to be 40 horsepower with only a moderate supply of water and up to 200 horsepower when the Avon was at its full height.' For the first two years of its operation Jones had to send his cloths to Wootten-under-Edge for finishing whilst he waited for the installation of gig-mills in his new factory. In 1802, a visitor described the mill as 'having many types of newly invented machinery and capable of carrying out every woollen process except the weaving.'

The local cloth workers, concerned that the new machines would put them out of work, began to protest and later turned violent. The shearmen, considered to be the elite of the industry, were particularly upset when the gig-mills were finally installed in the factory in early 1802. The gig-mill comprised a series of rotating cylinders into which teasels were

John Jones' new Staverton cloth factory built in 1800.

inserted and when the cloth was wound from one cylinder to another the nap was raised far faster than could be done by hand. This process had always been done manually by the shearmen whose worst fears, that mechanisation would take away their livelihoods, were now confirmed. Serious rioting broke out at the mill in 1802 when the shearmen, who formed a strong brotherhood, decided to take the law into their own hands in protest at the introduction of this new machinery. Staverton mill was attacked on the night of 4 July 1802 and accounts of the riot describe the events in quite startling detail. The disgruntled shearmen had congregated outside the village at 11p.m. and then marched through Staverton to mass on the high bank above the mill. By about 2a.m. the 100-strong mob began firing guns and throwing projectiles at the mill buildings damaging the walls and breaking some windows. The firing, with ball slugs and small shot, continued for about half an hour but fortunately no lives were lost. Closest to the action, the mill overseer's house had taken the brunt of the attack and its residents felt so scared and in such great danger that they hid under their beds to try and save themselves. John Jones the mill owner was warned of the attack and rode from his home in Woolley with a local detachment of the

tioned in front of local magistrates, Beaumont refused to give evidence and was promptly jailed for three weeks for contempt. This punishment was enough for him to change his mind and he agreed to give a certain amount of evidence to the Justices. He returned to work at Staverton mill but soon left again complaining to Jones that he had been threatened with his life if he continued to work. Jones, concerned that he would lose a vital witness, offered him protection and a huge increase in wages from 14s. to 21s. a week if he would cooperate. Beaumont accepted the offer, agreed to resume work the following day but failed to turn up completely disappearing from the district never to be seen again!

The riots and mill burnings continued and Staverton mill was attacked again in August when protesting shearmen were dispersed by the soldiers. Local magistrates, under pressure from the mill owners, decided to deal severely with the rioters and funds were made available to provide rewards for information leading to the conviction of offenders. Jones organised the mill owners who provided money to pay witnesses to testify against those responsible for instigating the troubles. The burning of Littleton mill in Seend had Jones involved again when he ordered the arrest of Thomas Helliker and arranged an identity parade of a number of the suspects. Mr Heath, the owner of Littleton mill, picked out young Helliker who was sent to Salisbury Prison to await trial for arson. The trial, in March 1803, found him guilty, he was sentenced to death and hanged at Fisherton Jail on 28 March 1803. His body was released and carried back to Trowbridge by the local cloth workers who arranged for his burial in St James' churchyard. He had become a martyr to the cause of the local woollen workers and many years later fresh evidence came to light which suggested that he had not been involved in the burning of Littleton mill and had been wrongly convicted and hanged. The rioting gradually died down by the end of 1802 and the shearmen's leaders decided to press their case in Parliament on the grounds that the new machinery being introduced was illegal under earlier employment acts. Jones fought the clothiers' case and told the Parliamentary Commission in 1803 that the new gig-mills were the source of all the unrest but the local clothiers were determined to keep them and also introduce new machinery as they thought fit. He also denied to the Commissioners that he intended to erect a weaving factory, another potential

Queen's Dragoon Guards under the command of Captain Quantock. Before they could reach the mill the rioters had dispersed but Jones, fearing further attacks on his mill at Staverton, arranged for the soldiers to be quartered in Trowbridge and Bradford-on-Avon and to carry out nightly patrols.

The seriousness of the rioting was recognised in a statement by James Read, a government official sent down to Wiltshire to monitor the troubles, who reported that 'not a single shearman was at work at Staverton'.

John Jones, who was also a local magistrate and leader of the local cloth manufacturers, managed to discover the names of the shearmen's ringleaders and wrote to the Home Secretary demanding that they be arrested and punished. He complained that the striking shearmen were forcing other workers to stay away and the situation had become so bad that he would have no option but to shut the mill down. To try and resolve the dispute Jones met a deputation of shearmen at his home in Woolley on 24 July and tried to negotiate a settlement. He offered to find new jobs for all those put out of work in the Staverton area and agreed to do no more gigging and shearing for other manufacturers. The shearmen would not agree to this compromise and insisted that Jones remove his machines from Staverton mill. This he refused to do and the meeting ended with no agreement being reached.

Frustrated by the whole affair, Jones wrote to the Home Secretary again complaining about the intolerable situation at his mill and the Government ordered him to take out an indictment against the shearmen for conspiracy. Witnesses were needed to betray the shearmen's leaders and Jones sought suitable candidates amongst his mill workers. A shearman named Beaumont, from Bradford-on-Avon, who had been intimidated by the other shearmen and forced to stop working, was recruited by Jones to testify against his 'brothers'. However, when ques-

Left: *View of the mill-stream and the sluice mechanism above the weir, 1890s.*

Right: *The Staverton token issued by mill owner John Jones junior in 1811.*

Below: *Rear of the cloth-mill showing the trash grills that protected the water-wheels.*

source of unrest, for to do this he claimed he would need a large four-storey building to hold 100 broad-looms and this would not be worthwhile. This statement, as later events were to prove, was a 'white lie' and intended to sway the verdict of the Commission. The result of the parliamentary hearings led to the old employment acts being repealed and thus the mill owners had nothing to stop them legally modernising the manufacturing processes in their mills and factories.

With the troubles at an end, Staverton mill was soon functioning normally but was running into financial difficulties by 1805 when the rating assessment for the mill that year was reduced from 1s.6d. to 6d. John Jones died in 1807 and was succeeded by his son who took over the running of the mill. He was soon to experience the wrath of the shearmen whose long-standing grudge against his father came to the surface again in 1808 when he was attacked and injured by gunfire as he rode to his home in Woolley. A reward of £500 to apprehend the culprits brought no results until four years later when two men were arrested and charged with attempted murder. They were James Ball, a shearman, who was suspected of being one of those who fired the shots, and William Tunbury, a slay maker, accused of attending a meeting of the shearmen's committee where the attempt on Jones' life was decided upon. The two men stood trial but due to lack of evidence and unreliable witnesses they were both found not guilty and freed and nobody was ever convicted of the offence.

In 1809 Jones enquired about buying a 20hp steam engine from Boulton and Watt and in 1810 he had a rank of weavers' cottages built on the high bank above the mill. This terrace of ten cottages, built of ashlar with pantiled roof, stood in a lane called Millbank and contained three storeys. The front of each house had a pair of large windows on the first and second floors and a single small window at the ground-floor level. At the back each had one large window on the second floor, a smaller one on the first floor and a square-headed ground-floor entrance door. The large upper windows were designed to provide a good degree of natural light essential to the intricate work of the cottage weavers whose hand looms were sited on the upper floors. Mill workers and weavers occupied these cottages into the 1890s and after Nestlé took over the old cloth factory in 1897 they were used to house their key workers in the first half of the twentieth century. They were finally demolished in 1966 by which time they were in a very poor condition and unfit for habitation.

Set at 9d. in 1810 the mill rate dramatically fell to 2d. in 1811 indicating that the business was in serious financial trouble and, in 1812, Jones was declared bankrupt. He died shortly afterwards and was buried in the family plot at Winsley where there remains today a fine Georgian monument to his mother. A year before his death he had issued two Staverton tokens with the face values of one penny and two and six. One of these was recently purchased by Trowbridge Museum for their collection of local coins and tokens. The tokens portrayed a picture of the mill on their obverse faces, with the words 'Staverton Factory, Near Bradford, Wiltshire' around the central design. The reverse face depicts the value of the tokens and their date of issue, 1811, between sprays of palm branches. Around the edge of this reverse face a legend proclaims 'Prosperity to the Woollen Manufactory' which was ironic as, at the time of their circulation, the mill was in serious financial trouble. The tokens were valid until December 1814, two years after the death of their issuer, but whether the new mill owner ever redeemed their value is not certain. Now very rare, the half-crown tokens are extremely valuable and only four are known to be left in existence.

Staverton cloth factory was offered for sale in 1813 and particulars of the sale document describe it as being powered by three water-wheels, designed by the famous engineer John Rennie, architect of the nearby Kennet and Avon Canal. Described as the 'most complete clothing factory in the West of England' the mill machinery included 24 scribbling and carding machines, one wool tucker, 42 shearing frames, 2 brushing machines, 1 napping machine, 6 fulling stocks, 3 indigo pots and 3 dressing gigs. There was room for another gig, and rasping and chipping machines which Jones had prepared plans for. The mill building was 120 feet long, 40 feet wide, and next to it was a recently erected stone building 144 feet long and 30 feet wide with three floors. The lower one was fitted for a hack stove and the upper two for weaving shops. The factory had every necessary requisite for carrying out the manufacture of fine cloths and Kerseymeres equal to the consumption of between 16 and 20 large bags of Spanish wool per week. Outbuildings consisted of a large dye house with four blue vats, two large wool furnaces, one cloth furnace and a scouring furnace. Close by was a very superior washing stage, wool store, raw cloth house, excellent streaming aqueduct, wool warehouse, oil warehouse, dye drug warehouse, sorting rooms, picking rooms, gig handle house with teasel loft, press shop, packing room, passing rooms and yarn room. Other facilities included weaving rooms with 40 spring looms, accounting houses, smith's and carpenter's shops, large wagon house and ten stall stables. Domestic dwellings attached to the factory were two complete houses for the foreman and superintendent and a mansion house for the proprietor with a walled garden and orchard, well stocked with choice fruit trees, and fishing rights on the Avon. The sale included the rack field adjoining the factory, 'an excellent close of pasture' with an area of about four-and-a-half acres. Water usage rights were exclusive to the factory and the bill of sale enthused about 'the abundant supply of work people from the neighbouring populous villages of Staverton, Holt, Hilperton, Semington, Broughton Gifford and Woolley.'

The mill was insured against loss or damage by fire to the tune of £17,150 and the new owner would take over all the valuable machinery on the premises 'which had recently been laid in with the greatest judgement, and is in excellent condition, at a fair evaluation.' Staverton mill came up for auction on Monday 15 February 1813 at the York Hotel in Bath but did not reach its reserved price, and at a second sale at the Swan Inn in Bradford-on-Avon on 22 June 1813 the firm of Joyce, Cooper and Co. from Freshford secured the mill for £14,000. They immediately installed a 14hp steam engine taken from their Dunkirk mill and the Staverton cloth factory was soon back in full production. The factory prospered and the following year was rated at one shilling. This rate increased to 1s.3d. over the next two years and from 1818 onwards was set at 1s.8d.

By 1816 the factory employed 119 men and 154 women whose working hours were 6a.m. to 7p.m. on weekdays and up to 2p.m. on Saturdays. Business was booming by 1817 and a salesman from the firm commented that 'money was plentiful, trade brisk, and scarcely a weaver in Trowbridge and Bradford was not working.' This prosperity led to further modernisation and a gas-lighting plant, designed by Boulton and Watt, was installed in the factory by the end of that year. Joyce left the partnership in 1820 and the business continued under Cooper Brothers. By the 1820s all of the cloth manufacturing processes had been mechanised except for the weaving which was still being carried out in the cottages.

Troubles flared up again in 1822 when local weavers went on strike in protest at their low wages and the mill owners, some with the 1802 riots still fresh in their minds, reacted strongly to this latest threat against their businesses and some of the weavers were jailed. In 1824 the mill was said to be creating employment for 1,500 local workers including the cottage weavers and other cloth trades. However, tragedy struck the prosperity of the industry on the night of 5 November 1824 when the mill was mysteriously burnt down. A newspaper report in the *Devizes Gazette* described the events of that evening in graphic detail. The report, published on 11 November, read as follows:

On Friday evening last, between the hours of seven and eleven, this noble building – the most extensive and handsome of its kind in Wilts, comprising no less than six different floors, and having 65 windows in the front – was entirely demolished by fire: together with its valuable machinery, and stock of cloth amounting to 600 pieces. And when it is added, that nearly 1500 hands were employed by its spirited proprietors – a great portion of whom must of necessity remain for a time unemployed – some idea of the extent of the calamity may be conceived.

The fire was first discovered at about eight o'clock, proceeding from a room on the first floor, used for separating the wool, having already made considerable progress: and not withstanding there was scarcely any wind at the time, with much rapidity did the fire extend, that by ten o'clock the roof fell in. This may, in great measure, be accounted for, from the large quantities of oil used in the process of manufacturing cloths, and with which, the floors and timbers were so saturated, that they burnt like paper. Soon after ten a few rafters only remained, and they fast hastened to the general ruin – the windows were entirely demolished – and the north side of the front fell in pieces of from ten to twelve feet. Before the engines could arrive from Bradford and Trowbridge, the fire had gained such an ascendancy, as to defy every effort to arrest it; the firemen therefore

Above left: *The cloth-mill's drying house.*

Left: *Mill outbuildings on the north side of the main mill building.*

directed their exertions to the preservation of the contiguous dwelling house of Mr Cooper, and other buildings, in which they happily succeeded. Information was immediately sent to the different insurance offices in which the property was insured; and the Norwich Union Company (and they only) have sent down their London Surveyor, who was at Staverton on Tuesday. The damage is estimated at about £18,000; and the insurances amount to £16,000; £4,000 of which is the Norwich Union, and £5,000 in the Imperial. Another factory is immediately to be commenced building; and on the very morning succeeding the fire, the proprietors proceeded to engage fresh shops, for the purpose of carrying on their business, and of employing as many as possible of the immense number of persons that would otherwise be dependent on the parish.

A malicious report was circulated that the building was wilfully set on fire by some of the workmen, on account of the erection of some new machinery – but this report is entirely destitute of foundation – the only probable cause assigned; is the falling of the snuff of a candle; as half an hour previous to the discovery of the fire, the man, employed for the purpose, had gone over the premises and reported that all was safe. Staverton is in the Parish of Trowbridge, about two miles from the town, and the same distance from Bradford. The proprietors, Messrs Cooper Brothers and Co. had only a short time previous, we understand, made improvements and additions to the premises at a great expense. The account books and a large quantity of finished cloth, we are happy to state, were saved. It will scarcely be credited that during the fire, a man named Bullock, employed in removing the furniture from Mr Edward Cooper's house, stole a silver spoon, and other articles, which were found in his house.

He has been committed to Fisherton Gaol, and we trust that he will meet with punishment due to so hardened a villain.

The mill was immediately rebuilt based on its original style and was able to reopen for business in 1825. Details of the reconstruction show a modification to the old design by raising the façade to six storeys and eliminating the attic and clock tower that featured on the previous building. A deep parapet around the pediment was inscribed with the date of the fire and the rebuilding and the top of the new mill was crowned by a huge stone phoenix, the mythical bird of rebirth, rising from a nest of flames. Iron floors, supported on iron columns, were fitted into the main building and the north-side outbuildings were raised to three storeys. Power for the rebuilt mill was still supplied by a combination of water-wheels and steam engines.

Business had not suffered unduly because of the fire and the factory was soon back in full production. The first Factory Act was introduced in 1833 and Staverton mill was visited by the inspectors that year who gave the business a good report saying that the employees 'were well clothed and respectable and the children were fit and healthy'. They noted the good relationship between the workers and Edward Cooper, the owner, who stated that he was employing from 400 to 500 in the factory with a similar number in support industries outside. Staverton mill had become the biggest in the area and one of the biggest in Britain with an estimated working capital of £200,000. The mill's power, in 1833, was provided by a 80hp steam engine and two water-wheels of 40hp each. An additional steam engine of 24hp, purchased from Sheppard's of Frome, was installed the following year and the first power looms to be used in the district were operating at Staverton by 1839.

Benjamin Cooper was head of the firm in 1835 when the bulk of the mill's output was being sent to Bristol and Liverpool for export to Ireland. Following the failure of the Hobhouse Bank in Bradford-on-Avon in 1842, Cooper Brothers went bankrupt and the mill had to put up for sale again. The bank had been supporting the mill with loans over the past five years and its sudden crash was a catastrophic blow for the Staverton business. Sale details show that the mill had been elaborately equipped, its inventory included a gas plant capable of illuminating 400 batwing lamps. £500,000 had been spent on modifications in recent years and the mill was said to be capable of producing 150 pieces of broadcloth a week with Venetians and black broadcloth, woven with a twill, being specialities at Staverton. The ground floor contained 18 pairs of iron-framed fulling stocks worked by hollow iron shafts and ten more worked by wooden shafts. There were 18 broad gigs and three washers, and outbuildings containing tucking and picking shops, a drying stove, a gig-mill with six broad and six narrow gigs, and a seven-year-old four-storey building full of power looms said to be capable of weaving any description of fancy patterns. Dye house, warping shops and warehouses made up the complex and the two water-wheels, rated at 20hp each, were still in use together with steam engines of 50hp, 36hp, and 24hp respectively. No buyer could be found and in 1847 the equipment was sold off. The complex of mill buildings stood gaunt and empty for the next 17 years and reports in the *Trowbridge Advertiser* in 1856, that the Government had acquired the property for a barracks, were quickly denied.

New purchasers were found in 1864 and the West of England Woollen Manufacturing Co. moved into the mill to set about making cloth by a new felting process. The idea was to manufacture cloth from carded wool without the spinning and weaving processes and this could be extended to make fine

Mill outbuildings on the south side showing the ranks of cottages on the high bank above.

cloth with the aid of newly invented machinery secured by patent. The only local director was Ezekiel Edmonds, of Bradford-on-Avon, whose own firm in the town had recently gone bankrupt. The new company's aspirations were short-lived and it went into liquidation in 1866 without any of the new cloth being produced. The empty factory was immediately purchased for £20,000 by a group of London businessmen who set up a new company called the Staverton Cloth Co. This new enterprise re-equipped the mill with modern machinery and went back to producing cloth in the traditional way, later installing looms with a Jacquard mechanism which could produce cloth with elaborate patterns. Business progressed well initially and the mill's new continuous production system became much envied by other local clothiers and mill owners. By 1867 the mill was employing 145 workers and was said to have plenty of work on the order books.

Shareholders were pleased with the first half-year returns and the company chairman, Mr Gibbons, expressed great confidence in the mill manager Mr W.C. Webb, who was apparently doing an excellent job. Several minor setbacks were also noted at the time, including problems caused by the annual flooding, one recent deluge uprooting the factory's new boiler and carrying it across several fields. Despite initial success the company went out of business in 1870 and Staverton mill was yet again put up for sale. The machinery in the mill was said to be largely new and it was clear that the factory had been well equipped with 31 broad power looms, 20 broad hand looms, two 400-spindle larks, six 200- and one 225-spindle mules, 6 carding sets with condensers, 10 broad gigs, 6 fulling stocks, 8 fulling machines, a hydro extractor, a tentering machine, wool-scouring machines, and dye house apparatus making up its range of cloth-making equipment. A Yorkshire clothier, James Hargreaves, bought the mill and ran it as a successful cloth-making business until 1891. By 1875, 250 local people were employed in the mill and, two

years later, Webb, the mill's manager, retained by Hargreaves from the previous venture, was accused of embezzling money and was put on trial. He was found guilty and sentenced to a term in prison.

A constant and adequate water supply to power the water-wheels had always been essential to the effective operation of Staverton mill and rights to retain this vital supply were protected by an Act of Parliament. The Trowbridge Water Acts of 1878 reduced the monopoly by the mill when water was taken from the Semington and Paxcroft Brooks to set up the new piped water supply system to the surrounding neighbourhoods. An earlier Water Act of 1873 had decreed that water could not be taken from these sources without the prior consent of the Staverton mill owner, and even with the necessary permission, no more than a million gallons a day. The 1873 Act allowed for Semington Brook to be widened and deepened, and a weir and pumping station installed with meter added to ensure the mill owner's rights were not being jeopardised. Staverton mill received a quarterly statement determining the amount of water taken and if the meter failed or the agreed amount was exceeded the mill owners received £20 and could claim compensation if the loss of water affected the mill's workings. The later Water Act of 1878 recognised these constraints on the water company who, in order to resolve the problem, proposed that Staverton mill be purchased together with its water rights. The mill owners would not sell but agreed a compromise by which the payments made for taking extra water from Semington Brook were increased to £35. Water supply problems occurred again in 1888 when the Staverton mill owners sued G.P. Fuller of Great Chalfield Manor for alleged interference with the flow of water to their factory. The problem had started when Fuller agreed to the tapping of some springs near Chalfield to allow a water supply to be piped to Holt but the Staverton mill owners complained that, as the overflow from these springs ran into a brook that fed the Avon, they could be affected by water level problems. The matter was eventually resolved when Fuller agreed to restore the works that had caused the interference, much to the dismay of the Holt residents who would now have to wait a little longer for their promised piped water supply.

James Hargreaves died in 1883 and the trustees leased the mill to his son and brother who continued to run the business successfully for the following eight years. The mill was put up for sale in 1891 as a going concern and was purchased by a London lawyer, George Phipp Eyre, who had taken an interest in the cloth manufacturing trade and was trying to develop a new wool scouring process. This process would de-grease the wool with the use of carbon bisulphate without added heat and he engaged a Huddersfield man, by the name of Armitage, to manage his new operation at Staverton.

Above: *Staverton cloth-mill in the nineteenth century.*

Right: *The stone phoenix and inscription on the rebuilt 1825 cloth-mill.*

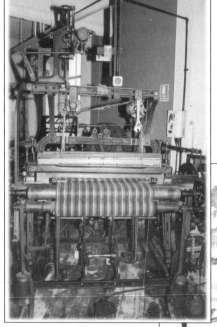

Left: *A small power loom.*

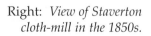

Right: *View of Staverton cloth-mill in the 1850s.*

Left: *Members of the Hargreaves family in the mill yard, c.1890.*

Left: *Detail of the mill sale document, 1813.*

Right: *Mill sale notice, 1891.*

Right: *Horse and carriage used by the mill owner and his family, c.1890.*

He, however, was soon in trouble with local people because of the terrible smell his new process created and within a short space of time his efforts had become a total failure and he put the mill up for sale.

No buyers were forthcoming for several years and the mill remained empty. In order to encourage a new buyer, the mill machinery was completely over-hauled in 1893 and the mill-stream, mill-head and mill-race were cleaned out at a cost of £2,000. Sale documents at the time described the mill in glowing terms and listed the extensive range of outbuildings and machinery much of which had been newly added during Hargreaves' 21-year occupancy. The main building was said to be practically fireproof with a large iron cistern, situated above the staircase, being constantly charged with water by a self-acti-vating hydraulic ram, near the mill-head, which fed a series of pipes and cocks on every floor and which could be brought into action in the event of a fire.

Water closets were provided on every floor for the workforce and two iron breastshot water-wheels, each 10 feet long and 16 feet in diameter, and esti-mated to generate 60hp, provided some of the power for the mill. The sale particulars went on to say that the mill was placed 'on a fine and never failing stream of the River Avon across which, at the east end, is placed a stone weir.' This was 'constructed at great cost, affording a fine head of water of great extent with a fall of about six feet, flowing under the arches of the mill.'

Mill buildings sited near the southern gateway consisted of capital stabling with slated roof for eight horses, a coach-house with provender loft above and an adjoining manure pound. Next to this was an open wagon lodge and two cottages containing four rooms each. A two-storey building with work people's dining-room on the lower floor and a loom shed on the upper floor adjoined another two-storey building, with iron-framed roofing, which contained a wool warehouse and a second loom shed. On the southern side of the site was a 'commodious dwelling house' that could house two families, with three sitting rooms, two kitchens, ample domestic offices, two staircases, 14 bedrooms, staircase to ser-vant's bedroom and a pump for supplying fresh spring water. Attached to this substantial dwelling was a walled garden with iron gateway entrance, a tool-house, vinery and forcing-house. Behind the mill owner's house was a 125-foot octagonal brick chimney shaft with moulded cap and square pan-elled base and a two-storey teasel-house and machin-ery store. The mill's engine-houses contained a 25hp condensing beam steam engine, a double-cylinder high-and-low pressure steam engine of 50hp made by Hall's of Dartford, and a 45hp condensing steam engine with wagon steam boiler. Boiler-houses contained a seven-foot-diameter steam boiler with sugar-loaf tubes by Horsfield's of Dewsbury and an Elephant boiler with six tubes made by Hall's, over

which were drying rooms and a second teasel room. Small buildings at the rear of the site contained scouring rooms, mechanic's shop, smith's shop and another cottage containing four rooms. To the north side of the main building was a complete gas plant, willey shop, tucking shop, dye house with two copper vats, press and spilling shops. Buildings inside the bottom gateway contained offices, passing and stock rooms, warehouses, and a cottage with entrance porch, two living-rooms and three bedrooms. An ornamental plantation, called The Island in later times, was studded with fine grown elms and shrubs and extended from the mill's tumbling bay right back to the weir. Outside the southern range of buildings was a close of rich pasture land, $4^1/_2$ acres in size, and used as the mill's rackfield. On the high bank overlooking the mill was a rank of three double and four single weavers' cot-tages, built by John Jones in 1810, each with a garden in front and serviced by a well of spring water in the adjacent field. The sale documents concluded that local labour was easily obtained 'at moderate cost' and coal supplies were readily available from Radstock and other well-known collieries which were in easy distance of the mill. These coal supplies were delivered by canal barge to the Staverton wharfes and by rail to local stations, particularly Holt, where it could be purchased for 4s.9d. a ton.

Besides the coal, other raw materials and finished goods could be afforded on the nearby Kennet and Avon Canal, and the main GWR line ran within a few yards of the property making it possible to arrange a siding to the mill at a very reasonable outlay. The extensive range of cloth-making machinery included 35 broad looms, some old, 2 narrow looms and a Jacquard loom, 17 carding machines with con-densers, 6 self-activating mules, 4 warping machines, 3 grinding frames, 2 snapping machines, and 3 spool-ing machines with 5 spool frames, 4 dressing gigs, 3 Yorkshire gigs, 4 milling machines, 5 cutting machines, 7 brushing machines, 2 washing machines and quilling, doubling, turning, crabbing and tenter-ing machines. Other equipment in the inventory were three hydro extractors, a yarn tester and snap-per, fulling stocks and tucking machine, emery frame, napping machine, bumbling machine, picking machine, willeying machine, and soaping machine. The dye houses contained an indigo-mill with two pots, five dye vats and five vitriol vats, and scattered around the mill in various buildings were large quantities of teasels in handles and iron frames, and numerous bobbins and spools.

The cloth firm of G. Lewis and Company moved into the mill in 1895 but, after initial success, their business was soon in trouble and they gave up cloth making in early 1897. Staverton mill came up for auction again in April 1897 with a reserved price of £10,000, later reduced to £6,000, but there were no bidders and the sale was adjourned. The West-of-

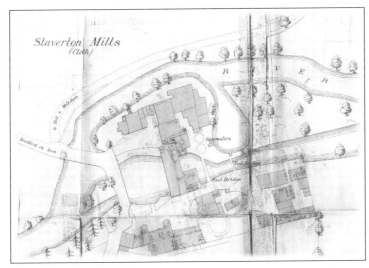

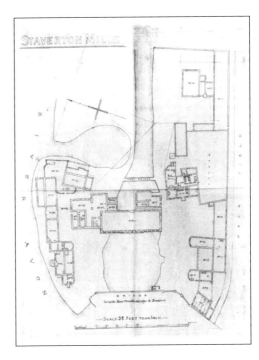

Above: *Plan of the cloth-mill in 1891 showing the newly installed gas plant.*

Right: *Plan of the cloth-mill in 1897.*

England cloth trade had been in decline for a number of years, local mills had been going out of business and the operation of a large cloth-making factory, like Staverton, was no longer an attractive proposition.

In August the mill acquired a new lease of life when a company called the Acetylene Light Syndicate, based in Trowbridge, began leasing part of the mill for the production of calcium carbonate. The idea was to bring the calcium carbonate into contact with water thus producing acetylene, a hydrocarbon gas, which had a greater illuminating power than any other gas and therefore a tremendous commercial potential. Large quantities of calcium carbonate would be needed to make the venture a viable business proposition so the empty Staverton mill was utilised by the syndicate to carry out initial experiments using its extensive engine power. The manufacturing process consisted of fusing coke with lime by intense heat in an electric furnace thus producing the required amounts of calcium carbide which would then be sold for £28 a ton to local power providers. A powerful water-driven dynamo was installed and 150hp brought into use to carry out the first trials which were reported to be a great success. The new process was patented by Hudson Maxim, brother of Hiram Maxim the inventor of the Maxim machine gun, and W.H. Graham, a young but thoroughly experienced chemical electrician. Hudson, an American, had recently invented an aerial torpedo designed to plant half a ton of dynamite on a battleship, at a range of nine miles, and like his brother had been experimenting in producing a new family of weapons for the American Armed Forces. Mr Graham, of English parents, had already invented an electric motor and was currently engaged in producing a storage battery which would revolutionize the clumsy and wasteful system of accumulators. The Acetylene Light Syndicate had been established in Trowbridge in early 1897 to manufacture generators, fittings and accessories for the new illuminant and boasted that their equipment, produced under the Gore-Pym and Crees principles, was the best apparatus of its kind on the market.

Whilst all this was going on negotiations had been taking place between the Anglo-Swiss Condensed Milk Co. and the previous owner, George Phipp Eyre, for the purchase of the empty Staverton mill and agreement for the sale had been completed by September 1897 with the tinned milk company acquiring the whole of the premises. The Acetylene Light Syndicate had to stop operations at the factory and, on vacating the site, announced that they would be continuing their business at other premises near Cradle Bridge in Trowbridge.

Staverton's long and illustrious connection with the cloth industry was finally at an end and the uncertainties of the last decade had created a high level of unemployment and hardship for village families who had relied on it for centuries to provide their living. Many Staverton families were forced to move away from the village to seek employment and the parish population dropped dramatically between 1891 and the end of the century. In the 1890s hopes that new cloth businesses would move into the village mill were dashed as the premises remained virtually unused so it was with great relief that locals learned of Anglo-Swiss' purchase of the site in 1897. Remaining Staverton families looked forward to the opportunities of gaining new employment and most prayed that the new milk-processing business would, at long last, provide a more secure and permanent industry in the village which had suffered badly through the unpredictable and unreliable cloth-making trade throughout the 1800s.

Left: The cloth-mill chimney which was replaced by the Nestlé chimney in 1914.

Right: The business card of G. Lewis and Co., 1895, listing the different types of cloth being made at Staverton.

Below: Villagers enjoyed boat trips from Couzen's moorings in the early 1900s.

Below: Landing stages at the moorings at the turn of the century.

Chapter Eight

Nineteenth-Century Staverton

The nineteenth century brought tremendous change to Staverton as the parish witnessed a dramatic rise and then decline in its population, there was the ongoing mechanisation and eventual loss of the cloth industry, and the beneficial effects of the Industrial Revolution which brought new modes of travel and trade in the form of the canal, railway and improved roads. The village acquired a new church, a Methodist chapel, its first school, a vicarage to house its first resident vicars, a new schoolhouse, and there began a growth in housing which continued into the twentieth century. The domestic arrangements of villagers were enhanced considerably towards the end of the century with the provision of piped water and gas supplies and the ever-increasing availability of affordable household goods and services being generated from the growth of new factories and businesses in the local towns, but, despite the benefits that all these changes were bringing they also created enormous social, health and economic problems and many ordinary Staverton families became the victims of the down side of the Industrial Revolution, particularly in the decades around the middle of the century. With the growth in population during the first half of the century came overcrowding and poor living conditions; the ongoing mechanisation of industry and farming caused unemployment and hardship. Together these factors lead to an increase in illness and disease and a doubling of the village mortality rate.

The nineteenth century began on an optimistic note for the people of Staverton. The community was heavily involved in the cloth trade with most villagers having some connection to the industry, either directly as weavers and mill workers or in the many supporting trades that serviced the cloth factory. The boom in the local industry and the plentiful work being provided by John Jones' new Staverton manufactory had encouraged more and more cloth-working families into the village putting a strain on housing and meagre parish resources. By 1821 there were 87 families recorded as living in the parish, most of them engaged in the cloth trade, many as weavers. The cloth workers and labourers usually had very large families and it was not uncommon to find eight or nine individuals living in the tiny cottages that made up the bulk of the village housing. In the 1820s nearly half of Staverton's families had at least six members, with 16 of the households comprising over eight. A further 24 had six or seven, with very few having less than four. The largest families at the time were those of Charles Willis, William Johnson, William Gilbert, James Edmunds and William Grigory, most of them using all members of the family to help with the spinning and weaving or working on the land. The arrival of the canal through the parish in 1801 provided new jobs for some villagers and a number of Staverton families, like the Birds, began to build up profitable little businesses from the coal and cargo-handling trade on the newly opened canal wharfes.

At the start of the nineteenth century the land that made up the parish of Staverton, 679 acres in all, was split into many holdings, some large and some as small as a few acres. Most of the land by this time had been enclosed with hedges and fences and some of the larger landowners had done deals with their neighbours to rearrange their fields into more compact and manageable units. The Tithe Maps of 1802 and 1812 list the biggest landowners as Nathaniel Bessey with 163 acres, Dr Harvey with 94 acres (most of it in or around the Down), the Revd John Lewis Bythesea of Wyke House with 74 acres, Walter Long with 43 acres and James Chapman with 24 acres. The Kennet & Avon Canal Company owned 32 acres, John Jones, the Staverton cloth-mill owner, had 19 acres, and the rest was in small lots of a few acres owned by a dozen or more villagers. Properly surfaced roads had not yet arrived and the maps indicate that the turnpike roads in and out of the village were just rough tracks running to Bradford-on-Avon, Hilperton and to Trowbridge via the Down which was still open land with, as yet, no houses appearing in Lower Wyke Road. The Enclosure Awards and Tithe Commutation Acts of 1815 and the 1830s considerably changed the land situation, large acreages changed hands and the number of major landholders in the parish dropped to about 20, the largest of these being new landowner John Keddle with 250 acres, most of it straddling

THE BOOK OF STAVERTON

each side of the track from the top of School Lane to the river bridge. His fields extended as far as the River Biss to the west of the parish and up to the present rail bridge across the Avon to the east. This considerable landholding was only interrupted by one small field, owned by Samuel Bird, between the present club and the Square, and the land around the cloth factory which was the property of mill owner Edward Cooper.

John Keddle did not work the land himself but leased it out to several village farmers, principally Thomas Hulbert, 186 acres, and William Dallimore of Staverton Farm, 62 acres. The second largest landowner, with 118 acres, was John Clark who had bought Wyke House from the Bytheseas in 1832, and possessed six fields that ran in a swathe from the River Biss across to Wyke Road, plus a further three at the southern end of the Down near the present-day Canal Road. He also owned four strips in Lot Mead, a divided field than ran northward from the River Biss, and a large field between Marsh Lane and the canal. Most of his land, 78 acres, was leased to Joseph Giddance in 1837 but he remained in occupation of the Lot Mead strips and some acres on the Down near Islington. Village tithes in 1837, amounting to £625, were being paid to the rector of Trowbridge, Revd Francis Fulford, who also received £16 annually for the tithes of the Staverton glebe land. Other substantial landowners were Herbert Bird, William Stancombe and Walter Long with John Cook and William Dallimore owning several small parcels of land to the south and east of the village. Most of Herbert Bird's land was located around Marsh Lane and the top of Wyke Road, William Stancombe's six large fields occupied the area which is now the Canal Road Trading Estate, and most of Walter Long's lay behind New Terrace, the fields behind Wyke House and two large strips each side of the canal off Marsh Lane. Herbert Bird was in occupation of all his land in the village and most of Walter Long's was being farmed by Ann Watts and Thomas Hayward. Smaller landowners around the village were James Chapman who had two large fields between Marsh Lane and the river, Richard Tucker with land at the top of Wyke Road and at Islington, and Mary Eggar with a modest acreage to the south of Victoria Road. Several tiny closes at the bottom of School Lane were owned by John Bailey and William Moody and Ann Rainer possessed one large field halfway between the canal wharf and the river.

Not all of the lesser landowners worked the fields themselves but leased them to smaller village farmers such as John Steeds, John Cadby, James Gye, James Norris and Samuel Hooper. One who did use her own plot was Betty Hudd who occupied a small piece of ground off Marsh Lane, which contained a cottage and an orchard. Several other large orchards were scattered around the village, one behind the Square owned by Herbert Bird, and one behind

Staverton Farm owned by John Keddle but being leased by William Dallimore. A number of smaller orchards lay behind cottages at the top of Wyke Road and were located on plots of land that stretched from Wyke House to the canal bridge. The landholdings around the village constantly changed hands throughout the nineteenth century as farmers either gave up or went out of business and ownership had altered considerably by the end of the century as large areas of the parish acreage were sold off to existing or new landlords. The title of lord of the manor was bought by Thomas Timbrell in 1809 although by then the estate had no land attached to it. The growth of the village population in the first decades of the century put a strain on the existing religious buildings in Staverton, prompting the building of a new Wesleyan Methodist Chapel in 1824 and the rebuilding and enlargement of St Paul's Church two years later.

By 1840 there were over 100 people living in the parish who were involved in cloth making including 24 weavers, 6 fullers, 3 millwrights and 70 cloth-mill workers. Many more weavers and cloth workers were living in Islington, just outside the parish, some of these producing cloth for, or working at, the Staverton Woollen Cloth Factory. However, the prosperity and reasonably good standard of living enjoyed by villagers in the previous century was to change dramatically by the middle of the nineteenth century for a whole host of social and economic reasons. The mechanisation of the cloth-making processes began to accelerate threatening the livelihood of local cloth workers, increasing unemployment, and, as there was no State aid at the time, causing tremendous hardships to some village families. In the first part of the century the restrictions placed on the import of foreign grain due to the Napoleonic Wars further compounded the economic problems by pushing up bread prices. Continuing mechanisation on the farms and the slump in food production and prices after 1820, which forced some farmers out of business, began to reduce the number of jobs available to farm labourers and those who managed to keep their jobs had to accept lower wages, which at the time were around eight shillings for a 60-hour week. Farm boys were paid about four shillings a week and women who helped out on the land received about a shilling a day when they were fortunate enough to be offered work. Many farm labourers were paid in kind with free housing in tied cottages and sometimes free produce from the farm such as milk, vegetables, eggs and cider.

Being in a tied cottage, however, could have severe disadvantages for farm labourers who were unable to seek better jobs and, if the farmer no longer needed their help, they could be immediately evicted causing extreme hardship to their families. Sometimes a displaced family would be helped out by relatives or neighbours but in extreme cases the only option was usually the workhouse. One such Staverton family was that of Thomas Gay, recorded as an agricultural labourer in 1841, who lived in the village with his wife Ann and their eight children. They later fell on hard times and Thomas was eventually to die in the Semington workhouse in 1878. Sometimes the children of destitute families were sent to the workhouse as were three children from the village in 1863 who had lost their mother and whose father claimed he could no longer look after them. Other large families in the 1840s were the ten children of fuller Isaac Waite and wife Louise. Farm worker Thomas Wicks and wife Sarah had eight children as did cloth worker James Ricketts and Ann, four of their offspring also worked in the cloth trade. Weaver William Linzey and Charlotte had seven children, as did cloth workers Samuel and Jane Marshman and James and Alice Walker. Many other families in the 1840s had at least six children such as William and Grace Rich and James and Gemima Gye (both men working as bargees on the canal), and two widows Ann Peglar and Elizabeth Hudd, the latter supporting her large family by gardening her cottage plot and selling the produce to villagers.

The reduction in farm jobs and the unreliability of regular work in the mid 1800s forced many who were not tied to seek alternative employment in the ever growing number of cloth-mills in the neighbouring towns, and the emigration of these job-seeking families began to reduce the village population through the latter half of the century. The momentum of the Industrial Revolution, with the introduction of steam engines and manufacturing machinery, also began to affect the village's traditional cottage industries which, by the end of the century, had virtually been put out of business by the cheaper mass-produced goods made by machines in the newly opened factories and workshops in the nearby towns.

Staverton had a number of cottage industries in the 1840s providing goods and services to villagers as their predecessors had done in the past centuries. John and Mary Edmonds ran a grocery store, John Parsons was a 'beer retailer' while Thomas Tratman and his young apprentice James Walker, looked after the village's black-

Front of Bear Cottage which stood opposite the Square.

Side view of Bear Cottage.

smithing requirements from a workshop near the Square. There were three shoemakers, John Gerrish, John Hacker and John Rison; clothes could be purchased from tailor John Ricketts, milliner Mary Bull, and James Walker's daughter who traded as a dressmaker. The village's building and furniture needs were supplied by carpenters Samuel Cooper and John Bailey, with James Pearce offering his services as plasterer. Other village services included auctioneer Benjamin Brown, engineer John Rich, and gardener George Davis. The turnpike house at the top of the hill opposite the church gates was occupied by widow Fanny Bailey who was responsible for collecting the tolls on Staverton's turnpike road. The Kennet and Avon Canal, at its peak in the 1840s, provided a living for over a dozen families, most of them bargees operating from the canal wharfes. A blacksmith's shop on the wharf, for the shoeing of the canal horses, was being operated by William Dyer. A grocery shop in the marsh was run by Ann Edmonds, Herbert Bird was publican of the King's Arms, and other 'beer retailers' selling home-brewed ale from their cottages were Ann Kite and Ann Newth. Ann Newth's husband John had the unusual occupation of an engraver, Elizabeth Hill ran a laundry service, and sons and daughters of some of these families were apprenticed at 15, such as William Gye and Richard Newth (to a carpenter and grocer) and Ann Edmond's daughter Mary (to a local milliner). A number of boys and girls from village families were in service in the 1840s, most becoming domestics in the larger houses in the village and the surrounding district. Cloth-mill owner Edward Cooper and his wife Mary, who lived in a house near the church gates and were one of the wealthiest village families, were sufficiently affluent to employ four female servants, Elizabeth Langley, Charlotte Rogers, Elizabeth Masters and Emma Elderton. Farmer William Dallimore, of Staverton Farm, employed agricultural labourers James Bull and Thomas Gay and was substantial enough to keep two young female servants to help with the household chores.

Health problems increased as a result of the dramatic population growth in Staverton in the 1800s, there were food shortages due to a series of bad harvests, increased unemployment and a drop in living

Right: *Farm horses in the stable yard behind Staverton Farm, 1940s.*

Below: *Staverton Farmhouse, home of the Blake family, 1910.*

Right: *Bringing in the hay on Staverton Farm.*

Below: *Staverton farmer Syd Yates and labourers set out to bring in the harvest.*

Above: *Staverton Farm's dairy herd in the 1940s.*

Left: *Aerial view of Staverton Farm, c.1950. The old cottages on the right occupy the land which is now the entrance to Elm Close.*

Below: *Aerial view of Staverton Farm buildings with the Old Bear in the foreground.*

standards, all of which combined to accelerate the village death rate, especially amongst the very young and the elderly. Poor diets and living conditions reduced resistance to illness and, although the horrific Black Death and smallpox epidemics of previous centuries did not re-emerge, other diseases were still rife and took a regular toll on the weak and frail. The sanitary arrangements were very poor at the time, the only toilet facilities being earth privies at the bottom of village gardens, which invariably seeped into wells and boreholes, which were main sources of water for the community. Added to the other contributing factors, this unhygienic situation helped to further increase the villagers' health problems and led to frequent outbreaks of disease and illness. Infant mortality rates amongst Staverton families in the first half of the century were very high with over 40 per cent of all deaths recorded up to 1839 being of children and young adults under the age of 20. Many families lost two or three infants within periods of a couple of years and quite a number of young women died in their twenties as a result of consumption and other illnesses, childbirth and the effects of difficult pregnancies. Childbirth, at the time, was a perilous affair, the babies were being born in cottages in unhygienic conditions, the births being aided by older family females or by employing the services of the village midwife who was looked upon as the local expert in these matters but who went about the business with no formal medical training. Many babies were stillborn, or died within a few hours or days of the birth, and some mothers perished during the birth or shortly afterwards mostly due to internal infections caused by the lack of adequate hygiene or proper medical care. Deaths of young Staverton women recorded between 1837 and 1843 included Elizabeth Edmonds aged 25, Elizabeth Deverill, 30, Elizabeth Browne, 28, Honor Gilbert, 19, Ann Edmonds, 23, Elizabeth Baker, 20, Jemima Powell, 27, Isabella, 28, and Ursula Brown, 20 – an average of almost two a year.

Infant deaths ranged from new-born babies only a few hours old up to children who had attained the age of five or six and even some village teenagers did not survive into their twenties with ten deaths in this age group being recorded between 1816 and 1850. The Gilbert family lost three of their children between 1825 and 1827, two of them just three weeks old, and a third, their 19-year-old daughter, who has already been mentioned. Other village families who suffered multiple bereavements of their young children were: the Gays whose seven-month-old son and nine-month-old daughter died within a space of three years in the 1820s. The Pocock family lost three children, two five-year-olds and one just a year old in the 1830s, and only two of Thomas and Mary Bull's children survived, one for three months and the other for two years, also in the 1830s. Nor did the infant death syndrome escape the wealthier

Staverton families, some of whom lost their offspring at very young ages. The cloth-mill owner Edward Cooper and his wife Mary mourned the death of their one-week-old son Henry in 1820 and the family suffered a double blow when a year later Edward's son Stephen and his wife lost their daughter Elizabeth at only nine months old. Herbert Bird's son, George, died aged 15 in 1825 and John Bird lost young Herbert Samuel, only two weeks old, in 1831.

The personal hygiene arrangements of many villagers during this period did not help the situation and normally amounted to the occasional bath in front of the parlour fire, the dirty water then being emptied into the back yard or by the roadside, further contaminating the underground water sources. Clothing was cleaned and washed infrequently and, when attempted, was a difficult and laborious operation, the garments first having to be soaked in tubs of water for several days without soap or detergent which was heavily taxed up until the 1850s and well beyond the meagre financial means of most ordinary villagers. Various scouring agents, including urine, were added to try and de-grease the soiled clothing, which was then vigorously rubbed and pounded before being rinsed in the river or nearby spring. Advances in medicine and medical care in the second half of the century gradually began to reduce the high mortality rate although Staverton, like many other communities during this time, still suffered frequent outbreaks of illness and epidemic especially amongst the young. Consumption, now known as tuberculosis, was still a fatal illness, which could affect all age groups and took a regular toll on those susceptible throughout the nineteenth century. It was still rife in the latter years of the 1800s and was responsible for the premature deaths of six villagers in the two years between 1875 and 1877, three of them being under 30 years of age.

Many deaths were put down to fever, such as those of four-year-old Martha Tayler and 21-year-old Frances Purnell in 1871, and ten-year-old Richard Taylor in 1872, but in many cases the fatal ailment was not really known and the cause of death only a guess. A particularly severe scarlet fever epidemic swept Staverton in 1877 affecting most of the village children and causing many deaths and long-term illness. In that year alone, nine village children all under five years old died from the fever including four young members of the Dallimore family, aged between one and four years old, who all died within days of each other. Two of the Barnetts' young daughters, Annie and Emily, aged three and four, succumbed to the illness, two-year-old George Powell did not recover from it, and several babies, four-month-old William Lloyd and eight-month-old Lucy Osborne, also became victims. Altogether, between the years 1813 and 1891, there were 134 deaths of village children under the age of five plus 22 in the age group 6 to 16, and 29 young adults

*Avonlea Cottage, the oldest house in the village, and
home to the Cooper family, cloth-mill owners,
in the 1820s.*

between 17 and 25, half of them females who had contracted fever, consumption or had childbirth complications.

Suicides were not uncommon especially amongst villagers who had fallen on hard times and young servant girls who had got themselves into trouble, as with 16-year-old Lily Barnett who threw herself into the canal in 1887 unable to cope with the disgrace. Many accidental drownings were also recorded, such as 21-year-old Samuel Powell who perished whilst swimming in the river in 1883 and James Hawkins, who had married Sarah Ann Miles in 1879, and was pulled dead from the canal in 1885. The rivers, streams and ponds around Staverton seemed to have a fatal attraction for some villagers, especially children, and many accidental and deliberate drownings were recorded in parish records in the eighteenth and nineteenth centuries such as the cases of Mary Watts, drowned in the Avon in 1783, and three village teenagers, Grace Bull and Sarah Silverthorne, both 12, and 14-year-old John Pullin who drowned in a frozen pond near the Down in 1791 after falling through the ice.

During the nineteenth century the interiors of the village cottages began to resemble the present-day homes with a number of distinct rooms such as a parlour, scullery and upstairs bedrooms. However, in the small weavers' cottages that made up most of the village housing stock, conditions were still very cramped and overcrowded with the large wooden hand looms taking up most of the upstairs which forced the often very large families to live and sleep together in the tiny space that remained. Kitchens, bathrooms and internal toilets were not yet a common feature, except in the larger houses of the wealthier families, and most of the domestic activities centred around the parlour with its open hearth for cooking and heating. By the early-nineteenth century, iron fire baskets were being introduced and coal began to replace wood and turf as the fuel for fires. Later in the century fireplaces improved with the addition of ranges, some quite sophisticated, and a whole variety of additional facilities became available on these including boilers for heating water and small ovens for baking. By the end of the century, home baking of bread was declining in favour of the local bakery and home brewing of ale was being superseded by the readily available supplies of beer and cider that could be purchased from or consumed in the village inn. Families relied on their garden plots and small orchards for the provision of vegetables and fruit and most villagers kept a pig in a sty or shed at the end of the garden, most treating the animal as an important member of the family. The pigs, after being fattened throughout the year, were slaughtered around Christmas time, quite an annual event in some households, and virtually every part of the carcass was saved and used. Blood was made into puddings and fat was collected in jars and used for cooking and as tallow for cottage lighting, besides providing a cheap and nourishing meal of bread and dripping for hungry family members. Part of the slaughtered pig was generally sold off to a local butcher or at the market, the money made from the sale being used to buy the next year's piglet. The arrival of the railway through Staverton in 1848 would later revolutionize villagers' travel habits, but until a small railway halt was provided in the early-twentieth century the old methods of horse and carriage, or more often Shank's pony, were employed to get to the nearest towns and railway stations at Trowbridge, Bradford-on-Avon and later Holt.

The railway did provide new job opportunities for some villagers, one of the first to be employed being James Hale, and in the latter years of the century quite a number of Staverton men and women were working for the GWR. Charles Turner took over the Old Bear Inn in the 1850s. Richard Hale was running a village shop, and up in Hilperton Marsh, William Shell was landlord of the King's Arms. Mary Ann Messiter dispensed beer from the Prince of Wales and George Purnell had a small shop on the Down. The first village school was founded in a warehouse on the canal wharf in 1850 and Staverton's river bridge underwent major repairs in 1852. Although the Staverton cloth factory ran into troubles in the 1840s and '50s, and even closed down for a while, the majority of villagers struggled on in the industry, many making cloth or taking jobs in the cloth-mills in Trowbridge and Bradford. Most of the remainder were labourers, some working as farm hands around the village, and a few still clinging on to their cottage businesses within the parish. The cloth-trade occupations varied from weavers to ordinary mill labourers and although work had been plentiful in the early decades of the century, it was not always guaranteed in the second half of the 1800s when the West-of-England cloth trade began to decline. Moses Barrett, Joseph Hiscox and Charles Powell are recorded as

Staverton weavers in 1865, James Turner as a spinner in 1861, and Charles Powell junior as a handle setter in 1866. George Powell, Martha Turner, William Woods, John and James Starr and John Samuel Moore are noted as cloth workers between 1861 and 1872. William Richman is described as a 'boatman' in 1864, probably working a barge on the canal. Richard Hale became a railway worker in the 1860s, and his daughter Elizabeth traded as a dressmaker in 1867. The local building trade was supported by masons Eli and William Lindsay in 1867 and Charles Powell offered his services as a carpenter in 1866. Two members of the Blake family, John and his son Maneah, were recorded as engineers in 1865 but whether they were freelance or connected to one of the local industries is not established.

Frederick Blake, Jesse Williams and William Summers, Joseph Osborne and George Davis were all farming varying acreages around the parish between 1862 and 1869 with Samuel Rudman, Wesley Perrett and Thomas Buckley also noted as Staverton farmers in the 1880s. John Osborne and Uriah Ladd traded as craftsmen in the building trade in 1868, the former as a carpenter, the latter as a mason, and another member of the Osborne family, James, earned his living as a hawker around the same time. Two other members of the Osborne family were employed in the parish in 1872, George as a milkman and John Henry as a day watchman, probably at Hargreaves' cloth factory. Village businessmen in the 1860s and '70s included John Collett, new landlord of the Old Bear, and Samuel Bird, a coal merchant, who operated from the Staverton canal wharfes alongside A. Cox and Sons, Walter Newth and William Watts who were all involved in the cargo-handling business on the Kennet and Avon Canal. Staverton had its own resident village vicar after 1861 when a new vicarage was built on the top road and Wyke House, home of the Trowbridge cloth-mill owners the Clark family, was rebuilt in 1865.

Staverton's weaving families were busy again when the village cloth factory reopened in the late 1860s and Walter and William Slade, Charles Powell, Jacob Rawlings, Joseph Jones and Arthur Davis are all noted as village weavers between 1873 and 1880. George Millard and James Powell are recorded as cloth dressers in the 1880s and many other Staverton men including John Fryer, Samuel Parrott, James and William White, Francis Silus Purnell and William Powell were all employed as cloth workers in the village cloth factory. Two village men had taken up clerical work in the 1870s and '80s with Mark Fryer working as an office clerk and Frederick Huntley Powell as a solicitor's clerk for a legal practice in the town. One unusual occupation noted from 1879 was that of artillery man, the profession attributed to James Hawkins, who lived in the parish and was probably attached to the military barracks in Trowbridge. Other craftsmen employed in the village cloth factory were engineer James Stokes, metalworkers Samuel and Berkely Munday and engine worker James Parfitt, the engines being the coal-fired steam engines which supplemented the water power in the cloth factory. William and Jane Linsey had taken over the Old Bear in 1880, Noah and Simeon Wakely traded as confectioners, Samuel Powell as a brewer and the King's Arms changed hands several times within a few years in the 1880s with Frank Gerrish, Abraham James and George Gibbs succeeding each other as pub landlord. In the late 1880s George Buckley was making mattresses. The Usher family and Herbert Vezey worked as leather dressers, James Hodges traded as a mason, Thomas Vezey as a gardener and James Chapman was a canal worker. William Blake had taken over the running of Staverton Farm from his father in the 1870s, Ann Taylor was the village shopkeeper in 1885, William Stokes took over the grocery store in Hilperton Marsh and Jesse Ovens became the new landlord of the Old Bear in 1895.

Despite the poor living conditions and difficult way of life during the nineteenth century, villagers were still able to enjoy themselves occasionally at the parish's annual festivals and celebrations. Plough Monday was one such event, held after Christmas to celebrate the coming of the new farming season, maypole dancing was an annual spectacle, and by the end of the century a parish feast was held every year in the village schoolroom. The most enjoyable event in the parish calendar was the harvest home supper laid on by the local farmers and landowners as a thanksgiving for the successful gathering in of the harvest. Every villager who had helped was invited to a sumptuous meal, served by the farmer, his family and servants, which was always supplemented with copious tankards of ale and home-made cider. Many an inebriated villager would stagger back to his cottage after this splendid day's feasting or collapse by the roadside or under a hedge where he was left to sleep it off.

The annual fairs and regular markets in the nearby towns were another source of entertainment for villagers, many spending the whole day enjoying the attractions on offer and taking the opportunity to purchase a wide variety of household items, food, clothes and even animals which could not be obtained in the village. Flower shows, carnivals, circuses, sporting events, fêtes and concerts, which became popular towards the end of the century, were keenly supported by villagers who later made up their own colourful floats on the back of horse-drawn carts and took part in the parades through the town. Apart from these activities the only other social life available to villagers, and then only the menfolk, was the visit to the local inns, which in the nineteenth century had no formal opening or closing hours, and which were a useful venue for swapping news and gossip and discussing all manner of topics from politics to gripes about the state of the village.

Staverton's first piped water supply came to the village in 1878 although some householders initially refused to be connected still preferring to draw their water from the various wells and pumps that were located near their cottages. It was to take a few more years to persuade every villager to accept the new water supply and several of them, like Mrs England in the Square, eventually had to be compelled to be connected by Local Authority Order in 1895. The first piped gas supply came to Staverton several years after the water, in 1880, and most cottages had been connected by the end of the century. This new power supply completely changed the domestic lives of villagers who, throughout the preceding centuries, had relied on candles, oil lamps, wood and coal fires for their lighting, heating and cooking. As a result of the new piped gas service seven gas street lamps were erected in the village in 1895 and Henry Taylor was appointed the village lamp lighter later that year. The new street lighting, however, did not please everyone and the newly formed Parish Council had to write to the village vicar, Revd Cavell, asking him to explain his comments in the church magazine in which he stated that 'the lamps erected by the Parish Council were more harmful than helpful.'

By 1891, the Staverton cloth factory was in serious decline and the Hargreaves family made plans to quit the business and put the mill up for sale. Prior to its closure there were still 30 cloth-making families living in the village and a similar number in Hilperton Marsh and the Down. Cottage weaving, however, had all but ceased and only four weaving families, those of Elizabeth Munday, Amelia Purnell, Ann and Martha Moody and Harry Giles, were still operating in the village. The remaining cloth workers included dyers Henry Purnell and Thomas Gay, cloth finishers and dressers Joseph and Jane Jones, Henry Taylor, May and Annie Dallimore, wool sorter Alfred Hale, millwright William Dallimore, and mill workers William Lane, Mary Taylor, Ann and Lucy Purnell, Nelson, Louis and Silus Purnell, George Ricketts, Henry and Martha Woodward, Arthur and Kate Chapman, Henry and Sarah Gay, and James and Charles Bennett.

The second biggest group of village workers were the farm labourers and, despite the steady reduction in agricultural jobs throughout the nineteenth century, there were still nine village men and boys working on the two or three farms that were operating around Staverton at the end of the century. Four members of the Purnell family, James, Edward, John and 12-year-old William were labouring on these

Wyke House, home of the Clark family, was rebuilt in 1865.

farms together with Fred Pearce, William Lloyd, William Woodward, Alfred Bennett and Edward Ladd. George Stevens, Frank Oram and brothers Charles and Henry Purnell were working at the nearby tannery, Richard Smith was a lath maker and his wife Bridget traded as a licensed hawker. Mason Alfred Barnett, his wife Sarah, and their four children, Edith, Henry, Florence and Clara, were living in Vine Cottage in the 1890s and he provided a local building service employing Herbert Oram and Edward Bennett as mason's labourers. Other villagers in the building trade were bricklayer Henry Stebbins, mason Frank Lloyd and, in Hilperton Marsh, carpenter and joiner James Osborne and plumber and glazier George Osborne. Staverton widow Mary Rison made straw bonnets for village ladies, John Pearce ran a boat-building business on the canal, Mary Hannum was a local dressmaker and James and Elizabeth Hudd sold flowers from their small nursery plot in Marsh Lane. A number of village women took in washing and provided a laundry service such as Mary Lloyd in Staverton and Eliza White, Elizabeth Chapman, Sarah Wiltshire and Anne Osborne in Marsh Lane and Wyke Road.

Many village youngsters were in service as parlourmaids, housemaids, cooks, nursemaids, gardeners and errand boys, and in 1891 over 20 Staverton boys and girls were working as domestics for the wealthier families in the village and in Hilperton Marsh and the nearby towns. Village vet Thomas Bazeley and his wife Fanny, who had bought the house and lands at Smallbrook in the 1880s, employed two servants, Martha Bishop and Ellen Cleverley. Parlourmaid Lydia Miles and cook Julie Usher looked after the Revd Cavell and his family at the vicarage, and clothier William Clark and wife Elizabeth, of Wyke House, were tended to by housemaid Jemima Pearce, parlourmaid Sarah Townsend and cook Lydia Newport. Coal merchant Samuel Bird and his wife Rosalie were served by Emma Emmans, Harry and Ann Purnell employed domestic Laura Jenkins, and widow Charlotte Mullins, in Wood Villa, was looked after by Alice Gaisford. Many other sons and daughters of village families were in service like Amelia Jones, Mary Powell, sisters Harriet and Mary Pearce, Florence Greenland

Above: *The Stevens family, c.1900.*
Albert and Martha (seated) *with*
baby Gertrude. Also in the picture
are Arthur, Charlie, Ethel and Bert.

Left: *Young Stan Bath who lived at*
5 Nasmilco Terrace.

Right: *Sarah Barnett who lived in*
Vine Cottage in the nineteenth
century.

Right: *The*
Taylor family,
c.1900.
Walter Taylor
and wife with
Victor,
Marjory and
Norah.

Right: *Some Staverton girls trained as nurses. Florence Barnett is on the left.*

Inset: *Nurse Florence Barnett.*

Right: *Edith Barnett became a nursemaid for the Sawtell family in the early 1900s. Seen here with young Geoff Sawtell.*

Below right: *Village mason Alfred Barnett and his family, Clara, Edith and Sarah, outside Vine Cottage in the 1890s.*

Below left: *Clara Barnett worked all her life at the Nestlé factory, c.1910.*

Above: *Clara Barnett as a young girl.*

Smallbrook House, c.1900, the largest dwelling in Staverton.

and gardener George Hancock. Henry and Lydia Taylor's daughter was a nursemaid, their young son an errand boy, and Old Bear landlords William and Jane Linsay employed Rhoda Kelson as their domestic. Some adults were also in service in the large houses of the local gentry such as coachman James Poplett, groom Everett Underwood and gardeners George Hancock, Frederick Morris and Thomas Vezey.

Many other occupations were taken up by villagers in the last years of the century like that of John Howland who had taken advantage of the new domestic fuel service coming into Staverton and had taken a job as a gasman. The village blacksmith in 1894 was Hedley Herbert Davis and Francis Merrett carried out his trade as a thatcher. Albert Browne and James Sartain set themselves up as dealers in 1898, Henry Taylor became an upholsterer, James Dyer had become a master farrier and Jesse Loxley a plasterer. At the turn of the century Edward Cleverley was a miller, Edward Salter a dairyman, and his son Albert a fireman attached to the Trowbridge brigade.

In the late 1890s there were just two main farms operating in the village, Staverton Farm and Smallbrook Farm. Thomas Candy was running Upper Wyke Farm, next to Wyke House, Sydney Crees had Lower Wyke Farm, and James Pike and Walter Greenhill were farming the lands around Hilperton Marsh. Wyke Road was beginning to fill up with houses, several long ranks being constructed in the late 1800s although the Down was still open land right up to Islington.

By the end of the nineteenth century the Church Vestry, which had looked after all parish matters for centuries, had lost most of its historic powers, and its influence gradually wained when County, Urban and Rural Councils were set up after the Local Government Acts of 1888. Staverton was made a separate civil parish in 1894, with a rateable value of £2,622, and the resulting boundary changes effectively reduced its size by a third to 446 acres. The introduction of the electoral system gave every resident the right to vote for their own local representatives and these elected bodies became the first Parish Councils. Staverton Parish Council was formed in 1895 with Ebeneezer Coleman as chairman, Henry Purnell as vice chairman, George Oram as clerk, and James Hale, John Hedges, William Lane and Joseph Jones as elected councillors. Ebeneezer Coleman was selected to represent Staverton on the Trowbridge Burial Board in April, George Oram was appointed assistant overseer of the parish poor, with a salary of £4 a year, and James Hale took over the vacant position of Parish Clerk. The Council hired the village schoolroom for their meetings at a cost of 1s.6d. and much of their initial business was taken up dealing with complaints about the bad state of the village's footpaths, drains and sewerage system. Harry Kemp was ordered to provide more closets 'at a suitable distance from his cottages' as there were only two to serve the rank of ten dwellings that sat behind Wood Villa opposite the Old Bear. Alfred Bennett became a Parish Councillor in 1897 when complaints were rife about the smell from Thomas Bazeley's pigsties at the bottom of School Lane, and concerns were being expressed about overcrowding at Turnpike Cottage, a situation that had also caused great social problems earlier in the century.

The Hargreaves family closed the Staverton cloth factory in 1891 putting many village cloth workers out of a job. Attempts by several other cloth-making firms to keep the factory going failed and by 1897 the site was again empty and up for sale. Cloth making had finally come to an end and many villagers, who had relied on the industry for their livelihoods in the latter decades of the century, moved on to find new work elsewhere. This mass exodus of village families dramatically reduced Staverton's population from nearly 350 in 1891 to less than 200 a decade later.

Aerial view of the village in 1968.

CHAPTER NINE

THE CANAL & THE RAILWAY

At the very beginning of the nineteenth century Staverton witnessed one of the engineering feats of the time when work started on the village's section of the Kennet and Avon Canal. The eastern and southern boundaries of the village were swarming with hundreds of navigators who had poured into the area to start digging out the cut and to build the bridges, locks and wharfes that would be needed to service this revolution in transportation. With no mechanical construction aids available at the time, all the work had to done by hand with the army of workmen having to move thousands of tons of earth, rocks and clay using only picks, shovels, barrels and horses. These navvies, as they became known, were rough hard-drinking men who often scared the locals. They moved from site to site living in hastily constructed crude wooden shacks which formed temporary ramshackle villages.

The original route of the canal, which would eventually link London with Bristol, was planned to pass close to Hilperton as it ran on into Trowbridge and would have bypassed Staverton as it snaked westwards and on into Bradford-on-Avon. However, this plan was changed in 1790 after a survey was carried out by the famous engineer John Rennie who needed to shorten the route in order to save on its building costs estimated at £214,000. This change of route would now bring the canal through Staverton, bypassing Trowbridge, and travelling on through Ladydown towards Bradford. Final approval for the construction came in 1793 but by then the cost had risen considerably to an estimated £375,000. Royal ascent was granted the following year with Rennie being appointed chief engineer, Dudley Clark the resident engineer and George Fletcher the superintendent of masonry responsible for building the locks and bridges. Work started on the Staverton section of the canal in 1800, was completed a year later, and the whole stretch from Devizes to Bath was open by 1803 except for the Caen Hill flight of locks which were not completed until 1810. The canal was constructed with sloping sides and a flat bottom and clay was used to line the cut and give it a watertight seal. This clay had to be puddled which involved it being mixed with water to make a crude cement, and then

The canal (1801) and railway (1848) dissected the village from north to south.

herds of cattle were driven along the canal bed helping to compact the mixture for the lining.

There were many obstructions during the building of the canal, including landslips, difficult rock formations and labour problems. Resident engineer Dudley Clark was sacked in 1800 for incurring too many expenses. Shortly after the opening of the canal in 1801 faulty stonework was discovered on some of the bridges and locks and by 1803 the Biss aqueduct was already in a bad state of repair. In 1804 Rennie asked for a further £140,000 to complete the whole canal, the extra money being needed to replace the poor quality stone in some of the locks and bridges, to repair leaks in several sections, and for

fencing the whole stretch, the cost of this being far greater than originally estimated. The Caen Hill locks were opened in 1810, the whole canal operating by 1811, and the total cost of construction had risen from the original estimate of £214,000 to just under £1 million.

The canal's potential for transporting goods was immediately recognised by local manufacturers who, up to then, had no option but to use slow and laborious land transport. Initial costs of carrying goods between Bath and London on the new canal were set at £2.9s.6d. a ton compared with £6 or £7 a ton overland. A small community soon sprang up around the Staverton wharf and the new canal way of life was written into the annals of the village history. The first barges on the canal were towed by gangs of men called bow hauliers but as soon as the tow-paths were completed mules, donkeys, and then horses took over the hauling task. Horse-towed barges moved from stretch to stretch at a leisurely two miles per hour with the towing animals being changed at

Top: *The Biss aqueduct, built in the Rennie style, 1801.*

Above: *Parson's Bridge before it was demolished and rebuilt over the marina entrance.*

regular intervals. The first narrow boats were built entirely of wood with the bottoms made from elm, because of its great resistance to rot, and the sides from oak which had to be treated with a mixture of cow hair, horse manure and tar to make them watertight. In the early days of the canal, narrow boats usually worked in pairs, the lead boat which was owned by the bargee being called a No.1 and the towed barge a butty.

Several links were proposed to the new canal including a branch which was planned to run into Trowbridge. This section, which would have left the canal near Ladydown and run into Islington, was started but never completed and evidence of its planned exit from the main canal can still be seen on the east bank just before the rear of Airsprung's factory. A Dorset and Somerset link to Frome, Wincanton and Sturminster Newton, which would have left the canal at the Beehive Inn, Widbrook, was commenced in 1803 but soon abandoned and some traces of the work can still be seen in the area. One branch of the canal which was completed was the Wilts and Berks which opened to canal traffic in 1810. It left the Kennet and Avon just below Semington Lock and ran via Melksham, Wootten Bassett and Swindon to Abingdon from where there were plans to link it into the Oxford Canal. This branch, initially very successful, was later abandoned and finally closed down in 1914. The busiest branch, and the one that would subsequently bring most of the trade to the Staverton wharfes, was the Somerset Coal Canal which was opened in 1805 and ran from the Dundas aqueduct at Limpley Stoke to the Somerset coalfields around the Radstock area. For many years it transported coal all along the canal and thousands of tons were offloaded at the Staverton wharfes to supply the woollen mills in the Trowbridge and Westbury areas which, by the early-nineteenth century, were converting to coal-fired steam engines for their power. Just like the other sections and branches on the Kennet and Avon Canal, severe competition from the railways after 1850 led to its decline and it was finally abandoned in 1907.

The Kennet and Avon Canal was initially very popular with local businesses and made steady trading profits in its early years. By 1818 over 200 barges were using the canal, nearly half of them with a 60-ton capacity, and average travelling time from Bath to Newbury was three and a half days. Some of the boats were huge, for example Bradford-on-Avon boatman James Long's barge *Trimmer* was 69 feet long and said to be able to carry 88 tons of cargo, and Charles Magg's boat was even longer at 70 feet with a 7-foot beam. The canal brought increased prosperity to the communities along its route and more than half the tonnage carried on it in the early years was Somerset coal, most of it being handled by Herbert Bird's business in 1821. Staverton wharfes became very busy and canal receipts for 1823 amounted to nearly £38,000. Passengers were also carried on the canal with services running between Staverton and Bath and a flyboat service to London. Flyboats were light craft which travelled mainly at night and operated on the Kennet and Avon from Bristol through to London and also on the Wilts and Berks section to Swindon. Average travelling time on these fast boats from Bristol to London was 36 hours, less than half the time a cargo-carrying barge took to cover the same distance. In the 1840s Drewe's, Shaw's and Parker's flyboats plied daily between Bath and London and these three operators handled most of the passenger and goods business on the canal. Best known was a flyboat called *Swallow*, known locally as the Scotch Boat, which carried some goods, mostly smaller packages, but which was really intended for passenger trade. It provided first- and second-class cabins, had a string band on board to entertain the passengers, was horse towed, and could travel between eight and nine miles per hour. Another small operator, Richard Bush, who also owned a beer shop in Bradford-on-Avon, ran an occasional flyboat service from Bradford Lock to Bath and Bristol and the other way to London, the latter service picking up passengers at the Staverton wharfes.

At its peak in the 1830s and '40s the canal was carrying nearly 200,000 tons of cargo annually, much of it loaded and unloaded at the local wharfes in Bradford, Staverton and Devizes. Staff on this section of the canal included 31 lock-keepers, 26 navigators, lengthmen and blacksmiths with each wharf equipped with stabling to house the canal horses which were the motive power to haul the barges. Amongst the goods carried on the canal, apart from the coal, were iron, building stone, slates, lime, chalk, timber, bricks, cement, grain, flour, tea, sugar, salt, tin plate and finished goods from a number of local industries. Coal, the major cargo handled at Staverton, was used to fire the first steam engines being installed in the local cloth-mills with one being in use as early as 1805 in Trowbridge and one in Staverton's cloth factory in 1813. Not only did the Staverton wharfes serve the immediate vicinity, but it was also cheaper for Westbury to obtain its coal from the wharfes rather than haul it by horse and cart from the Somerset coalfields. The availability of cheap coal gave the impetus to the construction of more new woollen mills in Trowbridge which were built to be steam powered from the start.

Constructed as a wide canal, the Kennet and Avon was 44 feet across and originally had a depth of 6 feet. The huge 70-foot barges being offloaded at the Staverton wharfes had to be first turned in a winding bay near Parson's Bridge before being towed stern first to the dock because they were too long to be turned in front of the wharfes. The coal being handled and transported on the Staverton stretch of the canal in the 1840s created profitable businesses for coal merchants John Bird and John Gye and

supported boat builders Samuel and Joseph Large. It also provided livelihoods for William Rolfe, John Pearce, John Kettlety, Eli Pickwick, Charles Wicks, Thomas Huntley, William Rich, James Gye, Thomas Hudd and Richard Hulbert, all recorded as Staverton boatmen in 1841. Two or three horse-drawn barges a day were pulling into the wharf to offload their cargoes of coal, most of it being transported by horse and cart to Trowbridge and Westbury to supply the cloth-mills and dye houses. One of the principal hauliers operating from the wharf were John Shallow and his wife who almost daily transported loads of coal to J. & T. Clark's factory in Trowbridge and to Salter's dye house in Duke Street. Other hauliers, such as Smith and Son, regularly delivered coal, coke, timber and other materials to businesses all over the district. The demand for coal from the cloth-mills was considerable and besides supplying Clarks' and Salter's mills, over 112 tons of coal a month from the Staverton wharfes was being delivered to Samuel Brown's factory in Trowbridge to fire his 20hp steam engine. Loads of Radford coal went to George Cadby's works in 1852, and most of the cloth-mills in Westbury were being supplied from Staverton in the 1840s and '50s.

The coal from the pits around Radstock came in a variety of different types and references are found to the Staverton wharfes handling small coal, black rock, coke and groze, most of the latter being used in the local cloth-mill's dye houses. Bird's wharf, on the south side of the road bridge, handled mostly Writhlington coal in the 1850s. Many other materials were hauled from the wharfes such as when John Gye's horses and wagons transported eight loads of redundant machinery from the empty Staverton cloth-mill to Westbury in October 1851, charging the customer 4s. per load. On the return journey the wagons brought back four loads of materials from Westbury to Staverton for 2s. a load. Gye and Bird kept quite a number of horses at the wharf, some as replacements to haul barges, and some as draught animals to pull the carts and wagons. Large quantities of hay, oats, beans and straw were needed to feed these animals and much of it was supplied by local farmers such as James Hooper who delivered a load of clover hay to Gye's in September 1852. Bargees regularly passing through Staverton in the 1850s were George Bunce, who often transported 65-ton cargoes of coal from Bristol to Crofton, and George Gye and George Beames, all operating 70-foot craft throughout the canal network.

Several other coal merchants had set up businesses at the wharfes after the 1850s and these included Arthur Newth, A. Cox and Sons, Walter Newth, William Wicks and Herbert and Samuel Bird, the latter employing father and son Edward and Edmond Powell as coal heavers in the 1870s. In the 1880s Robbins, Lane and Pinniger, based at Honeystreet, were the largest carriers on the canal and their barges

Left: *Canal Cottage in 1961.*

Right: *Broombridge, part of the Bird's coal wharf in the 1800s and later Avon's brush factory.*

Samuel Bird outside Elmfield, the Bird family home near the canal, which he built in 1906.

Star, *Speculator*, *Unity*, *Jane* and *Bissie* transported loads of wood, cut deals, elm boards, oak planks, cement, salt, and even manure, to the Staverton wharfes, one large consignment of building timber being delivered to James Hiscock.

The decline of the canal started with the opening of the railway in 1848 and four years later the Kennet and Avon was taken over by the GWR whose objectives were to gradually capture the canal's cargo business and move it onto their rail freight services. This severe competition led to further decline in the last half of the century and by 1900 the canal was virtually out of business as a going concern. Coal was still being handled at Staverton in the 1880s and '90s, 3d. a cwt screened and 2d. a cwt unscreened, and the Staverton cloth-mill sale notice of 1891 referred to 'plenteous' supplies of coal being available from the canal wharfes at 4s.9d. a ton. However, the severe competition from railway transport finally led to the cessation of the cargo business with the exception of several small operators who continued carrying goods on the canal into the 1930s. From the turn of the century up to the start of the Second World War, Robbin's boats *Argus* and *Jane*, and Noad's boat transported 500 sack-loads of grain from Avonmouth docks, twice a week, to Littleton flour-mill in Seend, the horse-drawn barges taking three days to complete the journey. In the 1920s and '30s Brown's barge *Irene* and Samuel Jackman's barge were still operating on the canal, on several occasions carrying loads of copper nails, paint, red lead, putty, linseed oil, tar and timber. The Staverton wharfes briefly enjoyed a new lease of life in the early 1900s when cases of tinned milk products from the newly opened Anglo-Swiss factory in the village were transported by barge to Bath and Bristol for distribution and export.

Returning barges brought back raw materials for the factory, some being stored in the wharf warehouse, which later became Avon's brush factory before being converted into a private dwelling. This building, located on the south side of the road bridge and now known as Broombridge, was originally stabling and a feed store for the coal horses. It contained a gas-driven chaff cutter which was given to Lackham Agricultural Museum. On the north side of the bridge there were coal stores and general goods storage; many of these original buildings remain. A small canal crane was in place on the edge of the wharf until the early 1900s and barge-towing horses were stabled in one of the buildings later used for storage by Nestlé. When the canal business finally ceased most of the wharf buildings were converted to private houses and some of the sheds and stores were used as farm buildings. A.H. and S. Bird continued to use the wharf on the Trowbridge side of the canal bridge for their coal business, and after the Second World War their horses and wagons were replaced by lorries operating from the yard until the early 1960s.

Canal lengthman George Parker and his family outside Ladydown Cottage in the late 1800s.

The first village school was started up in 1850, in a converted canal warehouse owned by the Kennet & Avon Canal Co., the building, now demolished, being adjacent to the present Wharf Cottage on the north side of the canal bridge. Walter Newth, a coal merchant and manager of the Staverton wharfes, arranged for the building to be leased from the company and he became one of the first school managers. A school building on the banks of the canal was not an ideal location and some parents expressed concerns about the dangers to their children, particularly one mother in 1864 who removed her son from the school with fears that 'he would fall into the canal and drown'.

The canal at Staverton did claim a number of lives over the years with accidental drownings and suicides, one of the most tragic incidences being that of six-year-old Thomas Parker who fell in and drowned in 1884. One of 13 children, he was the son of George and Nellie Parker who lived in a canal cottage near Ladydown Bridge. George was the lengthman on Staverton's stretch of the canal, whose job it was to daily walk the section checking that all was in order, that the water levels were maintained, and that there were no obstructions or leaks. The cottage, on the side of the tow-path, was provided by the canal company for the lengthman and his family and contemporary accounts describe it as having a beautiful arch of roses over the front door and a small garden plot at the back. When the canal went out of business in the early 1900s the cottage was abandoned, fell into ruins, and now only a few foundation stones remain in the undergrowth just off the tow-path below Ladydown Bridge where it was sited. Some who did accidentally fall into the canal were fortunate enough to be saved by the quick actions of nearby onlookers, as in the case of young John Hendry who was pulled out of the cut in 1889 by Herbert Vezey, who was later awarded the Royal Humane Society Certificate of Bravery. Despite the

Above: *The Vezey family outside Canal Cottage, 1920s. Pictured are Nell Vezey, Walter Vezey, Florence Foreman and Thomas Vezey.*

Edith and Walter Vezey, c.1930.

Left: *The wedding of Bert Foreman and Nell Vezey with bridesmaids Mabel and Dora Vezey, photographed outside Canal Cottage. The wharf crane can be seen in the background.*

Below: *Villagers setting off on a barge trip in the late 1800s. The wharf crane and Cox's warehouse can be seen in the background.*

tragic deaths caused by the canal it was also used for happier occasions. In the late 1800s, Staverton schoolchildren were treated to annual barge trips to Dundas organised by the Clarks of Wyke House. Coal merchant Samuel Bird also laid on boat trips on the canal around the turn of the century providing a horse to tow a barge brightly decorated with canopy and streamers, and with a string band on board, which took villagers on picnic trips to Dundas and Conkwell Woods.

The late Mabel Beaven (Vezey) recalled that when she was a young girl living in Marsh Road she often visited her gran, Miriam Vezey, who lived in the old canal cottage, just below Bird's coal yard, which had no electricity or running water, and she remembers water being taken from the canal and boiled up to wash the clothes. In the winter, when the canal froze over, her Aunt Nellie (Gibbs) used to love skating on its icy surface sometimes placing a lantern on the wall when it got dark so she could see to get back to the steps. Aunt Nellie, who lived her entire life in the cottage, married Bert Foreman, who owned a cold-meat shop in Church Street, Trowbridge, and he moved in with her after the wedding, later taking an active part in village life, at one stage serving a term as churchwarden at St Paul's Church.

Staverton's section of the canal runs from the accommodation bridge behind Hilperton Marsh Farm to Ladydown Bridge on the southern boundary of the parish. Travelling from north to south the canal runs through the Staverton wharfes which straddle the road bridge carrying the B3105 through the village and onwards to Bradford-on-Avon and Holt. This humpback bridge, which in recent times has carried vehicle weights far in excess of its original loading, used to carry the old red triangular load-limit signs which were removed by the Highways Department in the 1970s when the pedestrian footbridge was installed on the north side of the road bridge. Between the road bridge and Parson's Bridge there used to be a wooden swing-bridge which linked the lands of Upper Wyke and Smallbrook Farms, the only remains of this now being the stone abutments where the canal narrows at this point. Parson's Bridge, originally across the canal by the consortium, was replaced in 1990 by a modern road bridge which now services the marina development. The dismantled, 190-year-old over-bridge was reconstructed to span the entrance to the marina basins and carry the tow-path on the west bank of the canal. Careful examination of this old bridge reveals the grooves worn into the stonework on the arch sides, made by ropes in the old horse-towing days. Just in front of the modern road bridge, on the east bank of the

canal, are the remains of the winding bay referred to earlier and now incorporated into the boat yard and slipway owned by Hilperton Marina Holdings.

Below the modern glass-sided chandlery building are the remains of the canal bank where a boat-house, owned by the Clarks of Wyke House, used to be located and where members of the Clark family used to gather on summer evenings and take leisurely boat trips along the canal. The Hilperton wharf marina, established in 1982, created a base for modern leisure cruisers and narrow boats which could explore the waterway in far more comfort and style than the original bargees. A hire-boat company, Wessex Narrow Boats, set up by Graham and Mary Lee, was originally located here until moving to a new boat yard on the marina development in 1992. Wessex Narrow Boats, now under new ownership, have a fleet of ten luxury craft which are hired out throughout the year to holiday-makers who wish to spend a week or two exploring the peaceful and picturesque stretches of the Kennet and Avon Canal.

Samuel Bird, after whom the Old Bear Inn restaurant was named.

Following the canal southward from the new road bridge reveals an area on the east bank where the aborted Trowbridge branch of the canal was to exit the main waterway. This proposed branch, which would run to the north of Timbrell Street, never materialised because of the cost, and Trowbridge, a rapidly growing cloth town in the 1800s, was never directly linked to the Kennet and Avon. At the rear of the present-day Airsprung factory is another original canal over-bridge, Ball's Bridge, which carries the ancient footpath from Staverton village into Canal Road and then on into the town. The canal bends westwards at this point and crosses the railway and the River Biss on two almost adjoining aqueducts, the second one being built in the classic Rennie style. A little further on the canal leaves the parish boundaries at Ladydown Bridge and proceeds westwards to Widbrook and Bradford-on-Avon.

The arrival of the canal through the parish in the nineteenth century brought new business and employment opportunities to many Staverton families, some of whom made their fortunes from the coal trade they operated from the wharfes. The Bird family particularly were prominent in building up successful businesses and the canal in its heyday was providing work for lots of local people not only as wharf workers but in the many other trades that supported the canal industry. The availability of cheap coal was also the spur that accelerated the building of many new cloth factories in Trowbridge, and the Staverton canal wharfes played an important part in helping to create a golden age for local industry in the first half of the nineteenth century.

An engine of the Firefly class, the first engine through Staverton when the railway opened in 1848.

THE RAILWAY

Some 40 years after the building of the canal another major transport system came to the area. The railway, an increasingly popular mode of travel, was slowly creeping westwards and again the village of Staverton stood witness to history in the making within its borders. The WSWR (Wilts, Somerset and Weymouth Railway) had presented plans for a local railway system in 1844 and building began in 1845 after the necessary Acts of Parliament had been passed. The new line would run from Chippenham to Trowbridge dissecting the village to the west of what is now School Lane and only several hundred metres from the fully operational Kennet and Avon Canal which opened in 1801. The construction work would involve the building of a bridge to span the River Avon on the northern boundary of the parish and pass under the canal on the Ladydown side. Crossing under the main village road meant the construction of a road bridge near where the old school now stands and this must have caused great disruption to local movements at the time of its building in 1846.

By August 1848 the 14 miles of track from Thingley Junction, near Chippenham, to Westbury, had been laid and newspaper articles at the time described the grand opening of the railway on 2 September 1848 as an occasion of great interest and rejoicing, the innovation firing the imagination of most local people who marvelled at this modern mode of transportation. Isambard Kingdom Brunel, the famous railway engineer and architect of the new scheme, attended the grand opening and travelled on the first train down the line, a Vulture 2-2-2 of the

Firefly class, which was driven by Daniel Gooch, the superintendent of the GWRs locomotive department.

The line was officially opened to the public on 5 September 1848 and initially the timetable planned for five trains per day each way and two on Sundays. The planned branch line from Staverton Junction, which was later called Bradford North Junction, to Bradford-on-Avon remained unfinished, the reason for this was never fully explained although the probable cause was lack of sufficient funds to complete the work. Bradford Station had been built in 1848 and was ready and waiting for the line to be connected. The ensuing delay caused much fury in the town where the woollen-cloth industry was beginning to decline and the community was relying on the railway to generate fresh business and bring a new prosperity. It was nine years later, in February 1857, that the connection was finally made and during the long lapse much business had been lost to Trowbridge. About the same time as the Bradford link the branch line to Devizes was completed, connected into the main track from the junction at Holt. Initially, the new rail travel over Staverton's section of the line was so popular that in 1862 scheduled train services were increased to seven a day each way. Conversion to narrow gauge came in June 1874 and the original GWR broad gauge of seven feet and half an inch gradually disappeared from the railway network. In 1895 a connecting track was laid on the west side of Staverton Junction completing the triangle and creating a diversion route for the London to Bristol service which normally went through Box Tunnel.

The arrival of the railway brought new employment opportunities for villagers and a number of Staverton men and women made careers as railway workers with the GWR. Richard Hale became a platelayer in the 1870s and George Taylor, who started as a points man around the same time, had become a signalman by the 1880s. By the end of the century Thomas Barrow, Samuel Jones and Edward Hobbs had also become signalmen. Robert Purnell was an engine cleaner, Frank Gay a general cleaner, and William Lane and Alfred Nicholls were employed as railway labourers. James Hale was promoted to foreman in charge of a gang of platelayers which included Henry Gay, Henry Gumm and William Lane. Fred Stevens and Earnest Algar became porters on Trowbridge Station and James Andrews a brake man.

As Staverton moved into the twentieth century the railway was being used more and more, not only for passenger transport but also freight, and had taken most of the carrying business from the nearby canal which was, by then, in serious decline. The railway was used to despatch boxes of tinned milk from the newly opened Anglo-Swiss factory, the work being shared between Holt Station and the old Midland Railway terminus in Bath. Sentinal steam wagons and, later, Albion and Foden chain-driven lorries, ferried the factory's products to Bath and many stories were told by drivers of the troubles they sometimes encountered on the journeys. Many local roads at the time contained deep ruts, became very dusty in the dry summer months, and turned into quagmires in the winter. Steam wagons often got stuck on these uneven roads, or ended up in ditches, stranding their drivers for hours and delaying the delivery of goods to their intended destinations. Some drivers were lucky to escape serious injury or even death when their wagons ploughed through bridge parapets and hung perilously from the shattered stonework only inches from the deep waters below. From Holt and Bath the milk products were sent by rail to all parts of the country with many consignments going to the docks for export abroad.

The first steam motor-rail service was introduced in 1903, the trains stopping at Staverton to pick up passengers who climbed aboard from the track side on steps that were lowered from the carriages. This unsatisfactory method of boarding the motor rails was eliminated two years later when in October 1905 the village's own little station, Staverton Halt, was opened. The small station was located on the north side of the road bridge and initially contained only two 100-foot platforms, the wooden shelters and tall gas lamps being added several years later. Staverton's station soon became popular with local

Staverton's signal-box which used to stand on Bradford North Junction.

travellers and over the following decades was used by hundreds of villagers as well as Nestlé staff commuting to and from the factory. Milk-factory workers, who were given an annual treat by the company in the years preceding the First World War, sometimes used the railway service to travel on their day's outing to favourite seaside resorts on the south and west coasts and on one occasion for a day-trip to London. The factory also used the railway to deliver and despatch churns of fresh milk from Holt and Trowbridge stations where special sidings and covered loading bays were provided to handle the 17-gallon milk churns.

During the First World War rail traffic increased considerably with the movement of military supplies and equipment, war materials, troops and wounded servicemen, and in 1916 the royal train, carrying King George V and Queen Mary on a wartime visit to Trowbridge, passed sedately through Staverton Halt cheered by dozens of excited villagers who had heard of their visit to the town. In 1916 Nestlé drew up plans to install a factory siding and after long negotiations with the landowners, the Keddle family, secured the land they needed in 1917 for £1,160. However, the austerity of the war years and the recession that followed put a halt to the plan and it was to be many more years before the factory siding materialised.

Most villagers used the railway between the wars to get to work or to go on shopping trips and, during weekends and bank holidays, many took the train for days out at seaside resorts such as Weston-super-Mare and Weymouth. As a young girl at Staverton School Mabel Beaven (Vezey) remembered the fascination the village children had for the railway as they used to call out and wave to the engine drivers waiting on the line below the school for the signals on the junction to change. This fascination often got pupils into trouble and accounts in Staverton School's logbooks refer to some of them being 'severely scolded' by the mistress for absconding from the classroom to watch the trains go by, and several boys being 'severely punished' and threatened with expulsion for straying onto the railway lines. Mabel Beaven, when she left school and had completed an apprenticeship as a milliner, worked at a shop in Chippenham and had to catch the 7.30 train from Staverton Halt every morning and then wait in Chippenham Station until the shop opened. She would return to Staverton on the 6.27 during the week but on Saturdays the shop stayed open longer and Mabel had to catch a later service arriving back in the village after 9p.m. in the evening. No shorter working week in those days!

In 1933 the three signal-boxes on the junction were demolished and replaced with a single box on the up line between the north and south tracks and the old manual points and signals were converted to a motorised system. The long planned Nestlé

Left: *An engine in the milk siding at Holt Station.*

Below: *Staverton Halt, opened in 1906.*

Below: *Nestlé factory siding plan, first drawn up in 1915.*

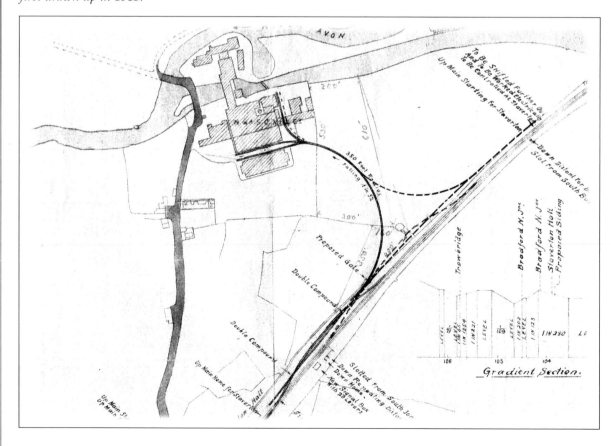

Above: *Nestlé factory girls Christine and Sheila Vines waiting for a train on Staverton Halt, 1966.*

Above: *Front of the milk factory showing the rail wagons on the siding.*

Below: *The siding running into the back of the factory.*

Below right: *A Foden chain-driven lorry in trouble on the river bridge, c.1910.*

An engine shunting on the factory siding.

siding came in September 1934 and at long last the company could bring raw materials and milk supplies straight into the condensery. First planned in 1916, but delayed for 18 years, the siding branched off the main railway line at the back of the factory and movements were controlled by a simple ground frame which had to be operated by the shunter driver. The original plan had been for the siding to sweep in from the Staverton Halt direction but when finally installed this had been reversed and the line came off the main track from the north. As the siding entered the factory buildings it split into several separate branches which serviced the warehouse, tin shop, process block and boiler-house. Simple points were installed to control the movements of the rail wagons, a turntable directed coal trucks to the rear of the boiler-house, and the lines which ran right to the front of the factory were terminated by large sets of buffers.

The siding allowed Nestlé to receive a variety of raw materials straight to the door and regular deliveries of commodities included tin plate from South Wales, box board for making the cartons, sugar, coal, and of course supplies of fresh milk. Finished products were also sent out by rail and in the early days the shunting of the wagons on the siding was aided by the factory horse, this arrangement however being very short-lived when the poor animal was invalided out of service after only two days having gone lame with a nail in its foot.

Rail traffic passing through the village increased enormously during the Second World War and at times there were more than 40 scheduled workings a day. Ambulance and troop trains frequently passed through the village together with freight wagons delivering war supplies to Army camps, Navy bases and embarkation ports.

The factory siding was also very busy bringing in raw materials and surplus milk to be made into products mainly for the Ministry of Defence and the Admiralty. Later in the war the siding was used to despatch Red Cross parcels for POWs, compo packs for the Armed Forces, which were packed at the factory, and to send desperately needed bulk milk supplies to the bombed-out citizens of London. Staverton Halt was also a hive of activity in the early war years becoming the stopping-off point for members of Nestlé's Head-Office staff sent down to the factory from London in 1939 to escape the threatened aerial attacks on the capital. Evacuees sent to the relative safety of the Wiltshire countryside at the start of the war also arrived by rail at Staverton Halt to be collected and accommodated in houses around the village. The shortage of petrol later in the war increased passenger use on the railway and many villagers and factory personnel used the trains to carry out their essential journeys.

In the years following the end of the Second World War passenger use declined mainly due to the more convenient and regular bus services that were beginning to serve the community. Nestlé staff from outlying districts continued to use the railway to get to work and a number of regulars used the service right up to the closure of the Halt in 1966. Some villagers still preferred to use the rail service in the 1950s and '60s for shopping trips to Trowbridge, Bath and Bristol and the occasional outing to the seaside. Some village mothers with young babies found it more convenient than the bus service in the 1960s and on some days quite a few mothers with prams and pushchairs could be spotted lined up on the platform waiting for the Trowbridge train to arrive.

A few villagers were fortunate enough to witness a rare and historic sight in 1963 when the famous *Flying Scotsman*, hauling a Pullman train, steamed slowly through Staverton Halt on one of its promotional trips. This was a rare event indeed as engines of this type rarely strayed from the main rail routes and hardly ever ventured on to small country branch lines. The railway decline reached a peak in the mid 1960s and Dr Beeching was called in to wield his now infamous axe. One of the casualties of Beeching's cost-cutting exercise was the branch line that ran through Staverton which was closed to passenger traffic in April 1966 and the village's station was closed down and demolished the following year. Nestlé's siding was also removed, in January 1967, to make way for further factory expansion and the main line between Bradford Junction and Chippenham was reduced to single track later that year. Staverton no longer had its own station and the era of rail travel from the village came to an end after 60 years.

Staverton could claim to have a royal patronage when, on a day in 1966, the royal train with the Queen and Prince Philip on board spent the night on the siding by Bradford Junction. Royal trains used this convenient and secluded stopping place on several occasions and Prince Charles was rumoured to have courted his future wife, Lady Diana Spencer, when the train had stopped overnight at Staverton in 1980. Reports in a national newspaper suggested that Lady Diana was driven to the village 'at dead of night', and under great secrecy, to meet up with the Prince aboard the royal train. Local reports describe her being smuggled through the chicken farm at the bottom of School Lane, by police and security men, for a rendezvous with the future king.

Despite the axe, in 1966 Staverton's section of the line remained open for passenger trains and became a vital diversionary route when adjoining branches of the network were taken out of use for essential maintenance or other disruptions. For instance, between 1986 and 1988 there were seven return workings daily on the line but by early 1990 passenger traffic on the Bradford to Chippenham line had dropped to only one return per day plus two at weekends. Freight traffic on the line also continued after the official closure but consisted almost entirely

The royal train on the junction near School Lane.

of stone trains rumbling slowly through the village carrying their cargoes from the Mendip Quarries and heading to destinations northward. This traffic was at its height in the 1970s when up to 14 stone trains, loaded and empty, passed through the village daily mostly during the hours of darkness. The signal-box on the junction was in use until March 1990 and was the last remaining manually-operated box controlling semaphore signals in Wiltshire. It had been planned to phase it out in 1984 when a new signalling scheme came into service transferring the control of Bradford Junction to Westbury.

Delays in the implementation of the new scheme kept Staverton signal-box open for another six years and traffic on the line continued to be controlled by Tyers Key Token instruments, one at the signal-box and the other at Chippenham Station. The old red-brick signal-box, which had controlled traffic on the junction since 1933, was finally closed down in 1990 and later demolished. By the early 1990s very little remained of the village's tiny station although observers could just make out the overgrown pathways which led down to the two small platforms, now just bramble-strewn piles of rubble. The golden age of rail travel from the village was long gone and very few traces of its existence and the important role it played in Staverton's history are left for future generations to study. Whether train services will ever return to Staverton is a matter of conjecture but recent Government policies to expand public transport services in rural areas have given a small glimmer of hope that Staverton Halt could be resurrected one day as part of the overall strategy for transport provision in the future.

Right: The notice on the Ground Frame which controlled rail traffic movements on Nestlé's siding.

The royal train entering Staverton over the river bridge in 1966.

A train steaming through Staverton Halt in the 1950s.

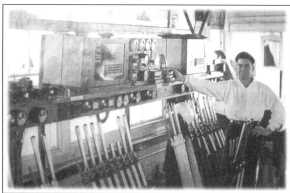

Above: *The last signals were pulled in Staverton's signal-box in March 1990.*

Right: *Lighting the gas lamps on Staverton Halt, 1966.*

Right: *The last tickets issued for Staverton Halt before its closure in 1966.*

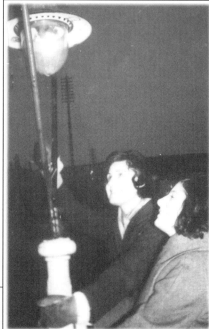

Left: *Gang of Great Western Railway platelayers working on the railway near Staverton. William Lane is third from the right.*

CHAPTER TEN

A CENTURY OF NESTLÉ AT STAVERTON

The closure of the village cloth-mill in 1891 was a devastating blow for many families who had been employed in the cloth trade as they now faced the prospect of losing their livelihoods. There had been over 30 cloth workers living in the village prior to the closure with a similar number in Hilperton Marsh and, despite the aspirations of several smaller cloth-making firms to keep the factory going between 1893 and 1897, cloth making in Staverton came to an end when G. Lewis and Co. vacated the premises. Many Staverton cloth-making families were forced to leave the village and to seek employment elsewhere while those that remained waited anxiously for the opportunity to secure work with the business that would take over the site.

The Nestlé connection with Staverton began in 1897 when the Anglo-Swiss Condensed Milk Co. purchased the empty cloth-mill site for £6,000 and began converting its old buildings into facilities for producing tinned milk products. Anglo-Swiss had been founded in Cham, Switzerland, in 1866 and moved into the UK in 1873 setting up condenseries at Chippenham, Aylesbury and Middlewich. In the 1890s the company, whose business had expanded rapidly, looked for a fourth site on which to open another milk factory. The old Staverton cloth-mill was an ideal spot with its complex of easily converted buildings, an abundant local supply of fresh milk, and a readily recruitable workforce of local people who were desperately seeking new employment. The old mill, at the time, was powered by three coal-fired steam engines and two iron breast-shot water-wheels that could generate 60hp when the water level in the river was at a suitable height. Anglo-Swiss soon replaced these unreliable water-wheels with a 43hp Vortex water turbine but, as later events were to prove, this was equally as unreliable as its predecessors. With the necessary conversions under way, the company began to recruit its first workforce in December 1897, the first hourly paid worker to be engaged being Staverton resident James Bond whose job it was to drive the factory steam engines. Henry Purnell was taken on as a stoker, Arthur Baldwin was engaged to look after milk deliveries, and James Beaven was given the job of pan man processing the vats of condensed milk. Wages for these first three employees were around £1 for a 60-hour week and Fred Rogers, manager of the Chippenham factory, was put in charge of Staverton Condensery assisted by his son Donald. The first tins of sweetened condensed milk, in a 12oz size, came off the production line in March 1898. The cans needed for this were made at Chippenham and transported 11 miles to Staverton by horse and cart, the journey usually taking a whole day to complete. Local farmers were contracted to supply fresh milk and this was delivered by horse and cart in 17-gallon conical churns each weighing over 2 cwt when full. All the manufacturing operations were done by hand in those early days and by the end of the first year the workforce had increased to around 140 with male workers being paid £1 a week and women 10s. a week. Production increased slowly and by 1901 200 local farmers were delivering their milk to the factory, contemporary accounts describing the long lines of horse-drawn wagons, loaded with churns, stretching along the road, their drivers waiting patiently to be called forward for offloading.

In 1902 the first tins of unsweetened condensed milk rolled off the production line and Anglo-Swiss, the pioneers of this new product in the UK, began to sell it under the now famous brand name of Ideal Milk. With two products now being made, the workforce steadily increased under the watchful eye of George Hussey, the factory's first timekeeper and unofficial labour overseer. Fred Rogers, the manager, made a weekly journey on his bicycle from Chippenham to Staverton to bring back and pay out the workers' wages. He later used the railway for this journey before acquiring one of the early Ford cars and was on hand to witness the first telephones being installed in the Staverton factory in 1903.

Nestlé came onto the scene in 1905 when they merged with Anglo-Swiss to form the Nestlé and

Above: *A horse and cart taking churns of milk into the condensery, 1899.*

Above and left: *The first products made at Staverton's milk condensery in the early 1900s.*

Anglo-Swiss Condensed Milk Co., which had a combined workforce of 3,000 nationwide. Henri Nestlé, a Swiss chemist, had started a baby-food business at Vevey in Switzerland in 1867 and, like Anglo-Swiss, his company had grown rapidly by the turn of the century and was keenly competing with its rival for the condensed milk market in the UK. Local accounts of the 1905 merger refer to Staverton factory being made 'spick and span' for the visit by 'top-hatted gentlemen' from the Swiss Nestlé Company. The merger was enthusiastically welcomed by the Staverton workforce who were more than pleased with the celebration bonus which varied from £1.15s. in cash to a £5 company bond.

The first production of skimmed condensed milk commenced in 1906 and the surplus cream from the separation process was made into butter with over two tons a day being produced by 1908, most of it being sent to London to be sold on the wholesale markets. By 1906 the increased levels of production prompted the building of Staverton's first tin-making plant which was set up in one of the old outbuildings, and by 1910 the company's four English condenseries were producing 225,000 cases of tinned milk each year.

The workforce continued to grow and the first social activities were organised for the employees, including the formation of the factory's first soccer team and an annual outing, paid for by the company, which took the Staverton and Chippenham workers to favourite seaside resorts for the day and, in 1907, to watch the opening of the White City in London. The eagerly awaited day of the annual treat started with the Chippenham contingent boarding an excursion train at 6a.m. and travelling to Trowbridge Station where they were joined by their colleagues from Staverton. Each worker received 6d. to spend on the trip and this was invariably used to purchase, amongst other things, two pints of beer and an ounce of tobacco. In later years the workers travelled on solid-tyred open-topped charabancs to the chosen annual destinations.

The factory began making tinned milk for the Admiralty in 1910 and the company's English Creamery Butter, produced under the supervision of Herbert Griffen, was packed in 2lb rolls in salted and unsalted varieties, and sold for 5d. per pound. Skimmed condensed milk was produced and sold under the Blue Joss, Teapot, Cow's Head and Milk Jug labels as well as 50 or more others which were supplied by the buyers who required their own brand labels on the tins. Richard Wells, who had joined the factory as a fitter in 1900, was appointed 'in charge of the control and maintenance of all mechanical equipment' in 1912 and this position became the forerunner of later factory chief

Left: *Nestlé factory girls on the bridge in front of the old mill, 1905.*

Below: *Nestlé factory girls, 1906.*

Below: *Lil Purnell was a nurse in the First World War and later became the factory nurse.*

Above: *Staverton factory hot-room girls, c.1919.* Left to right, back row: *Nellie Parker, Rose Charnbury, Lil Purnell, Isobel Gliddon, Maude Davis, Dorothy Fralley, Winnie Randall, Gladys Lane, Elsie Landsdown, Clara Barnett, Kit Lane;* centre: *Rose Jones, Ethel Gray, Win Chapman, Gladys Hale, Violet Sharp, Florence Lane;* front: *Florence Whatley, Daisy Bowyer.*

Below: *Nestlé workers with bicycles on the hill leading up from the factory during the First World War.*

Workmen building Staverton's tin shop in 1913.

engineers. One of the first concerns in his new role was to resolve the problem of the factory's main steam engine constantly breaking down and halting production for many hours on several occasions. The water turbine, described earlier as 'unreliable', proved this to be the case when, during these major breakdowns, it could not be operated if the water level in the river was too high. He was also involved in another major construction project at the factory and oversaw the completion of a rank of six workmen's cottages adjoining the old weavers' cottages in Nasmilco Lane. These new cottages were needed to house some of the factory's key workers and their families and added to the nine existing cottages, built by John Jones in 1810, which sat on the high bank overlooking the factory. He also supervised the construction of a brand new custom-built red-brick tin shop on the south side of the site which had three floor levels and lifts and toilet blocks at each end.

Business was booming by 1913 and to meet the growing demand for the company's products, factory extensions were needed. The boiler-house was enlarged and two new Babcock water-tube boilers, with mechanical chain-grate stokers, were installed together with a 120-tube economiser. A new factory chimney was needed to service the modernised boiler-house and the German firm of Alphons Custodis began its construction by the end of the year. Shop floor wages had risen to £1.2s. for a 55-hour week for men and 65d. a week for women. Foremen's pay varied from £1.16s. a week for process and filling staff to £2.2s. a week earned by the maintenance-shop foreman. The new chimney was completed by early 1914 except for the water tank, which was built in Dortmund, Germany, and had to be shipped over to the UK and erected on site. Unfortunately, when the tank was lifted for connection to the chimney it would not fit and modifications had to be carried out on site, the work finally being completed by April 1914. The 172-foot-high chimney had a 6ft 6in. diameter at the top and a 40-cubic-metre capacity water tank fitted halfway up the stack, the whole construction costing £1,056.

Prior to the start of the First World War the factory was employing 116 men and 140 women and employees with more than ten years' service were now getting six days' paid holiday a year including Christmas Day and the annual outing day. Staff salaries varied by rank with chief clerk Frank Brewer earning £15 a month, Reg Mundy, the factory's general foreman, receiving £14 a month, and a junior clerk £6 a month. Donald Rogers, the acting factory manager, received the usual senior management benefits such as free housing and a company vehicle which he exchanged in 1914 for a brand new Studebaker car costing £295.

The outbreak of the First World War in August 1914 stimulated a huge demand for tinned milk products and the factory output immediately came under the control of the Ministry of Munitions and the Admiralty who increased their orders to over 6,500 tonnes of Ideal Milk a year. Several key Staverton workers had been drafted for active service at the start of the war and a number of men had volunteered for the Armed Forces in the first few weeks of the conflict. By October the factory was facing difficulties meeting the sudden increase in demand, machines began to break down through overwork, milk supply problems were being experienced, a fever epidemic had caused high absenteeism, and call-ups were taking away many operators. A total of 17 key men had already been called up by December and the factory began sending letters to the military authorities requesting their return. Most of the factory's production was going to the war effort and the company, considered a vital war industry, had issued war badges and certificates to their factory employees designating them 'essential war workers' and immune from call-up. The workforce increased to 289 in 1915 and Donald Rogers, who had looked after the running of the condensery almost from its opening in 1897, was appointed Staverton's first resident factory manager.

The factory's manufacturing difficulties continued as 1915 drew to a close and the demands by the Ministry of War to release more Staverton men for active service increased. Management reported that the factory was suffering from 'loss of expertise', replacement of male labour was impossible because of the war, and efforts became intense to prevent more 'badged' men from being called up. Urgent requests were made to the military to return some of Staverton's essential workers to help resolve the factory's running problems, and in early 1916 Herbert Griffen and five other men, including 16-year-old tin-shop worker Gilbert Griffen, who had disguised his age in order to join up, were eventually released and returned. However, efforts to get tin-shop fitter Howard Purnell returned ended in failure and he was killed in action at the Battle of the Somme some months later, the first Staverton man to make the 'supreme sacrifice'. Some 24 factory men had already been called up by March 1916 and the female workforce had to be increased to 170 to replace them. The stubborn resistance to more call-ups incurred the wrath of the military authorities who accused Staverton factory of 'being unpatriotic, the funkhole of Wiltshire regards recruiting' and Staverton itself as being 'a shirking ground for young men of military age who are badged but not indispensable'. Nestlé and Anglo-Swiss responded to this unfair criticism by stating that 24 Staverton men had already enlisted and 19 were already engaged on active service. The company as a whole had 435 men serving 'with the colours' and £10,000 a year was being paid to their dependants with each enlistee's family receiving 12d. per week plus an additional 2d. for each child. As more troops were lost in combat, so the military became desperate for replacements and all war badges were withdrawn making every factory male, of service age, available for call-up.

Wages had increased again by May 1917 to 3d. per hour for men and 2d. an hour for women with both receiving an additional 40d. per week war bonus. Staff received additional payments of between £5 and £10 per month to compensate them for the long hours some of them were being forced to work. In the last year of the war local appeals were being made for war funds and the factory responded with a generous donation of £500 for the National War Bonds Aeroplane Appeal, donations to local hospitals and financial support for the Staverton and Hilperton Nurse Funds. A worker's health scheme was introduced in early 1918 with each employee paying $1/2$d. a week out of their wages to Trowbridge Cottage Hospital in return for free medical attention, and wages increased again to 3d. an hour for men and 2d. an hour for women, both receiving an extra 55d. war bonus and married employees with families getting an extra 5d. a week for children under the age of 14. Staff salaries varied from £22 a month for senior office workers to £12 a month for a junior clerk, and foremen were paid between £2.5s. and £2.10s. a week, plus a £1.6s. war bonus, depending on departments. Fresh milk intake was averaging 18,000 gallons a day in the peak, most of this being turned into Ideal Milk for the Admiralty who were supplied with 14 million tins a year throughout the duration of the war. The Allied build-up for the final offensives of the war required massive troop reinforcements and every available man in the country was being called up to serve in the trenches.

Despite this drain on Staverton's male workforce in the last three years, more call-ups were issued to factory men in the summer of 1918 and, exasperated by the effect this was having on what had always been recognised as an essential war industry, the factory wrote another strong letter to the military authorities complaining that the further demand on its manpower resources was now seriously affecting the operation of the factory. Outputs and quality were being jeopardised due to the loss of skilled operators, and concerns were expressed that this could lead to a failure to deliver vital goods ordered under war contracts. Requests were made to stop recruiting at the factory which would be left with only one fitter if all the others, who had already received their call-up papers, had to go. Women and girls had been brought in to replace the enlisted men and this had led to more production problems as some of the females were finding it difficult to cope with many of the heavier jobs normally carried out by the men. The problem had become so acute that the factory manager, Donald Rogers, was constantly involved with trouble-shooting on the shop floor and had been unable to take a day off in the last three years. Despite the factory's protestations more Staverton men were called up in August, including two of the three fitters left, and by the war's end over 75 men, most of the male workforce, were in khaki.

The sudden end of the war in November 1918 was greeted with sighs of relief by the beleaguered Staverton workforce who could now look forward to the factory returning to normal despite mourning the loss of 11 of their colleagues. With the war finally at an end the company celebrated the Allied victory by giving every Staverton worker a £5 Victory Bond and declaring a day's holiday for all on 19 July 1919. Victory parades took place locally, the factory entering a patriotic float, and Donald Rogers and wife treated all the local children to a lavish tea party in the village schoolroom, each child receiving a commemorative mug, and sports and entertainment followed for the rest of the village.

By the end of the war 6,535 cows were supplying milk to the condensery, most of it being delivered in the 3,600 17-gallon churns owned by the factory, and an average 4,500 gallons a day were being delivered by rail, mostly into Trowbridge Station where it was collected by horse and cart from a special siding and brought to the factory. In November 1918 Donald Rogers purchased Wood Villa, the detached house opposite the Old Bear, and when the deal was completed he was given permission to install an inside toilet and a bathroom. The property, owned by Samuel Bird, was bought for £445 after previously being rented by the company for £18 a year as the factory manager's residence. Besides obtaining a new house Donald Rogers traded in his old Studebaker car, which was valued at £340, and purchased a brand new black and dark-green Paige

Nestlé office staff, 1919. Left to right, back row: *Arthur Francis, James Parker, Albert Stevens, Fred Roberts, ?;* front: *George Hussey, F.H. Brewer, Charles Gibbs.*

motor car for £875 commenting that 'it maintained a good grip on the road and there was very little vibration when driving.'

In 1919 the workforce numbered 313, the working week had been reduced to 48 hours and wages had further increased to £2.12s. a week for men and £1.13s. a week for women. Foremen were being paid between £4 and £4.15s. per week depending on their scope of job, and staff salaries had increased by ten per cent. Arthur Baldwin, one of the first employees to be engaged in 1897, was still foreman of the milk receiving room, Herbert Griffen was in charge of separating and William Purnell ran the sterilising room. The filling was supervised by Albert Matthews, the wet room by Herbert Bainton, and the packing room by John Brown. One of the highest paid foremen was George Wickham, in charge of the tin shop, and another long-serving employee, Herbert Gay, who had joined the company in 1899, was fitting-shop foreman under Richard Wells, the mechanical overseer. Bill Weston had taken over as the factory's general foreman, in charge of labour, and James Beaven was now senior pan man. The factory's first milk-collection lorry fleet came in 1919 with the purchase of two three-ton Albion trolleys which had solid tyres, a 13-inch wheelbase, and were geared to a top speed of 15mph. The vehicles had open cabs, two-side paraffin lamps, cost £495 each, and when a third arrived in early 1920 the first milk collections started from the farms. By the end of the year the fleet had built up to a dozen Albions and these were duly placed in the charge of the garage foreman, Charles Endru.

Signs of a post-war depression began to appear in late 1920, the demand for Admiralty milk dropped off and volumes fell to 271,000 cases. Sales of tinned milk fell resulting in a cut back of production and the laying off of 35 women workers at the end of 1920 and a further 32 the following January.

Demand continued to fall and, in an attempt to prevent more lay offs, the factory's working hours were temporarily reduced to 40. Since the end of the war raw material costs had risen sharply, by 500 per cent for some commodities, the factory began to run into financial difficulties, and the situation became so

serious by the end of the year that urgent measures were taken to reduce costs and all employees were asked to take a ten per cent pay cut. The problems continued through 1922, sales fell another 20 per cent and the year ended with only 136,000 cases of tinned milk being produced, half the amount of the previous year. The situation improved slightly in 1923 with volumes reaching 236,000 cases and with it an increase in the workforce to 255. Edward Watson became the new foreman of the wet room, Arthur Stevens the foreman of the filling room, and Harry Kemp had a similar role in the sterilising room. Herbert Griffen still supervised the small amount of butter now being made and the expansion of the lorry fleet operations required more help with vehicle maintenance in the form of garage lad Cecil Horner. The economic situation fluctuated over the next few years and improved slightly in 1925 allowing a small increase in the workforce to 302. Fresh milk intake was running at four million gallons a year in the mid 1920s, all this being made into products, but another slump in 1927 led to 51 workers being laid off and the workforce reduced to 227, the lowest it had been since the First World War.

The bubble finally burst in 1929, the world sank into depression, exports dried up, foreign markets disappeared, there was a run on the pound and unemployment shot up to over two million, all this affecting the factory whose outputs dropped to 192,000 cases, the lowest it had been for many years. Staverton factory, however, managed to weather the storm, James Homewood took over as factory manager in 1930 and the first tins of sterilised cream were produced, effectively ending the butter-making operation although a small amount was still produced up to the start of the Second World War. The new product gave the factory a much needed boost as it struggled through the depression, helping to retain most of the workforce. Although home markets were still depressed, the new sterilised cream had great export potential particularly to the United States.

Things began to pick up again after 1930 and by 1932 the factory was manufacturing canned milk in seven different sizes as well as producing cocoa tins in quarter, half and 1lb sizes. The factory regularly supported the local carnival in the 1930s by entering colourful floats, and the factory football team played competitive matches in the Trowbridge and District League and later the Bath League winning several trophies. By 1934 the workforce averaged 320, two extra can sizes were introduced, and outputs reached 700,000 cases helped by a reduction in the sale price by 1d. a tin. Pan men, the best paid factory operatives, were earning 7d. an hour, labourers 5d. an

Above: *Aerial view of the mill and factory, early 1920s.*

Right: *Workmen building the new red-brick process block in 1934.*

Above: *Factory carnival float in the 1930s.*

Right: *George Gibbs, Anglo-Swiss night-watchman at the turn of the century.*

Staverton victory parade, 1919.

hour, women 3d. an hour, and young boys and girls 2d. an hour. The factory's milk-collection lorry drivers, under foreman John Morris, averaged £3 per week, production foremen earned around £4 a week and George Gibbs, in charge of the laboratory, did marginally better at £4.10s. a week, although junior lab assistants were some of the poorest paid workers with several on the lowest factory wage of 62d. a week. Bill Weston was now titled 'labour overseer', directly responsible for the workforce who were working under foreman Ernie Hillman (tin shop), Frank Hinton (packing), Syd Wainwright (filling), William Purnell (sterilising) and Bill Pullen (milk-receiving room). Frank Beaven looked after the boiler-house, Archie Hillcoat the fitting shops, with Donald Sartain and Arthur Stevens in charge of sweetened and unsweetened filling lines.

The biggest factory expansion to date came in 1934 when some of the old mill buildings on the south side of the site were demolished to make way for a brand new red-brick processing block which was erected at the front of the factory and completed in 1935. New plants and equipment were installed including new stainless-steel vacuum pans, new filling machines, and updated labelling and packing lines which used fiberite cases to replace the old wooden boxes which had been used since the opening of the factory in 1897. The rest of the manufacturing equipment was transferred from the old six-storey cloth-mill building which was later brought down to two storeys. Blackfords of Calne carried out the work, the first task being to remove the large stone phoenix which crowned the top of the old mill building and which commemorated the rebuilding after the 1824 fire which had almost destroyed the whole structure.

This first major expansion of the condensery also included the installation of the long-planned railway siding, first proposed in 1916, and the factory was now able to receive milk in rail tankers as well as many other raw materials such as tin plate from South Wales and coal from the Somerset collieries. In December 1935 the company changed its name to

Nestlé Milk Products Ltd and the Anglo-Swiss name, connected with the factory since its foundation in 1897, would no longer be used.

The workforce increased again to 255 in 1937 and annual fresh milk intake exceeded five million gallons. Fred Price became the new factory labour overseer, Bert Lane was appointed chief clerk, and in September 85 employees from all over the company attended the first long-service presentations at the factory at which 38 men and 8 women from Staverton, whose service ranged from 39 years to 25, several starting their careers at the factory when it opened in 1897, were presented with silver tankards and clocks by the managing director, J.W. Gwynne.

When the Second World War broke out in 1939 the factory was again put on a war footing and all of its production was put under the control of the Ministry of Food and allocated by priority. Outputs were running at around 886,000 cases a year and much of this would now be directed to the rapidly expanding Armed Forces and to build up food stocks in anticipation of a long, drawn-out conflict. At the start of the war, and faced with the threat of massive air attacks on London, the company's Head Office was dispersed and some departments were relocated to Staverton where they were housed in the old office block which had been empty for years and only used in recent times as a churn store. The building was hurriedly refurbished and the Gay family, who had been living in part of the block, were rehoused. The accommodation was taken over by the night-watchman to increase the factory's security. Managing director J.W. Gwynne also joined the Head-Office staff at Staverton for a while and many of the Londoners were found accommodation in the village for the duration, several families being put up at Smallbrook House. In May 1940 volunteers were sought amongst the workforce to form a village Local Defence Unit, the forerunner of the Home Guard, and by the end of July Staverton's makeshift army

Nestlé's first milk collection fleet in the factory yard, 1920. The three-ton, solid-tyred Albion are loaded with 17-gallon churns each weighing nearly 2½ cwt when full.

Left: *Butter department workers, 1930s.*

Above: *Commer milk-collection lorry offloading churns in 1935.*

Left: *Nestlé office staff, 1935.*
Left to right, back row: *George Lovelock, Annie Pain, Walter Hart, Albert Stevens, ?, Betty Watkins, Jack Whitmarsh;* seated: *Phil Bryant, Jim Price, Richard Wells, James Homewood (factory manager), Norman Obourn, Bert Lane, ?;* sitting: *Gladys Hitchins, Nancy Bleasedale.*

was undergoing training in 'musketry and squad drill'. By August the volunteers had been split into two squads, Numbers 34 and 35, and had passed out in basic weapons training and been fitted with uniforms and boots. A guard room and armoury was set up on the ground floor of the old cloth-mill, fitted out with bunk beds, and Staverton's 'Dads Army' went out on nightly patrols and practised fire-fighting drills in the event of an attack. In November 1940 the Staverton detachment became part of B Company, the 4th Wilts. Home Guard, and took part in exercises under the guidance of Lt Ron Brewer and Sgts Gibbs, Lees, Moore and Taylor. Platoon NCOs were appointed in August 1941 with Cpls Whitmarsh, Lyke, Lloyd, Vezey, Potter, Harrison and Johnson sewing two stripes on their uniforms and Messrs Malyn, Barnes, Drewett, Culverhouse and the Norris brothers becoming Lance Corporals.

Ron Brewer had taken over as factory manager in 1940 when the workforce reached 400 in the peak, production exceeded one million cases, and the factory was using 8,600 tons of coal and over 460 million gallons of water annually to make their products. By 1942 the only tinned milk being produced was condensed and unsweetened, five million gallons of fresh milk was being handled annually, and the factory began packing rolled oats, milk powder and condensed milk in tubes, 75,000 of the latter being produced that year. Factory men were called up to serve in the Armed Forces, some women were drafted into the nursing volunteer schemes, and the vacancies were filled temporarily by older men and women and factory pensioners who were recalled.

The factory Home Guard platoons carried out nightly patrols and, apart from the odd fright at dead of night, their soldiering skills were never tested in anger. Ex-Home Guard members can recall a few hilarious moments from those tense days such as the night a patrol out searching for escaped POWs had just returned to the guard room in the factory and were unloading live rounds from their rifles, when one of the platoon accidentally fired his weapon. The bullet smashed through the old iron stove in the room, ricocheted off the wall dislodging a large chunk of masonry on its way which fell to the floor almost hitting the night-watchman's sleeping dog but failing to rouse it. Fortunately, nobody was injured in the incident but jokes about Nestlé's highly alert guard dog lasted the war out. Later, during an exercise to capture Atworth, strange noises were heard coming from a small building on the outskirts of the village. Fearing that the enemy were lurking inside, the intrepid Bill Gliddon crept up to the shed with rifle poised and threw open the door. He was, however, forced to make a hasty retreat after discovering that the enemy was really a very irate lady who had been peacefully 'going about her business' on her outside closet! On another occasion a patrol was moving up the Holt road at dead of night when they

heard loud tapping noises, like weapons being cocked, coming from a field up ahead. Everyone dived for cover fearing they had run into a group of enemy paratroopers and, after a whispered debate on what they should do next, a very reluctant scout was gingerly sent forward to draw the enemy fire. There were huge sighs of relief on hearing the news that the enemy force was merely a horse in the field tapping its itching hoof against the base of a tree. The final flurry of activity for the factory Home Guard came in June 1944 when they were put on high alert during the D-Day landings, but as the Allies pressed for final victory in 1945 they were stood down and Staverton's courageous Dads Army were finally disbanded at the end of the war.

Wages increased steadily during the war and by 1943 men were earning an average of £4.9s. per week with female employees on £3.4s. The workforce remained around 350 and due to the call-ups and retirements several new foremen were appointed to fill the gaps. Walt Vezey took charge of the milk dock, Bert Lloyd became the warehouse foreman, Graham Hale was in charge of sterilizing and Mrs Beaven became the first forewoman to be appointed and put in charge of the condensed milk filling and packing line. Coal supplies for the factory's boilers totalled 7,000 tons a year, over 5,300 tons of this being delivered by rail, but shortages of other raw materials, particularly petrol and rubber tyres, began to restrict the operation of the milk-collection fleet. Special wartime packing work was carried out at the factory including Nestrovite, dried egg powder, Red Cross parcels for POWs, and Army compo packs containing processed meat, fish, egg, jam, vegetable salad and baked beans for the British and American Armed Forces.

By the end of the war production was running at a million cases a year and fresh milk intake had exceeded five million gallons although, after 1946, dispatched milk began to increase dramatically reducing the amount available for manufacturing into finished products. Jack Whitmarsh took over as labour overseer, Alfie Earl became the factory chemist, and in 1947 the workforce had to be reduced to 227 when production dropped to just over 500,000 cases of tinned milk. At the end of the war the condensery became involved in the packing of Australian Food Parcels, a sub Post Office was set up in the factory to despatch the gifts all over the UK, and by the end of 1949 over 816,000 had been packed at Staverton. For their involvement in the Australian Food Parcels Scheme the factory was honoured by a visit from the Duchess of Gloucester in March 1948 when she toured the factory, watched the parcels being packed, and spent several hours chatting to the workforce. Company social events, suspended for the duration of the war, resumed in the late 1940s and at the 1950 annual Hayes Gala Day Staverton factory press operator Iris Brewer won the company beauty

Nestlé veterans, 1937. The members of Staverton staff receiving mementoes were: Messrs H.G. Bainton, F. Beaven, H. Beaven, A.J. Bennett, E.G. Bennett, W. Chapman, F.W. Endru, R.T. Fido, H. Francis, C. Gibbs, G. Gibbs, H. Griffin, G.F. Hale, V.R. Hale, A.E. Harrison, F. Hutchings, H. Lane, R.S. Moore, H.H.P. Perry, E.W. Potter, H.J. Price, W.J. Pullen, W. Purnell, D.R. Sartain, A.W. Stevens, C.B. Stevens, R.W. Taylor, W.J. Taylor, R.G. Wells, A. Vincent; and Misses D. Bowyer, F. Lane, K. Lane, E. Lansdown, E.L.M. Osborne, E.M. Pearce, M.E. Purnell, E.M. Taylor.

Nestlé Home Guard unit, 1941.

contest and 35 other Staverton employees won prizes, mostly in the gardening classes. Village factory workers built up quite a reputation for their gardening skills and throughout the 1950s and '60s won many awards at the annual company gala days.

Bert Griffen was promoted to tin-shop foreman in 1950 and Len Wells, son of the factory chief engineer Richard Wells, was appointed foreman of the maintenance department which in 1951 was employing 34 craftsmen including two tin smiths, a carpenter, mason, painter, turbine operator and two electricians. Archie Hillcoat was in charge of the four tin-shop fitters and Bill Fry was charge-hand of the boiler-house and its nine stokers. Harry Beaven, one of the factory's longest-serving employees, retired in 1952 at the age of 71 having completed over 50 years' service. Harry came from a long line of Beavens associated with the factory starting with his father-in-law who had been caretaker for Hargreaves in the cloth-mill days, continuing in a similar role when Anglo-Swiss took over the site in 1897. Harry's father, James Beaven, was one of the first Staverton residents to be employed in the condensery and worked as a pan man until his retirement in 1927.

Output dropped to 443,000 cases in 1953 and the workforce stood at 270. Further changes came to the supervisory structure with Arthur Harrison becoming filling-room foreman, Bert Ransome maintenance foreman to replace the recently promoted Len Wells, and Eric Morris was put in charge of the factory's lorry fleet.

Major alterations were made to the factory frontage in 1953 when the high wall surrounding the site, a legacy of the old cloth-mill days, was reduced to low level and topped with railings. At the same time extensive repairs were made to the bridge arches over the mill-race which flowed under the road to rejoin the river at the front of the factory. 1954 was a better year for the factory with volumes increasing to 690,000 cases and the workforce growing to nearly 300 in the peak. Wages had risen to £7.10s. a week for men and £4.4s. a week for women over 21. Production continued to increase in the 1950s and totalled over 800,000 cases in 1955. The workforce stood at 314 in September but dropped back to 256 by the end of the year when the flush was over. In all 21 personnel made up the main office staff and the average weekly hours worked by men, including overtime, were 57, with women and girls averaging 42. Fresh milk intake, some of it in rail tankers, had reached $8^1/_4$ million gallons by 1956 with over a million gallons of this subsequently being dispatched. Output for the year totalled 863,000 cases of which 170,000 were exports. Nearly half this volume was being produced as Ideal Milk, 33 per cent of it as sterilised cream, sweetened condensed had fallen to 18 per cent of the total filled, and a small amount of skimmed made up the balance. Production levels and workforce numbers remained fairly constant in

the latter part of the 1950s and into the early 1960s. Ron Brewer, factory manager since 1940, retired in 1960, and his place was taken by two temporary managers, Tim Lester and Geoff Buckingham, before Harold Ives took up the position in 1962. Bert Rawlings was made tin-shop foreman in 1960, Ted Barnes took up a post in the factory's general stores, Les Matthews was put in charge of the process floor in 1961 and Don Weston the tin-shop fitting staff.

Two John Thompson boilers were installed in 1962, one of the old coal-fired boilers was converted to a steam accumulator and the factory switched to burning oil after bulk storage tanks were installed behind the boiler-house. The factory's milk-collection lorries, now mostly Commers, were picking up about 40 loads of milk a day, 15 tons of sugar a day was being handled in 2-cwt sacks, and the tin shop, equipped with five body makers and three high-speed presses was using three million sheets of tin plate annually – enough to make 50 million cans and 100 million ends. The five filling machines available, with a filling rate of 150 tins per minute each, fed three main packing lines whose labelling speeds varied from 200 to 400 tins a minute. Chippenham factory closed down in 1962 and for a while was used as a finished-goods store for Staverton's products now being filled, labelled and packed under the supervision of new foreman Bill Glover who replaced Frank Hinton after his retirement in June. Richard Andrew was appointed assistant factory manager in early 1963 and Joe Groom took over from Bert Lane as chief clerk in March. The strain of handling the heavy 2-cwt sacks of sugar was finally removed in 1963 when two 15-ton bulk sugar silos were installed in a room below the old sugar loft. The recently revamped factory canteen was serving a range of hot meals and drinks to the 300 Staverton employees, with breakfast and a cooked tea costing 6d. and lunch 7d. Tea and coffee could be purchased for 1d. a cup.

Since the early 1960s the factory employees had been trying to start up a social club and in 1964 the redundant old office block was used as a social amenities building after being equipped with a snooker table, table-tennis table and dartboard, although the management would not allow alcoholic drinks to be dispensed on the premises. A keen and active social club committee organised annual indoor sports competitions, coach trips to Europe, dances, socials, bingo sessions and children's Christmas parties. Soccer and cricket teams were formed and, as well as organising matches with other local clubs, annual soccer and cricket matches were played against teams from Head Office with mixed success. The highlight of the social club year was the annual flower show and gala day, held on the factory grounds, organised jointly with the West Wilts. Chrysanthemum and Dahlia Society, and culminating in a grand dance usually attended by a well-known band or group. These popular annual

Right: *The Duchess of Gloucester meeting the Staverton workforce during her visit to Staverton factory in 1948.*

Left: *Milk tipping department, 1953. Ernie Matthews is on the right.*

Right: *Tug o' war contest at a Nestlé gala day in the 1950s.*

Below: *Parade of beauties vying to win the Miss Nestlé title, 1950s.*

events attracted large crowds, senior management from Head Office and other Nestlé centres, and continued throughout the 1960s and early '70s. Staverton factory snooker teams regularly won the Worth Tournament, hosted by Aylesbury factory for many years, and the factory fishing team generally came out winners against the opposition when fishing in the River Avon from the factory grounds.

The working week was reduced to 40 hours in 1965 and wages for a basic week were £11 for men over 18 and £8.5s. for women. Employee numbers averaged 300, Eric Sykes had been appointed factory chemist and Eddie Gamble became the new foreman in the packing room supervising the finishing of the four main products, sweetened condensed, Ideal Milk, sterilised cream and skimmed milk. The year 1966 was a significant one for Staverton factory with the construction of a new road-transport-orientated warehouse behind the red-brick process block, the demolition of the old weavers' cottages on the high bank above the factory, and the removal of the railway siding, used extensively since 1934, to make way for a new Culinary Products Plant. Work started on the construction of the £750,000 Crosse & Blackwell factory in February 1967 when the first piles were driven and hundreds of contractors' lorries removed tons of soil and clay from the site and delivered the building materials. Designed by London-based architects, Beard, Bennett, Wilkins and Partners, the new plant was constructed by Laings and a new car park, on land at the back of the milk warehouse, new effluent disposal plant, and improved mains water supply had to be provided to service the new plant. Adverts went out to recruit workers to man the plant and potential female employees were offered £11.2s.6d. for a 40-hour week, working on alternate shifts and with free transport to and from the factory. Meanwhile in the condensery, operations continued as normal and Harold Scrine was made foreman of the processing block, Jack Smith foreman of the warehouse, and Ray Thompson took charge of the factory's stores.

The Culinary Plant was completed in early 1968 and the first tins of spaghetti rings in tomato sauce rolled off the production line in March. Baked beans and tomato soup followed in April and all these products were packed under the C. & B. label. Fred Debnam was appointed culinary manager, Steve Beard culinary engineer, and Bill Glover became the first Culinary Plant supervisor. At the start the plant was equipped with four production lines, ran on two nine-hour shifts, and the maintenance department went on to three shifts in November. A twilight shift was started later in the year, staffed mainly by women who worked from 5p.m. to 10p.m. and received £5 a week. In order to supply the new plant with cans, the tin-shop operation had to be reorganised and extended and the body makers were resited on the two lower floors. The ground floor was for culinary cans, the middle floor for milk cans and the press shop was set up in a converted materials store across the yard from the tin shop. The advent of the Culinary Plant increased the factory's workforce to 450 and men's wages increased to £12.10s. basic plus £4 for those who worked shifts. During the year Martin Spearey joined the factory engineering team, initially seconded to culinary, but later put in charge of the factory engineering services department. The euphoria of all the exciting events that had been happening in the factory during this time was somewhat subdued later in the year when serious flooding swamped the factory, water covered the bridge parapets and the low-lying offices to a depth of four feet. It was the biggest flood for many years and disrupted both the movement of transport and employees for several days and caused severe damage to office equipment and fittings.

Steve Jones became the milk products manager in 1969 and Herman Kuratle joined the factory's engineers, both arriving at a time when the milk canning business was beginning to decline. Demand for tinned milk had fallen and more and more supplies of fresh milk were being directed away from the area reducing the manufacturing availability at

Marion Moody testing milk in the factory laboratory, 1953.

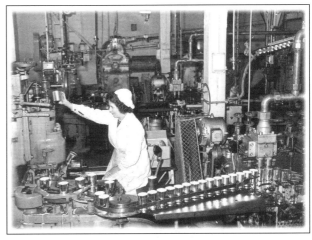

The factory filling room, 1953.

Above: *Labelling tins of milk, 1953. Glad Otterwell is the lady checking the labels.*

Inset: *The milk processing floor, 1953.*

Right: *Packing tins of Ideal Milk, 1953.*

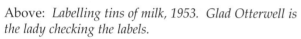

Left: *The factory press shop, 1953.*

Left: *Nestlé and Anglo-Swiss soccer team, 1906. Left to right, back row: H. Garrett, S. Davis, H. Beaven; centre: G. Wickham, R. Wells, H. Griffen, J. Vince, T. Hannam, H. Purnell, W. Clift, T. Fido (trainer); front: B. Clift, T. Wells, A. Matthews (captain), W. Chapman, A. Stevens.*

Right: *Nestlé factory soccer team, 1932–3.*

Left: *Nestlé factory soccer team, 1970s. Pictured, back row, are: Pete Bristow, Doug Loud, John Trueman, ?, Mick Stovold, Ian Diamond, John Shearer; front: Dave Akerman, Bill Pickett, Pat Emery, Pete Lavis, Tony McLean, 'Tich' Mead.*

Staverton factory flower show, 1960s. Left to right: Bill Weston, Arthur Taylor, Edgar Jacobs.

the factory. The company, aware of the declining situation for some time, made contingency plans and, having recently acquired an interest in the French Chambourcy yogurt business, decided to set up a chilled manufacturing operation at Staverton's under-utilised milk-canning factory. John Richardson was sent to Staverton in 1971 to commence trial yogurt production and a small amount of manufacturing equipment was installed alongside the milk processing plant in the red-brick process block which later became known as Y Plant. The inevitable came in 1972 when the company announced plans to close the milk cannery after further decline of the business and evaporated-milk production ceased in July followed by sweetened condensed at the end of the year. The last delivery of fresh milk from the farms came on 31 March the following year and immediately a £500,000 refit began to convert the redundant milk factory into a yogurt manufacturing plant, the transition being completed with very little structural upheaval and loss of employment to the workforce. The first commercial chilled products made in the new plant were fruit and natural yogurts, in conical waxed pots, and fresh single and double cream. Meanwhile, Colin Heavens took over the production manager's position in the Culinary Plant which had started to produce private-label products for the major supermarkets and export spaghetti rings for Findus.

The newly operational Chilled Products Plant ran into its first difficulties in 1975 when the loss of private-label fruit yogurts caused a reduction in output, although some small volumes of desserts, recently introduced, helped to soften the impact, and the year's total of chilled manufacture came out at just 43 million pots. The following year both plants increased their outputs, Chilled Products producing 49 million pots. The factory workforce now

Right: Staverton factory carnival entry 'The Ideal Island' in 1970. Left to right, standing: Margaret Perry, Frances Read, Jenny Lavis, Mo Dobson, Pauline Doddington, Sue Garrett, 'Busty' Wilson; seated: Rita Marshmont, Christine Jolly, Di Lavis.

numbered 500, the highest it had been since Nestlé took over the site. Findus took over Chambourcy management control in 1976 with Roger White becoming the regional manager and Ron Channon the depot manager at Staverton where the chilled products were now being filled into pre-formed plastic pots. The tin shop was being managed by Ron Coleman and its six body makers and eight presses were producing 123 million cans and ends annually from eight million sheets of tin plate.

Chilled volumes increased to 63 million pots in 1977 with small fruit yogurts being the dominant product sold, accounting for 36 million pots of the total which included 15 million pots of desserts. By 1978 Nestlé had acquired the major interest in Chambourcy and production of yogurts and desserts slowly increased from 67 million pots in 1978 to 72 million in 1980.

Investment in the site had also increased with £2 million being spent on improvements between 1978 and 1980, some of this finance going towards the reforestation of the factory's island, with 300 new trees and shrubs, and modifications to the factory chimney which was fitted with a venturi to help resolve a smuts emission problem. The continuing steady growth of both manufacturing plants through the 1970s had increased the workforce to over 600 by 1979 and total factory output had reached 50,000 tonnes annually. The Culinary Plant was producing around four million cases a year by the end of the 1970s and plans had been made to streamline the factory's can-production operation with the provision of a Littel tin-cutting plant, the construction of which started in 1979. Costing £1 million, the large square Littel building was sited behind the tin shop and the hi-tech, ultra-modern plant would convert tin plate from large coils into cut sheets for can making, not only for Staverton but other canneries in the Nestlé group. Completed in 1980 and handling ten-ton coils of tin plate purchased from steel mills in South Wales and the Low Countries, the new plant would initially cut 20,000 tons of plate a year with an annual value of £10 million. Each coil, three miles long and costing £4,000, would produce enough tin plate for

The flooded River Avon in 1960, one of the highest floods recorded in recent times.

200,000 can bodies or 750,000 ends and Staverton would also supply Omagh, Ashbourne and Dalston factories. By 1980 the chilled dessert range had expanded to include four varieties of A La Creme, Fruit Sundaes, Flanby Desserts, Supremes and Sundae Specials which accounted for 12 per cent of the year's 76-million-pots output. This ongoing growth necessitated the provision of two more filling machines, which increased the total to ten, seven of which were Hamba machines. Culinary volumes dropped slightly in 1980, some of it due to the decline in 8oz sales and to respond to this trend in the market the plant's second 8oz line was converted to 15oz.

Several new products were launched in both plants in 1981 with Chilled introducing Bonjour yogurts and Culinary developing a new potato-based product, Saucy Spuds, for which special dicing machines had to be installed. The revolutionary new product, however, failed to live up to expected sales, and was subsequently withdrawn from the market after a relatively short life span. Yearly investment in the factory continued with £275,000 being spent in 1981, most of it to provide bigger cold stores for the expanding Chambourcy business. After the last few years of steady growth Chilled ran into difficulties again in 1982 experiencing a drop in volumes to 58 million pots, this was due to a price war with competitors, loss of business from the large multiples, and unusual seasonal conditions which suppressed sales in the summer. Culinary volumes remained just under 5 million cases although baked beans sales had increased to 2.7 million cases. The rising cost of fuel oil prompted the factory to convert to the

cheaper gas burning for the boilers and a gas terminal building was provided near the bridge over the mill-stream opposite the boiler house.

Chilled sales increased again in 1983 and output reached 65 million pots helped by the installation of the first ERCA filling machine that could produce 20,000 pots an hour in a variety of pack formats. All Bonjour yogurt manufacture was taken over from the French factory and Mike Corcoran became the Chilled production manager with John Richardson taking on the role of development manager concentrating on some of the new products in the pipeline which included Waistline yogurt, Chambourcy Trifles, Black Forest Desserts and whole milk yogurt.

Culinary Plant volumes exceeded five million cases for the first time in 1983 helped by two new products, wholewheat pasta in sauce and Waistline tomato soup. Modifications were carried out in the baked-beans factory with a new filler and seamer and a new rotary sterilizer being installed, and the packing room was extended to house the new Iwema shrink-wrap packing lines that would eventually replace the cardboard cartons used to pack the tins in since the plant opened in 1968. The tin shop was also upgraded with the first hi-tech soudronic can-making machines being installed together with three new high-speed presses. 18,000 tons of tin plate were being used annually, enough to make 245 million cans and ends, some of them in the new trial tin-free steel, and altogether investment in the site in 1983 exceeded £2.5 million. Output increased to 97 million pots in the yogurts and desserts factory in 1984 helped by the launch of Nouvelle yogurts which

125

Above: *Crosse & Blackwell culinary products plant constructed in 1967.*

Above and below: *The first products produced in the Crosse & Blackwell plant, 1967.*

Left: *Factory fitter Bill Vezey, 1969.*

accounted for 12 million pots of the total sold. Cheesecakes in blackcurrant, strawberry and black cherry flavours came into production followed later in the year by Robot yogurts for the children's market. In the C. & B. Plant, new products included Spicy Shells and flavoured soups and further modifications of the tin shop had increased its equipment to seven can-making lines and eight high-speed presses. Factory floor wages had reached £100 for a 40-hour week with additional payments of £20 for shift working and £34 for permanent nights.

The phenomenal growth of the Chambourcy business continued in 1985 with 125 million pots of yogurts and desserts being produced, and new Burdosa whipping machines and Cetra packing lines heralded the first manufacture of chocolate mousses. However, severe competition in the market, intense pressure on prices by the major supermarkets, and a flood of cheap imports from the EEC countries badly affected Culinary Plant outputs which dropped by a million cases resulting in production being halted for two weeks in September to try and reduce the build-up of finished goods in the warehouses. Despite this setback, modifications continued in the C. & B. Plant with the installation of a new ACE materials handling system, and Healthy Balance Baked Beans and Dinosaur Pasta in sauce were introduced to try and regain some of the lost sales. Yogurt and desserts production continued to increase through 1986 helped by the launch of White Chocolate Mousse, Hippopotamousse and Um Bongo desserts, and the year's output reached 173 million pots. Chambourcy telesales and sales administration departments were relocated to Staverton, Alistair Inglis took over as Chilled Products production manager, Ian Grant as Chilled engineer, and Terry Foulkes became the Chilled Products development manager.

Chilled Products Manufacturing, originally set up in the old milk condensery in the early 1970s, had grown into a massive operation over the last 15 years and had begun to outgrow its limited and outdated production facility at the factory. Company commitment and investment in the chilled business, with its anticipated future growth, would require an expansion of its operations at Staverton and by 1986 plans were made to provide a brand new manufacturing facility which would cater for the business' needs into the twenty-first century. Preparatory work on the new multi-million-pound complex began during the year and Staverton factory witnessed the biggest changes to its operation since Anglo-Swiss took over the site in 1897. Work on the new Chilled Products factory, to be designated D Plant, commenced in June 1987 with the driving of 600 piles and the removal of 50,000 tons of soil and clay from the two areas that would house the new manufacturing facility and the new car park. D Plant was erected on land behind the cold stores which was the existing factory car park, and a new enlarged car park was laid out on the vacant land adjacent to the south side of the Culinary Plant. A new access road into the factory had to be provided, requiring the demolition of three of the existing six Nasmilco Cottages, and a 50-metre-wide steel and concrete platform was built across the mill-stream to provide extra turning space for the large refrigerated lorries using the cold store loading bays. Meanwhile, production continued in the cramped Y Plant and a 40 per cent increase in desserts production pushed the chilled volumes to over 200 million pots. New products were introduced including the revolutionary flower-flavoured yogurts, with essence of geranium, rosehip, elderberry and apple, orange and lemon mousse, chocolate Hippopotamousse, Pot au Choc and cream desserts, and a fifth ERCA filler was installed with additional Burdosa whipping equipment, a new packing line and CIP unit. The tomato soup lines were removed in the Culinary Plant and number six production line was converted to a two-shot solids filler to produce the new Fred Bears product, a mix of beans and pasta shapes in a rich tomato sauce.

There were also other new pasta shapes, Treasure Island and Mr Men, healthy pasta was added to the healthy balance range, and Culinary volumes improved marginally to 4.3 million cases. A second Littel tin-cutting line, transferred from Dumphries factory, was installed at the end of 1987 and the tin shop with its four soudronic lines and ten presses was handling 21,000 tons of plate. Clare Hunter became the new quality assurance manager in June 1987 and Alan Axford took on the job of Culinary Plant engineer.

Construction work on D Plant continued through 1988, the installation of the new effluent and water-treatment plants and electrical sub-stations, sited at the rear of the factory near the railway bridge, was commenced in the late summer and a new garage was built behind the culinary warehouse. Chilled volume rose again to 225 million pots, aided by the introduction of B Actif yogurts and Bonjour Rich & Creamy, and John Brittain was appointed technical manager of Culinary and Frozen Foods with responsibilities for the whole of the Staverton operation. Harold Ives, Staverton's factory manager for the past 27 years, retired in February 1989 and was replaced by Longbenton's factory manager, John Stewart, who took over a factory undergoing massive development and major changes to its whole operational infrastructure. £17.5 million had already been invested in the new Desserts Plant, £7.75 million on the building and £9.75 million on its manufacturing equipment; the production plants had undergone major modernisation work in the previous few years and the entire factory's business, management and operation was going through a period of intense restructuring. Many new chilled products were being developed and manufactured including low-fat varieties of yogurt and yogurt mousse, and

Right: *Thelma Roberts and Sue Garrett packing Alphabetti Spaghetti in the Crosse & Blackwell plant, 1970s.*

Below: *Nestlé factory workers in 1968.* Left to right: *Tegwyn Light, Harold Scrine, Kath Purnell, Bert Rawlings.* Inset, top left: *John Brewer;* bottom left: *Jack Whitmarsh;* bottom right: *Fred Debnam.*

Below: *A bevy of Nestlé office girls in the mini-skirt days, 1970.* Left to right: *Dawn Westall, Pauline Doddington, Elizabeth Massey, Diane Lavis, Jenny Mizen.*

volume had reached almost 250 million pots. Culinary was concentrating its production on four main lines, the new ACE sauce-making system installation had been completed, and outputs for 1989 had increased to 4.2 million cases. Management restructuring under John Stewart resulted in the appointment of Alistair Inglis as site production manager, responsible for the factory's three manufacturing plants which were now being run by plant managers Pete Lavis in Culinary, Colin Smith in the tin shop and John McNicol in Chilled Products. An in-depth review of the company's can production operations indicated that their continuation in can-making was no longer viable due to excessive costs and the ongoing decline in canned food sales, the decision was reluctantly taken to close down Staverton's tin shop and press shop at the end of 1989. In future, all can supplies for the Culinary Plant would be purchased from outside suppliers and the first consignments of cans and ends from CMB were used in the beans factory in early 1990.

Staverton factory workers Jack Osborne and George Taylor, 1970s.

The face of the factory was radically altered in 1989 when the old red-brick chimney, built in 1914, was demolished and replaced with a shorter and thinner modern metal stack. Despite protestations from local environmentalists and industrial archaeological groups that the chimney should be preserved, the demolition had become necessary as the old chimney had outlived its use, it had begun to erode badly and could no longer cope efficiently with the modern fuels now being burned in the factory's boilers. The new slender metal stack, erected slightly to the north of the old chimney, was 50 metres high, contained three separate flues, and contributed to the visual changes being created by the factory's extensive modernisation programme designed to equip the site for the business challenges of the new millennium. D Plant became operational in April 1990 and dessert production was transferred from Y Plant into the new facility during the year. Staverton's new dessert factory was fitted with the most up-to-date, hi-tech manufacturing equipment available and was the most modern chilled products factory in Europe.

By 1991, 70 per cent of the chilled volume was being produced in D Plant. The extensive list of Chambourcy's products now included a range of set, stirred, natural and fruit yogurts including Rich & Creamy, Disney and Honeypots, and a growing number of desserts such as Chocolate and White Chocolate Mousses, Hippo Mousses and Hippo Mud, Hippo Yogurt Mousse, Rich Fruit Mousse, Pot au Creme, Milky Bar Dessert, Milk Jelly and Aero Mousses in three flavours. Non ERCA products

included Cream Viennas, Dalky Supremes, Black Forest, Le Grand, Almond & Toffee Cup, Chocolate & Coconut Cup, cheesecakes in three varieties, Chocolate Bavarois, gateaux and liquid-chocolate desserts. Private-label products were being produced for Gateway, Tesco, Sainsbury, Asda and Marks & Spencers. 30,000 litres of fresh milk, from selected farms, was being used daily and total chilled output for the year was 233 million pots. The Crosse & Blackwell product range comprised standard and healthy balance baked beans, a range of pasta shapes including healthy balance and wholewheat, tomato soups, Fred Bears and fun pasta. Disney products were launched during the year and the plant was producing private-label baked beans and pasta for Sainsbury's and a range of pasta products for Tesco. Culinary enjoyed a better year in 1991 with production reaching $4^1/_2$ million cases, the highest output since 1984. The company changed its title to Nestlé UK Ltd at the start of 1992 and the remaining Chambourcy Head Office, based at Croydon, moved to take up residence at Staverton factory in April joined by Chilled Foods' general manager John Brittain and business financial controller Mike Bracey. They were accommodated mostly in the main office building and old office block, which had been extensively refurbished for their arrival.

New cloakrooms and toilets for the Chilled workforce, installed at the entrance to D Plant, came into use in September and new laboratories, canteen and wages offices, provided at the rear of D Plant, were opened in 1992. Working hours for all factory staff were reduced to 37, and John Stewart, Staverton's factory manager for the past three years, left to take up a position at Head Office in August and Bernie Owens came to Staverton as the factory's new technical manager.

Yogurt production ceased at Staverton in early 1993. Y Plant was closed down and all private-label yogurt production was transferred to France. Rolo dessert was launched, another new Hamba filler was installed, auto-packing machines were introduced, and two 15-ton liquid-chocolate storage tanks were installed in D Plant to receive bulk chocolate from Rowntrees and other suppliers. A new HiCone packing line got under way in Culinary in March, bean supplies in two-ton 'big bags' were on trial, and the first eurocan production commenced in October. Holbrooks baked beans were developed to try and capture the lower end of the baked-beans market, and another baked-beans label, Thunderbirds, was launched, backed up by an extensive advertising campaign, to attract younger consumers in the children's sector of the market. The environmental impact of the factory was also being studied in depth and, to help reduce air emissions from the boiler-house, a new Beel industrial boiler with Hamworthy Low Nox burner was installed during 1993 as part of the project.

The regular launch of new Chambourcy desserts was essential to keep the market vibrant and retain market share, and exotic new desserts, some based on well-known company confectionery brands, continued to flow from the factory's product development department. Dairy Box and Black Magic desserts were launched in 1994, together with Hippo Jelly, and exports increased to 5,200 tons per year. Despite many attempts to revive the ailing Crosse & Blackwell canned-food business in recent years, sales continued to decline and Culinary outputs dropped alarmingly to 2.7 million cases in 1994. The Culinary business was running into serious problems and decisions were finally made by the company to pull out of the canned-food market announcing in September their intention to close the Culinary Plant at Staverton in early 1995. Staverton's Crosse & Blackwell Plant, which had been operating on the site since 1968, ceased production in February 1995 with the loss of 145 jobs. In its 28 years of manufacturing it was estimated that 112 million cases of Culinary products had left the plant, 182,000 tons of beans had been filled and 62,000 tons of tomatoes had been used to make the sauces. The company tried to sell the operation as a going concern but when this proved unsuccessful the manufacturing equipment was sold off or scrapped. This dramatic loss of one of Staverton's major manufacturing operations reduced the factory's workforce to 400 and left the Chilled Products plant to continue the long-standing Nestlé connection with the site. D Plant dessert volumes increased slightly to 232 million pots and Toffee Crisp and Munchies split-pot desserts were launched and produced on new HitPak machines at 4,000 pots per hour. The frontage of the factory was irrevocably changed at the end of 1995 when the facing buildings, the redundant red-brick yogurt process block and the tin shop were demolished leaving a large vacant area which was subsequently grassed over and landscaped.

The Nestlé logo replaced the Chambourcy brand name on chilled desserts in 1996 when 233 million pots, including the recently launched After Eight, were produced by a workforce which now numbered 360 including the 127 business and commercial staff on the site. The factory was producing 18,000 tons of chilled desserts annually for the UK market with an additional 5,000 tons being exported mainly to France, Italy and Spain. During the year personnel manager Olive Smith retired and was replaced by Sarah Bettes, and Peter Borra became the factory's operations engineering manager. Further operational changes came in 1997, the factory's centenary

year, with the boiler-house, staff shop and distribution operations being contracted out and David Findlay being promoted to factory manager.

Three new desserts, Yorkie Chocolate, Yorkie Raisin & Biscuit and Aero Cappuccino joined the chilled products range and another split-pot dessert, Lion Bar, began manufacture in September. Real Chocolate Mousse, made with Belgian chocolate, and Aero Light were also developed and the year finished on a high with a weekly production output record being set at 6.75 million pots, and the business set for another good year with volumes up on 1996.

The chilled operation at Staverton had grown into a considerable business and was now the centre for Nestlé Chilled and Herta products. It had also become the UK centre for imports and distribution from 18 European factories and provided sales, administration, distribution and technical support for the range of Buitoni pastas and sauces. A fitting tribute to Staverton's 100-year contribution to the business success of the giant Nestlé Company came in its centenary year with the announcement that Cereal Partners would set up operations at the factory and produce breakfast cereals in the converted and modernised redundant Culinary Plant building. The timely arrival of this new business venture confirmed the Nestlé Company's commitment to continue operating on the Staverton site and the considerable investment that had been put into the factory in the last decade would ensure that a major food manufacturing operation would remain in the village well into the twenty-first century.

Staverton factory's Breakfast Cereals Plant, costing £35 million to build and equip with the latest hi-tech, computerised manufacturing systems, produced its first packs of Coco Shreddies in November 1998, and the production of Cornflakes followed three months later. The plant, under the expert guidance of factory manager Peter Smith, steadily increased its production over the next couple of years and by the year 2001 had a workforce of 90 and an annual output equivalent to 200 million breakfasts of Frosted, Coco and Standard Shreddies and Frosted and Choco Cornflakes, the latter manufactured mainly for the major supermarket chains. A new wheat biscuit product, Sporties, was launched in 2001 and the plant now exports a small volume of breakfast cereals to the Republic of Ireland. Containers of Argentinian maize and English-grown wheat are offloaded into silos inside the 36-metre-high process tower at the front of the factory from where the grain is put through the various manufacturing stages that convert it into cooked grits. From the final stages at the base of the tower the product moves through the forming, toasting, coating, filling and packing processes finishing up in the plant's warehouse at the end of the building where it is loaded onto lorries for distribution across the UK. Output at the plant has more than doubled since it

Above: *The old factory chimney was demolished in 1989 and replaced with a modern metal stack.*

Above: *Cereal Partners factory at Staverton, opened in 1998.*

Above: *A view of the factory frontage which used to be the old six-storey cloth-mill in the 1800s.*

Aerial view of the Staverton factory site in 2000.

started up in 1998 and further growth over the next few years will be catered for by the utilisation of a third production line which is already in place.

Martin Cruft became Chilled Products factory manager in 2000 when the business was undergoing major reorganisation, with most of the sales, telesales and administration departments being transferred to Croydon and York. D Plant continued to make chocolate and flavoured mousses, Rolo, Milky Bar and Nesquik desserts, and new products, Smarties in a split pot and Viennois, a mousse-based soft-centre dessert in vanilla, chocolate and coffee flavours, were introduced in 2001, most of the latter being exported to Europe. Volumes remained around the six million pots a week level, this being produced on the plant's three ERCA, two rotary and one Hamba filling lines. Sue Ballantyne replaced Debbie King as human resources manager and QA and applications manager Terry Foulkes was succeeded by Roger Emery in 2001 and Helen Fell in 2002. Chilled operations managers between 1998 and 2002 were Sandy Taylor, Phil Wright, Roger Emery and, at the time of writing, Kris Swinnerton.

The reorganisations at the factory at the turn of the century steadily reduced the workforce to 225, Andrew Vick took over as Chilled factory manager in 2002 and some production, such as Aero Mousse, was transferred to the Nestlé chilled factories on the Continent, although Staverton continued to manufacture a large volume of chocolate and fruit mousses for the major UK supermarkets.

Nestlé's factory remains an important village food production business, providing employment for many local people and making a considerable contribution to the economy of the area, as it has done for over 100 years, and with the success of the Breakfast Cereals Plant on the site, and the streamlining of the Chilled Desserts operation, should continue to do so for many more years to come.

Left: *Villagers' outing to Gough's Caves, Cheddar, c.1913.*

Right: *Albert Matthews and young Bert Ransome.*

Above: *Village street scene, early 1900s. The Old Bear is on the right and Wood Villa on the left.*

Wilfred Stone with churns of milk, Lower Wyke Farm.

Haymaking at Lower Wyke Farm.

CHAPTER ELEVEN

THE LAST ONE HUNDRED YEARS

At the start of the twentieth century, Staverton was a small community slowly starting to recover from the events of the previous decade, which had witnessed the final closure of the village cloth factory as a result of the dramatic and irreversible decline of the West-of-England cloth industry. Many village cloth workers had been thrown out of work, cloth weaving in the village had all but ceased, and numerous Staverton families had been forced to leave the parish to seek employment elsewhere. The impact of these events was clearly evident from the sudden decline in Staverton's population, which fell from 347 in 1891 to less than 200 at the turn of the century. Prior to the closure of Hargreaves' factory there had been over 30 cloth workers living in the village but ten years later only three remained. Two of these, Joseph Jones and Eliza Webley, were weavers who still made cloth in their Staverton cottages although the material they were producing was now being sent to other cloth-mills in the area.

One glimmer of light to the beleaguered Staverton families at the close of the nineteenth century was the purchase of the empty cloth-mill site by the Anglo-Swiss Condensed Milk Company bringing with it the hope and anticipation that the new business would create badly needed employment opportunities for local people. This, in fact, did turn out to be the case and by 1901 over 30 people in the parish were employed in the slowly expanding milk condensery which had arrived on their doorsteps four years earlier. Staverton residents Henry and Herbert Purnell had already established themselves as foremen in the condensery and three other members of the Purnell family had acquired jobs with Anglo-Swiss. A total of 17 of the newly employed milk factory workers lived in the Marsh Road and Wyke Road areas of the parish, one of the first to be employed when the condensery opened in 1897 being Arthur Baldwin who was taken on in the milk receiving department. By 1901, George Gibbs had already attained the position of foreman, his son Charlie was working in the factory laboratory as a milk tester, and the factory caretaker Herbert Gay was housed with his wife Alice and their six sons in one of the several cottages within the factory complex.

The mass exodus of many of the village cloth workers at the end of the century had left many cottages and houses empty and this situation was gradually relieved when new families began moving into the vacant properties. Some of these were staff and engineers from other Anglo-Swiss factories who had been sent out to Staverton to help get the newly converted milk condensery up and running. New residents Frank Couzens, a retired metropolitan police officer, and his wife Emma moved into Ivy Cottage and they later set up and ran a successful boat mooring and hire business on the river in front of the Anglo-Swiss factory. A number of Staverton men found work with the Great Western Railway Company, whose Chippenham to Bath and Westbury line ran through the village, and by the early 1900s the most successful of these, James Hale, had risen to the position of foreman platelayer. Henry Gumm, William Lane and Henry Gay were also platelayers, Fred Stevens was a porter at Trowbridge Station, and Samuel Jones and George Taylor had become signalmen working the box on Bradford Junction.

With similar effects to that of the ailing cloth industry, the number of agricultural jobs had also decreased since the 1800s, mostly due to the ongoing mechanisation of farming and the consolidation of the land within the village into two main farm units run by William Blake and Samuel Rudman. By the early 1900s the number of farm labourers living in the village had more than halved to only six, these being Edward and William Purnell, Alfred Bennett and his son, James Gerrish and William Lloyd. Some villagers found work outside the parish in the new industries in Trowbridge and the neighbouring district. These included the newly opened mattress factory which employed three members of the Taylor family, Harry, Herbert and Walter, Bowyers bacon factory where Louis Purnell worked as a lard melter and Beavens Tannery at Holt which employed George Stevens as a 'Skinyard Labourer'.

The Industrial Revolution and the demise of the local cloth industry had also taken a toll on the traditional cottage industries and by the turn of the century most of the village trades and crafts, the backbone of the community for centuries, had disappeared. Some did continue in business such as stonemason Albert Barnett who lived with wife Sarah and their four children in Vine Cottage and employed several village men as masons' labourers.

James Sartain, living in Mill Terrace, traded as a cattle dealer, his daughter Gertrude as a dressmaker, and Alfred Haseldon, lodging in Ivy Cottage, offered his skills as a civil engineer. There were two small confectionery shops in the village in 1901, one at West View Cottage run by Fred Stevens' wife Elizabeth, and the other, just across the road, was looked after by Mary Bennett. James and Fanny Bond ran the Old Bear, employing young Stanley Bath as the inn's horseman and no doubt had dealings with Justly Missen, a brewer's traveller, who lived with wife Sarah and their four children in Wood Villa, the house immediately opposite the pub.

Right up to the end of the nineteenth century, the only building between the Square and the canal wharfes, apart from the Victorian village school, was Staverton's vicarage built in 1861, but in the early 1900s two more substantial houses were added alongside the road from Staverton to Hilperton Marsh, the largest of these being the 22-room Smallbrook House built for veterinary surgeon Thomas Bazeley and his family. The second dwelling, Elmfield, an elegant red-brick property, was constructed in 1906 for coal merchant Samuel Bird and its position close to the canal wharfes reflected the Bird family's long-standing connections with the canal coal trade from which they had built up a very profitable business. The Bird family had started up the business almost from the opening of the canal in 1801 and successive generations of the family had continued to operate from Birds' Wharf right into the twentieth century. Vet Thomas Bazeley also farmed the land at Smallbrook, ran a smallholding with pigsties at the bottom of School Lane, and was later appointed Chief Veterinary Inspector for the recently formed Wiltshire County Council.

Gradually, throughout the early years of the 1900s, and up to the start of the First World War, Staverton and its villagers began to settle into the new way of life created by the considerable changes that had been thrust upon them by the events of the late-nineteenth century, and locals began to enjoy the various social activities that were being organised again within the parish. An annual parish dinner took place in the schoolroom, trips and outings were arranged that took villagers in open-topped chara-bancs to favourite tourist spots such as Cheddar Caves, Stonehenge, Wookey Hole and Weston-super-Mare, barge trips on the canal were a favourite and villagers flocked to the regular fairs, flower shows and carnivals in the local towns and villages. Many enjoyed boating on the river, setting off from Couzen's Moorings and sailing as far as Bradford-on-Avon, the occasional village football match was well supported, as were the village fêtes, and many

Staverton men spent their leisure time fishing off the banks of the Avon and the canal. Public transport was slowly becoming available and the opening of Staverton's tiny railway halt in 1906 allowed villagers to park up their bicycles, the main form of mobility up to then, and travel in greater comfort and speed to such far-flung places as Bath, Bristol, Weymouth, Chippenham and London. Many took advantage of the regular motor-rail service to make shopping trips to Trowbridge, although the usual way of getting there in those days was to walk the footpath that led from the bottom of School Lane and across the fields to enter the town near the Conigre.

The Parish Council, still in its infancy, was beginning to establish itself as the recognised village authority and councillors Alfred Bennett, James Hale, William Lane, James Gumm and Henry Purnell were forced to take official action when the sewerage ditch in School Lane became a health hazard and complaints were being made about the bad state of Henry Taylor's closet in the garden of Rose Villa. Annual payments were authorised to the Trowbridge Burial Board and Trowbridge Fire Brigade, who received £2 a year from the village, and Henry Purnell was elected Staverton's representative on the latter in 1902.

The lighter side of parish life was savoured in 1902 when villagers commemorated the Coronation of King Edward VII with a lavish dinner in the schoolroom and Staverton's school pupils, much to their delight, were given a whole week off and treated to a celebration tea party on the same afternoon as the parish meal. George Wickham, Albert Matthews, Harry Beaven and George Kemp were councillors between 1904 and 1910 and William Stokes was appointed Parish Clerk in 1905 after James Hale resigned because of ill health. Parish business during this period included the purchase of a new ladder for the village lamp lighter, the provision of allotments behind the Square and complaints about the poor water supply to the village, many being convinced that the constant low pressure was caused by the factory continually drawing water from the small-bore main.

The number of motor vehicles on the roads was slowly increasing and concerns were expressed about 'the great dangers of motor traffic passing through the village' prompting the installation of additional street lamps at the canal bridge and river bridge, these two spots considered to be the most hazardous in the village. As well as the extra lamps, the first road signs were erected warning motorists of the school and the difficult bends in Staverton.

Edward Drayton became the village lamp lighter in 1910 and two years later a rank of workmen's cottages were constructed next to the old weavers' cottages in Mill Terrace which was subsequently renamed Nasmilco Terrace after Nestlé and Anglo-Swiss, the owners of the properties. The public footpath that ran from the river bridge and across the fields to Whaddon was diverted in October 1911. This track originally left the road just above the bridge, ran through the factory gate, across Nestlé's factory yard and on towards the railway bridge. The new route would start 115 yards further up the hill and run down the new road recently constructed by Nestlé, and this change was agreed with apparently no local opposition. The following year a proposal by Melksham Urban Council to extend their area and include Holt and Staverton brought vigorous protests from villagers who feared that the move would increase the rates. The new Council elected in 1913 comprised the village vicar, Revd Isherwood, Donald Rogers, the milk condensery manager, and Samuel Bird who joined re-elected councillors Albert Matthews and William Stokes, their four-year term of office taking them into the traumatic years of the First World War.

The First World War was an anxious and difficult time for most Staverton families as husbands, fathers, sons and brothers answered the call to arms and enlisted for active service in the trenches of northern France and other theatres of operations. Village street lamps were extinguished in early 1915 at the request of Southern Command and were not relit again until the war was over three years later. Initially, the impact of the far-off war was hardly noticeable to villagers who were shielded to a great extent by the 'protection' of many of Staverton's menfolk who worked in the milk factory, a large percentage of the parish population at that time, and who were badged as essential war workers and technically immune from call-up. This situation however, was to change dramatically later in the war when the Ministry of Munitions, desperate to replace the ever increasing losses of fighting men, withdrew the badges rendering every able-bodied male up to 45 liable to call-up. Many Staverton men found themselves involved in the later stages of the war, some to come back terribly wounded and a few never to return at all.

A number of Staverton men had been drafted for active service at the start of the war and two of them, Herbert Griffin and Howard Purnell, became subjects of a fierce tussle between the military authorities and Nestlé who requested their return.

Herbert Griffin, foreman of the milk-cleaning department, was eventually returned with five other key workers and 16-year-old Gilbert Griffin who had disguised his age in his keenness to join. By early 1916, over 30 Staverton men had been called up and the strenuous efforts by Nestlé to get Howard Purnell sent back ended in failure; he was tragically killed in action in October 1916 during the latter stages of the Battle of the Somme.

The impact of the war and its ever increasing drain on local manpower did not only affect the milk factory but also other Staverton businesses. Smallbrook farmer Thomas Blease was forced to sell his herd of 22 milking cows, 40 pigs and 700 chickens in June 1916 after his 19-year-old cattle man, Stanley White, was called up for military service and an appeal tribunal had refused to grant a temporary exemption. Farmer Blease claimed that he couldn't continue to farm without him and the war situation had made it impossible for him to recruit and train a suitable replacement. Soon after the outbreak of the war the Blease family had been instrumental in rallying villagers to support the war effort on the Home Front and Tom Blease set up a scheme to collect eggs for the war wounded. He organised and managed a local depot at Smallbrook Farm which received donations of eggs from towns and villages all over West Wiltshire, and by June 1916 over 83,500 had been collected and dispatched to Red Cross hospitals in England and France. Most of the eggs were given by local farmers with over 10,000 being donated by the Blease family themselves. Despite the untimely closure of the

Above: *Pte Howard Purnell, killed at the Battle of the Somme in October 1916.*

Left: *4th Battalion Wilts. Regiment at the start of the First World War. Howard Purnell is fourth from the right, second row down.*

Frances Purnell

Smallbrook egg collection depot other village fund-raising activities continued and the Blease family were always at the forefront of organising and taking prominent roles in the many concerts, fêtes, musical evenings and whist drives that took place in Staverton and adjoining villages throughout the war years. The Hilperton Marsh fête in August 1915, held in a field next to Maxcroft Farm, raised the remarkable sum of £160 for blinded servicemen. Over 2,000 attended the event, many travelling on their bicycles from the towns and villages around the district, where they enjoyed such stimulating activities as climbing the greasy pole, skittling for a pig, china smashing, knocking the pipe out of Kaiser Bill's mouth, cork stabbing and donkey cart rides. Regular concerts took place in the village school to raise funds for war charities such as Vegetables for the Fleet, and Trowbridge Red Cross Hospital, which were always well supported and made much needed sums of money varying from £10 to £20, the latter being recorded as 'a record for such events' in contemporary accounts. Ethel, Tom and Bertie Blease always played leading roles in these productions with their songs, monologues and recitations and their well received acts on stage were often supported by Nellie Isherwood's recitals on the violin and singing performances by Miss Tucker and the Bird sisters, Milly and Lilly.

Collections of produce, sweets, clothing and other comforts for the troops were made throughout the war period and other practical activities took place around the village to aid the war effort. The village school was closed for three weeks in 1916 so that Staverton pupils could assist with annual haymaking, the fodder being badly needed to help feed the thousands of horses being used by the Armed Forces in France, and in 1917 special school days were allocated for blackberry and fruit picking to provide treats for the soldiers in the trenches. Many wartime appeals were generously supported by both the Nestlé factory and the villagers, the National War Bonds Aeroplane Appeal received a £500 donation and Trowbridge Cottage Hospital and the Staverton and Hilperton Nurse Funds also received regular contributions.

As the war progressed, villagers found themselves facing the inevitable consequences of the deepening conflict and, whilst endeavouring to carry on their daily lives as normally as possible, began to suffer from the shortages in the shops, the loss of their menfolk to the military, and the anxieties and uncertainties brought about by the horrific stories and mounting casualty lists coming back from the battlefields. Village businessmen like Simeon Gilbert, who had recently taken over the Old Bear,

and Edward Ransome, the new owner of the village shop, began to feel the pinch as the war's austerity measures began to bite, and the milk factory struggled to replace the lost male workers.

In the final year of the war nearly 100 men from the parish and the milk factory had been called up, nearly half the local male population, and some families had already received the terrible news that their loved ones had been killed in action. By the war's end in November 1918, seven men from the parish and another eight who had been working at the milk factory had made the supreme sacrifice and Staverton mourned the loss of so many of its young men. The names of Captain Harold Clark, of Wyke House, L/Cpl Albert Ash, Cpl Alec Hudd, Pte Frank Holloway, Pte William Gay and Seaman Stanley Gardiner were added to that of Pte Howard Purnell on the war memorial, and Pte William Bennett, L/Cpl Stanley Gosnell, Gunner Arthur Griffen, Pte Gilbert Griffen, Bdr Albert Johnson, Pte Arthur Millard, Rifleman Albert Pocock and Driver Stanley Reeves were remembered on the Nestlé Company's Roll of Honour. These courageous men had fought and died on the battlefields of the Somme, Ypres, Bethune, Passchendale and Cambrai and their loss was a devastating blow to many families in Staverton and the neighbouring villages. Of the many that did return from the trenches, some had received dreadful injuries that would affect them for the rest of their lives, and a few were decorated for their courage under fire such as Cpl George Gibbs, serving with the 1st Wilts, who was awarded the Military Medal for his conspicuous bravery during the battle for Thiepval in 1917.

With the most costly war in history at an end village life gradually returned to some semblance of normality although the loss of so many husbands, fathers, sons and brothers would have a lasting impact on Staverton families for generations to come. Almost everybody in the parish turned out for the Victory Parade in Trowbridge in 1919, Staverton's patriotic horse and cart float being escorted by dozens of cheering village youngsters as it made its way into the town. Afterwards, Donald and Amelia Rogers treated all the local children to a sumptuous tea party in the village schoolroom. War trophies, in the form of several German rifles, a pair of wire cutters, and a Maxim machine gun were presented to the village by the officers at Devizes Barracks and were put on display in the village school.

In the early 1920s Staverton was a close-knit community of cottages clustered around the church and the pub with just two houses and the vicarage lying outside the perimeter of the Square. Victor Blake was running Staverton Farm following the death of his father William, Thomas Blease had restarted farming at Smallbrook, and Lionel Gay had set up a haulage business operating from a property in the Square. At Hilperton Marsh Eliza Hedges ran

Top: *Staverton's float in the Victory Parade, 1919.*

Top left: *Edward Ransome outside his sweet shop, early 1900s. The lady in the picture is his mother-in-law Mrs Andrews.*

Above: *Village fête, 1915. Young Kathleen Wells presenting a bouquet of flowers to Mrs Palmer.*

Above: *Interior of the Staverton Reading Rooms, early 1920s.*

Right: *Staverton Reading Rooms, 1919.*

a shop, James Hudd, William Stokes and George Tucker traded as nurserymen and florists, Alfred Bird farmed at Maxcroft, and William Macey and George Drewett were beer retailers dispensing alcohol from the King's Arms and the Prince of Wales pubs. The land in the Hilperton Marsh area was being farmed by James Pike, Henry Pocock, Harry Norris, Sydney Crees at Lower Wyke Farm, and Frank Yates, the latter being recorded as a 'cowkeeper' in 1911. A.H. & S. Bird maintained their coal business on the canal wharf although the coal trade on the canal had virtually ceased by the mid 1920s.

With the rigour of the war years behind them villagers set about raising money to meet 'a long felt want' for Staverton people, the provision of a recreation room in the parish. The closure of the Red Cross hospital in Trowbridge at the end of the war had left a number of wooden huts vacant and a group of workers from the milk factory started a scheme to purchase one of them and reconstruct it in the village for use as a community hall. The cost of buying the redundant hut was £100, which was quickly met by a generous donation from Nestlé & Anglo-Swiss who also arranged for some of their workers to lay the foundations and erect the building on a plot of land near the railway, owned by farmer Victor Blake, and leased to the village for a nominal rent of 1s. a year. A village collection raised a further £63 and a committee was formed, comprising Ethel Blease, Lilly Purnell, Mrs Beames, Mrs Beaven, Mrs Endru, Donald Rogers, Frank Holloway, Richard Taylor, Richard Wells and George Wickham, who would manage the amenity. Donald Rogers, manager of the Nestlé factory, was elected chairman, Tom Blease vice chairman, and Henry Beaven became the first hon. secretary.

The new Reading Rooms were furnished at a cost of £140, water and gas supplies were connected and a garden laid out at the front of the building, its plants and flowers being donated by W.J. Stokes and Son of Hilperton Marsh Nursery. With everything finally ready the new Staverton Reading Rooms were opened in September 1919 by Mrs G. Palmer and a year later a second Red Cross hut was acquired and equipped with a full-size billiards table and well stocked library. The cost of purchasing the huts and fitting them out had left the project with a fairly large deficit and to redeem this situation the committee set about organising a fête and sale of work to be held in the field behind the school. It was a very successful event raising over £130 to clear the outstanding debt and leaving a small surplus in the funds as a future nest egg. The many sideshows at the fête included a pretty Britannia stall, in red, white and blue, run by Ethel Blease and her helpers, which contained a large assemblage of fancy goods, many of them made by the village school pupils. A miscellaneous stall, run by Maria Endru and team, was well stocked with produce donated by local tradesmen, the vegetable

Above: *Staverton snooker champions, 1923.* Left to right, back row: *Bert Matthews, Jack Purnell, Jack Osborne, Les Matthews, Ken Fryer;* front: *Bill Wickham, Roy Osborne, Albert Matthews, Len Wells, Curly Drewett.*

Below: *Staverton football team, 1920s.*

stall, set up by Tom Blease, was overflowing, and the tea stall, managed by Lilly Bird and her ladies, catered more than adequately for everbody's refreshment needs. Four separate skittle competitions, with prizes of a pig, two cockerels and two cheeses, were won respectively by Richard Wells, Albert Bath, Reg Moore and Frances Purnell.

Richard Taylor was in charge of the darts competition giving prizes of two more cockerels, and two rabbits in a hutch, donated by Tom Blease, was the prize in the rings game. Donald Rogers gave a silver wrist-watch as a prize for guessing the weight of two boxes, and Nellie Isherwood, the vicar's daughter, attracted a stream of inquisitive customers to her fortune-telling tent. Other attractions included guess the weight of the cake won by Elsie Barnes, sweets in a bottle won jointly by Alice Purnell and Carl Endru, a hoop-la stall, and a competition to win a tongue, donated by Bert Foreman and won by Lilly Purnell. The event finished with a concert and dance in the schoolroom, the main entertainment being a ventriloquist act performed by Herbert Sydee of Melksham.

By 1921 the Reading Rooms were the social hub of the village, membership had increased to 130, and sports teams had been formed such as Staverton's chess team of Bertie and Tom Blease, Alfred Bennett, Graham Hale, Percy Norman and Bert Lane, who won their first match 5-4 against a Church Institute team from Bradford. Over the next few years Reading Room teams built up a formidable reputation locally and won many matches and competitions with their billiards, skittle, darts, whist and chess teams, and outdoor sporting activities were enhanced with the laying out of a tennis court and cricket pitch on land at the bottom of School Lane. A ladies' sewing group, run by schoolteacher Maria Endru, also met regularly in the Reading Rooms throughout the 1920s.

Village fêtes and flower shows were commonplace during the summer months of the early 1920s, they were organised by the Reading Rooms' social committee, still headed by chairman Donald Rogers, assisted by vice-chairs Tom and Bertie Blease and Victor Blake, with Richard Wells as general secretary. The 1922 event was reported as 'a highly creditable show' and attracted 44 exhibitors in the fruit, vegetable and flower classes, in which Gladys Hale and Henry Purnell took the prizes for best asters, dahlias and roses. Vegetable classes were won by Herbert Bainton (carrots and onions), Nelson Purnell and Bert Lane (potatoes), John Purnell (marrows), Les Naish (lettuce), George Davis (shallots), Gladys Hale and Henry Beaven (cabbages), with best apples going to Ernest Cleverley. Herbert Bainton was awarded a special prize for his runner beans, the judge George Tucker remarking that 'they were the finest he had ever seen'.

The fête had the usual attractions and games with competitors vying for cockerels, a hare, a pig and a goose, besides the usual prizes of a cake, sweets and produce. Entertainment was provided by Beaven's brass and reed band, and the whole afternoon was deemed a great success raising over £85 for Reading Rooms funds. Throughout the 1920s and '30s, the Reading Rooms were well supported by villagers who also enjoyed the regular concerts, musical evenings, dances and many other social events that took place in the hut. Staverton's billiards, snooker and skittle teams made their mark in the local leagues, winning a number of trophies in the years between the wars, and village and factory football teams played matches on a pitch near the canal, later at Hilperton Marsh, and won several trophies in the Trowbridge & District and Bath Soccer Leagues. Highlight of the year for villagers was the annual Trowbridge carnival and for many years Staverton regularly entered a colourful village float usually built on the bed of a Nestlé milk-collection lorry.

The post-war depression brought back haunting memories of the 1890s to some Staverton families who feared another village recession when the milk factory began laying off many of the workforce in 1920 and 1921, most of them were women and girls who lived in the parish. The local employment situation remained precarious over the next five years and again caused alarm in 1927 when the factory was forced to lay off another 53 local workers, the workforce dropping to 227, the lowest it had been since the First World War. Some found alternative employment, many village families experienced hardships, but after 1930 the economic situation started to recover and village life slowly returned to normal. Another disastrous event that disrupted village life for a while in 1925 was an outbreak of foot and mouth disease on Staverton Farm forcing farmer Victor Blake to have his herd of 70 milking cows slaughtered and burnt, the outbreak also worsening an already difficult time at the Nestlé factory.

Another social problem facing Staverton through the 1920s was the ongoing erosion of village roads and houses, and the Parish Council found themselves having to deal with many complaints about the poor state of School Lane, full of deep ruts and potholes, and the nuisance being caused by gypsies who were frequently using the lane as a camp-site. Notices were placed at the top of School Lane warning them to keep out. Several of the old weavers' cottages in the Square were in a very bad state of repair, several on the south side in a very dilapidated condition with no doors or windows, which had become a haven for tramps. Plans were submitted to replace some of the older village properties by building new homes on Blacklands, each costing £450 and made available to rent at 10s. a week, but it would be a number of years before these finally materialised. By 1929 the dilapidated cottages in the Square were in such a bad state, labelled 'a disgrace to the parish' by the Council, that a closing-down order was served on their owner, Mrs Stevens, who had failed to take any action on them for over six years, and they were finally demolished the following year. The removal of these old cottages, which had originally been built right up to the edge of the road, considerably improved the visibility on the sharp bend by the Square which had been the site of several serious traffic accidents. By 1930 the village housing situation had become a serious social problem and the Parish Council complained that 11 properties in the lower part of Staverton 'were no longer fit for habitation'. Letters were sent to the local housing authority, and West Wilts. MP Robert Grimston was approached to see if he could help to rectify the worsening housing situation in the village.

Wyke House, and its adjoining land and properties, home of the Clark family since 1832, was bought by McCalls cloth-mill owner, John Gordon Hammond in 1931. His eldest son Roger became the chairman of the company and his other son, John, joined the RAF as a pilot and was tragically killed during the Second World War. The two farms attached to Wyke House in the 1930s were being run by the Stone families, Wilfred in Upper Wyke Farm

Above: *Stevens family wedding party outside Staverton School, 1928. Left to right, back row: Henry Purnell, Louis Stevens, Kit Purnell, Arthur Stevens; front: Joan Stevens, Jean Endru, Joyce Stevens, Martha Stevens, Joan Beaven, Betty Stevens.*

Above right: *Farmer Blake's car outside Staverton Farm, 1920s.*

Left: *Molly Tucker outside Lower Wyke Farm, 1927.*

Above: *Florence and Grace Barnett, 1925.*

Left: *William Purnell.*

Nestlé outing to Weymouth, 1925. Sammy Norris' charabanc in Salisbury. Jim Rawlings and young Les Rackley are on board.

and Cecil at Lower Wyke Farm. A 1925 proposal that Staverton and Hilperton should come under the control of Trowbridge Urban Council was vigorously opposed by villagers, who feared it would increase the rates, but their efforts were to no avail, and in October 1932, Staverton, the population of which had fallen to 216, was forced under the Local Government Act of 1929 to accept the change. Many stormy meetings took place with local officials, and villagers, incensed that their wishes had been denied, immediately organised a petition of protest.

William Stokes, the Parish Clerk for the past 26 years, retired from the position in 1931 and Albert White was appointed as his replacement. The long awaited new houses on Blacklands came in 1933 and again villagers were up in arms because the Parish Council's request that they should be allocated to village families, had been completely ignored. Explanations from the housing authority stated that the new Ministry of Health regulations debarred people who were already housed and angry villagers, annoyed that outsiders had been given preference to the newly erected dwellings in New Terrace, sarcastically labelled the properties 'the cuckoo's nest'.

The Parish Council, infuriated and dissatisfied with the outcome, immediately put in another request for more housing with the priority being given to village families who were struggling to survive in 'appalling living conditions' in condemned Staverton cottages. Melksham RDC took over as the lighting authority in 1933 and over the next couple of years villagers made many complaints about the continuing gypsy encampments in School Lane which were causing quite a considerable nuisance.

Staverton became part of the Bradford & Melksham RDC in 1934 and remained under its authority until the formation of the West Wilts. District Council many years later. Village housing continued to be a concern and, although 12 new houses had been promised in the 1933 building programme, only eight had actually been provided, the problems being compounded by the demolition of seven of the older village cottages with two more scheduled for removal. This time the local housing authority acknowledged Staverton's predicament and a row of houses was built in School Lane in 1937.

Jubilee celebrations to mark the 25 years of King George V's reign took place in May 1935. Sports events were organised, village children were given a tea party, each received a commemorative medal and chocolate presented by Phylis Blease and Revd Isherwood, and adults were treated to a celebration supper in the school.

In 1936 the village mourned the death of one of its most respected and long-serving Aldermen, Henry Purnell, who had given a great deal of his time and efforts to village life and had been a Parish Councillor for 41 years, most of that time as chairman. The first electricity supply was laid into the village at the end of 1937 and, not long afterwards, electric street lighting replaced the old gas system rendering the village lamp lighter, Edward Drayton, redundant after 27 years of dedicated service.

Pilot Officer John Hammond of Wyke House was killed when his fighter crashed in the Second World War.

The new Council, elected in 1937, comprised Victor Blake, Simeon Gilbert, Richard Scrine and Fred Taylor who were immediately confronted with complaints about the terrible smell of sewerage coming from the back of the council-houses which, according to the village vicar, Revd Francis Maunder, was so bad 'he couldn't open the vicarage windows because of it'. The Council again responded by requesting a proper sewerage system for the village and took measures to clean out the open sewerage ditch that ran alongside School Lane.

The threat of war in 1939 prompted the building of a village air-raid shelter behind the school and Revd Maunder was placed in charge of air-raid precautions. Most villagers and their children were fitted with gas masks in preparation for the forthcoming conflict, blackout rules were introduced, and volunteers were sought to become village fire watchers. Just after the outbreak of war in September 1939 the village street lights were closed down and the first evacuees began to arrive in the village, 20 of them being accommodated at Smallbrook House. Although difficulties were being experienced in securing volunteer fire watchers, piles of sand were placed by the church gates, the Old Bear, and the top of School Lane to help dampen any fires caused by enemy air raids. Villagers prepared themselves again to live through another world conflict, the milk factory was immediately put on a war footing, and hurriedly prepared to take in some of Nestlé's London Head Office staff who were being sent to the relative safety of a rural factory. Most were found accommodation locally, several were put up in the now very crowded Smallbrook House, and many became so fond of the village and its idyllic way of life that they stayed on after the war and made Wiltshire their home. After one year of war the village air-raid shelter was still unfinished, village men were gradually being called up to serve in the Armed Forces, and those remaining joined Nestlé factory workers in forming a Staverton Home Guard unit. Walter Ludlow replaced the Revd Maunder as the village air-raid warden and took charge of a stirrup pump kept in the Old Bear, and provided to help fight any roof fires that broke out. Gangs of construction workers descended on the village to build a line of pillboxes along the river and railway approaches, the section through Staverton forming part of the GHQ defence line designed to stop the enemy advancing into the Midlands if an invasion had been successful. Fortunately, these pillboxes were never used in anger but often doubled as shelters and look-out posts by the Staverton Home Guard when out on patrol or conducting a defensive exercise.

The air-raid shelter was finally completed by the end of 1940 and the Revd Maunder took over as Parish Clerk when Albert White, who had been doing the job for the last nine years, was called up for military service. Concerns about the increase in traffic through the village, and its dangers to locals because of the wartime 'no lights' restrictions, spurred the Parish Council into requesting a 30mph speed limit through Staverton, but this was turned down by the local Highways Authority.

Albert Bath in his garden behind Coalash cottages.

Staverton villagers, as they had so magnificently done in the First World War, held many fund-raising events to support the Red Cross and other war charities. The Blease family again took the lead and organised whist drives and other events throughout the war years. A whist drive held in the Reading Rooms in 1942 raised £19 for POWs and the sick and wounded, and a similar event in 1943, organised by Phylis Blease, made over £100 for the Red Cross Rural Pennies Fund. A Staverton children's carnival in support of Salute the Soldier was another of the regular events and the villagers' superb support for the war effort was rewarded with a Wings for Victory plaque in 1943 which was displayed alternately in the school and the Reading Rooms. Nestlé workers did their bit for war charities and the factory was able to make contributions of £1,350 to the Rural Pennies Fund and £1,400 towards the War Weapons Appeal. Another village event organised by Phylis Blease in 1944 added another £127 to Red Cross Funds and an additional £40 was raised on the same evening by auctioning a variety of goods, this sum going to help the sick and wounded and POWs.

House numbering was introduced for the first time in Staverton in early 1942, and in 1943 plans were approved to build ten more houses in School Lane. By 1944, however, only two of the ten had been built due to the shortage of building materials, and it was to be several more years before the full quota of new dwellings in School Lane was completed.

During the war years the Reading Rooms remained the social focal point of the village under the chairmanship of Richard Scrine, and later Fred Taylor, treasurer Fritz Endru, and secretary Bernard Taylor. Rosie Scrine dispensed refreshments, cups of tea and ginger beer to members in the evenings, the village Scouts and Guides met there, and during the day the hut doubled as a classroom for 28 of the 38 evacuee children who were staying in the village.

Wartime entertainment laid on for villagers included film shows, table tennis exhibitions, whist drives, jazz bands, dances, socials, children's Christmas parties and, on one occasion, a circus. Just like the First World War 20 years earlier, many village men had to leave their families to fight for their country and by the war's end three more names of men from the parish, Pilot Officer John Hammond, of Wyke House, Sgt Herbert Slatford, of Marsh Road, and Pte Reginald Carter, who lived in the Square, joined those of the earlier conflict on the list of village war dead.

Throughout the five long years of the war Staverton remained virtually unscathed, apart from the sadness at the loss of its young men. The nearest it came to enemy action was in 1942 when a stray German bomber, fleeing from a raid on Bath, attacked Holt, laced Whaddon with incendiaries, and jettisoned a bomb onto the side of the canal near the village blowing a large hole in its bank. Trowbridge was also attacked on several occasions, bombs falling on Kemp & Hewitt's cloth-mill and the barracks in Frome Road. When the war ended in 1945 villagers celebrated the victory in Europe and held a grand carnival and fête at Wyke House to raise money for a village war memorial. The event, opened by Mrs Gordon Hammond, commenced with a carnival procession, organised by Mrs Cook and Kath Taylor, followed by a fancy-dress parade and baby show, run by Mrs Walt Vezey and judged by Dr Margaret Hammond. Miss Beames supervised children's sports and Dorothy Bird looked after the tennis tournament. There were numerous sideshows, skittling for a pig run by James Beaven, and a refreshment tent staffed by Phylis Blease and helpers. The organising committee comprised Harry Beaven, Ted Malyn, Phylis Blease, and Jean Beaven aided by Mrs Cook, Mrs Vezey, Kath Taylor, Miss Beames, Betty Ludlow, Margaret Tucker, Geoff Woodman, Bill Wickham, Tom Applegate and the village vicar.

The following July a grand flower show took place in the grounds of Wyke House in aid of the Staverton Playing Field Fund. This one, organised by Roger Hammond, and opened by Lady Sybil Phipps, started with a carnival procession, followed by a fancy-dress parade, baby show, comic football match, and finished with a fireworks display in the evening lit up by Tom Blease. Added attractions included a rifle range, treasure hunt, and the usual sideshows and stalls. The previous year's organising committee was strengthened with help from Cecil Jacobs, Cliff Tucker, Ernie Potter and Stan Bath. It was the first of many village events, including a house-to-house collection, to raise money for a Staverton playing-field and by 1953 the fund stood at over £600.

In 1946 the new Parish Council of Stan Bath, Albert Scrine, Fred Taylor and Vic Tucker, chaired by Tom Blease, helped to organise the distribution of Australian food parcels to needy village families who had experienced a difficult time during the war years. Staverton's soccer team, temporarily disbanded during the war years, was reformed in 1948 using the King's Arms as a base, and under the guidance of secretary Ernie Potter, treasurer Cecil Jacobs and team captain Bill Gliddon, resumed competitive matches in the Trowbridge & District League. The Reading Rooms continued their sporting activities under a new committee led by chairman Fred Taylor, secretary Richard Scrine and treasurer Bernard Taylor, and the hut's billiards, snooker and skittle teams strived to win honours in the local leagues. Staverton's sporting claim to fame came in 1948 when the Old Bear's darts team, captained by Bill Fielding, reached the final of the *Sunday People* National Darts Tournament and travelled to London to take on the Red Lion pub team from Boreham Wood. The Old Bear team of Bob Allsop, Fred Razey, Alan Greenman, Bob Allison, Bill Alford, Ted Malyn, Reg Moore, Stan Bath, Gordon Dickson, Alan Cruse, Charlie Smith, Dick Gilbert and Bill Fielding had won through to the final by beating the Bennet Inn from Timsbury in the Wiltshire County Finals and a Royal Oak team from Bath in the Western Counties Area Final. Farm labourer Bill Fielding, dressed in traditional Moonraker's smock for the occasion, and the rest of the Old Bear team put up a tremendous fight in the finals for the Lonsdale Trophy narrowly losing 2-1 to the lads from Boreham Wood.

With the completion and occupation of the new

Staverton ladies' darts team, 1930s. Left to right, back row: Ethel Beaven, Ethel Matthews, Win Matthews, Bessie Wells, Rosie Townsend; front: Hilda Wickham, Maggie Brown, Laura Hart, Edith Wickham, Annie Wickham, Iris Feltham; centre front: Norah Chapman.

houses in School Lane and New Terrace Staverton's population in the late 1940s had increased to 288 and most of the old condemned cottages in the lower part of the village had finally been demolished. Farmer Victor Blake represented Staverton on the Rural District Council, and Dorothy and Bill Bird opened up a grocery store and sub Post Office in Marsh Road. Richard Gilbert temporarily took over the running of the Old Bear from his father before handing over to new landlord Frank Harrison in 1950, and Wickham's ran a small confectionery and tobacco shop from the cellar of 14 Nasmilco Terrace in the 1940s, later moving to a wooden building on land at the bottom of the lane.

Villagers celebrated the Coronation of Queen Elizabeth II in 1953 with sports and games for the children, each being presented with a coronation mug, and a dance in the Reading Rooms at which Ernie Pearce became the star attraction by enthralling everybody with his polka dancing. Money left over from the coronation fund was used to purchase and install a wooden bench on the top road near New Terrace and thoughts were turned again to the provision of a village playing-field for which fund-raising had been going on since the end of the Second World War. Plans to build a hard-surface tennis court were dropped because of the cost and it was eventually decided to provide village children with swings, a slide, and a roundabout on a piece of land behind the school leased from the County Council. The old village air-raid shelter, constructed behind the school in 1940, was finally filled in in 1955 and in 1957, after repeated requests by the Parish Council, the sharp bend by the Square was improved and the pavement widened. By the end of the 1950s Hector and Mary Wright were running a grocery store in Avonlea Cottage, a Staverton Over 60s club had been formed with 25 members, and the first licensed bar came to the Reading Rooms in 1958, initially run by the

Chapel concert, 1934. Left to right, back row: Daisy Townsend, ?, Maisy Parsons, ?, Grace Escott, Den Drewett, ?, Doug Wickham; front: Roy Parsons, Ivy Townsend, June Woodward, Betty Ludlow, Margaret Tucker, Keith Tucker.

Drewett family and Mrs Applegate. In 1959, the Parish Council, now chaired by John Blake, joined the campaign for flush toilets to replace the old bucket lavatories in the village school and these were installed a year later. Staverton's first WI Group was formed in 1959 by a number of village ladies, led by Phylis Blease who subsequently became its first president. Other founder members included Alice Purnell, Vera Malyn, Gladys Rose and Eileen Gamble, and in later years the village branch had their own unique WI banner in blue and white skilfully made by Eileen Curtis.

The village housing stock further increased with the construction of two bungalows at the top of School Lane, and two cottages opposite the Methodist Chapel. Around the same time major improvements were made to the road that ran down the hill to the river bridge with the high wall on the factory side being removed and a pavement provided. Bob Hughes took over as chairman of the Reading Rooms in 1960, Richard Beaven replaced Arthur Ransome as secretary, the first bingo sessions at the hut started in 1962, and the same year the Staverton B ladies' skittle team won the Melksham and District League championship. A Nestlé sports and social club was formed in the early 1960s, housed in one of the old factory outbuildings, equipped with billiards and table-tennis tables, a darts board and a variety of social activities were organised for workers over the next few decades. Indoor sports tournaments were held annually, soccer and cricket teams were formed and they played friendly matches against local opposition and other Nestlé factories. Outings and coach trips to Europe were also regular events, along with weekly bingo sessions run by Percy Strugnell which were well supported, as were the dances, socials and annual children's Christmas parties. The main event in the factory's social calendar in the 1960s and '70s was the annual Nestlé flower show, held on the factory grounds, which

Old Bear dart's team, 1948. Left to right: *Bob Allison, Bill Razey, Reg Moore, Alan Greenman (?), Gordon Dickson, Bill Fielding, Ted Malyn, Bob Allsop, Stan Bath, Bill Alford (?), Alan Cruse (?), Dick Gilbert, Charlie Smith.*

drew large crowds and ended with a grand dance, the music always being provided by a well-known band or group. Villagers who worked at the factory used their famous horticultural skills to good effect yet again and won many honours competing against the professional gardeners of the West Wilts. Chrysanthemum and Dahlia Society who co-hosted the show. Fishing contests took place from the banks of the river within the factory grounds and Staverton's keen angling team won many matches against visiting teams, occasionally pulling out record-breaking catches.

Staverton's tiny railway station became a victim of the infamous Beeching axe in 1966 and after 60 years of providing a transport service for generations of village people, was closed down and its two short platforms and wooden shelters demolished.

The Parish Council in 1965 comprising John Blake, Phylis Blease, Mrs Yandall, Walt Ludlow and Arthur Bodman, were becoming greatly concerned about the traffic situation in the village, requesting a speed limit through Staverton, a safer pedestrian route across the blind canal bridge and general highway improvements. Over the next two years a pavement was built along the frontage of New Terrace and the section of bendy road between the vicarage and School Lane straightened and widened. The largest housing development to date came to the village in 1965 with the completion of Elm Close, a cul-de-sac of nine houses and nine bungalows built on a piece of land opposite the Old Bear which was originally an orchard and allotments. Nestlé celebrated the company's centenary in 1966 and this coincided with a massive new development of the Staverton factory, the expansion necessitating the demolition of the rank of old weavers' cottages which had sat on the high bank above the factory since 1810. A huge new Crosse & Blackwell Culinary Plant, costing just under a million pounds, was erected at the back of the site and came into operation in March 1967 creating 150 extra jobs for local people. The siting of the new building also required the removal of the factory railway siding, installed in 1934 and extensively used during the war years, and another important part of Staverton's railway history came to an end. Nestlé's new million-pound development also brought considerable benefits to the village, the most significant being the construction of a new sewerage disposal plant which was linked into the antiquated village system, and at long last Staverton was able to breathe a sigh of relief that its long-standing sewage problem had been resolved. The village's piped water supply, another constant problem in the past, was also greatly improved with the laying of a new large-bore water main through the village. Urgent requests for a pedestrian footbridge over the dangerous canal bridge continued, the provision of a pavement down the side of School Lane was pursued and safety concerns about the

Staverton Club billiards team, 1951. Back: *Jack Jones, Jack Osborne;* front: *Stan Norman, Dick Scrine.*

state of some apparatus in the play area resulted in the children's roundabout being immobilised and later removed.

The Reading Rooms, now under the chairmanship of Jack Osborne and new secretary Edgar Jacobs, celebrated its 50th anniversary in 1970 with a dance and social, the evening's fun and games being provided by local entertainer Razz Ingham and his 'zany' band. Some of the founder members and trustees were guests of honour and were praised for their past involvement in keeping the very active and well supported village social amenity running for the past half century. The recreation rooms, still housed in two First World War wooden huts, had become the social centre of the village and the prowess of its billiards, snooker and skittle teams was recognised and respected by their opponents in the local leagues which they occasionally won. However, the wooden structures were beginning to deteriorate badly and after the celebrations the committee and trustees began giving serious thought to replacing the old huts with a modern club building. An annual skittle KO tournament was started in 1972 with teams from all over the district being invited to compete for the Brian Jacobs Memorial Cup, a trophy presented to the Reading Rooms by the Jacobs family in memory of their young son who was tragically killed in a road accident in the village the previous year.

Revd Maunder, the village vicar and Parish Clerk for the past 31 years, died in 1971 and Pam Hatton joined the Council as its new clerk together with new councillor Ken Knight who replaced the late Arthur Bodman. The long awaited pedestrian footbridge over the canal was started in 1972 and completed a year later, considerably improving the safety of villagers, who up to then had 'taken their lives in their hands' when trying to negotiate this very dangerous stretch of the road. The new Parish Clerk resigned after only one year in the job, was replaced by Marsh Road resident Geoff Woodman in March 1972, and Edgar Jacobs of School Lane became a councillor just before Laurie Bird replaced Mrs Yandall who was

forced to give up through ill health. The Hammond family sold Wyke House and its remaining lands in 1971, after which the fine old mansion was demolished, and the grounds it had stood on later became the Tudor Drive housing estate.

By 1974 the Reading Rooms committee had raised enough finance to rebuild the recreation centre and work commenced later that year to pull down the old wooden huts and replace them with a modern stone-built structure. The work, costing £15,000, was completed by the end of January 1975 and the newly named Staverton Club was officially opened by Phylis Blease who commented that 'the people of Staverton are lucky to have a club like this to pursue their interests and activities.' Three founder members of the Reading Rooms, including 93-year-old Harry Beaven, were guests of honour at the opening ceremony and joined with new chairman Vic Harrison, secretary Edgar Jacobs, and treasurer Bernard Taylor in drinking a toast to the future success of the new club.

Later that summer the first 30mph speed limit was introduced in the bottom part of Staverton, an abatement order was placed on Barry Meeres' poultry houses at the bottom of School Lane after the village had been plagued with swarms of flies, and the village bus service was improved with 14 stops daily in each direction, travel on the service in 1976 costing 12p to Trowbridge, 7p to Holt, and 19p to Melksham. Frank Harrison, landlord of the Old Bear since 1950, left the pub which remained closed for a number of years before being reopened by new landlord Laurie Bird in the 1970s. Persistent requests by the Parish Council, which went back ten years, for a pavement in School Lane, were finally heeded by the Highways Dept and this was constructed and completed in early 1977. The big Staverton event for that year was the Queen's Silver Jubilee and a meeting was held in February when representatives from all village organisations formulated a programme of celebrations. Jubilee day events were planned for 7 June with a big fête at Nestlé's factory, the presentation of Jubilee mugs to all Staverton children, followed by village parties and other Jubilee celebrations. Money left over from the Jubilee fund was used to place a Silver Jubilee bench at the entrance to Elm Close and the Staverton WI planted a Jubilee rose garden on the grass verge opposite.

Villagers continued to complain about the fly nuisance from the chicken farm and residents in the lower end of the village near Nestlé found their properties, cars and gardens being showered with black oily smuts from the factory chimney. Nestlé were quick to respond to this latest pollution problem and in 1978 a special venturi cap was fitted to the top of the tall factory chimney, the company assuring villagers that this would eliminate the problem.

Two new detached houses were built on land adjacent to the Old Bear pub in 1979 and farmer John

Left: *Townsend family wedding party outside their house in the Square, 1950s.*

Below: *Outdoor staff at Rodwell Hall, 1931. George Smith is on the extreme left, back row.*

Above: *Staverton football team, 1936.* Left to right, back row: *Bill Potter, Taffy Lyke, Frank Branding, Bert Stevens, Lou Stevens, Ken Fryer, Tommy Cooper;* middle: *Albert Matthews, Cliff Tucker, Bill Purnell, Les Matthews, Bill Wilkins, Jack Drewett, Bill Weston;* front: *Bill Wickham, Bert Ransome, Jack Osborne, Stanley Gane, John Bull, George Taylor.*

Below: *Nestlé workers skittles team, 1956.* Left to right, back row: *Bert Rawlings, Lou Cleary, George Pope, Fred Hurkett, Bert Ransome, Ray Jacobs;* middle: *Bert Escott, Ivor Price, Jack Osborne, Fred Taylor;* front: *Arthur Tanner, Dave Pope.*

Wedding of Nancy Selman and Jack Perry outside St Paul's Church gates, 1953.

Blake, Parish Council chairman, retired after 18 years' service to the community along with Edgar Jacobs, who had been a councillor since 1973. The steady growth of the village and the subsequent increase in its population over the last two decades qualified Staverton to increase its number of councillors to seven and the new Council elected in 1979 comprised Phylis Blease, Bob Beaven, Ken Knight, Laurie Bird, Pete Lavis, Michael Blake and Ernie Hawkins, the latter having recently taken over the village shop at Avonlea Cottage from the previous owners, the Staceys. One of the first priorities of the new Council was to take action on the ever increasing dangers of traffic speeding through the village and in 1980, after exerting much pressure on the Highways Authority, managed to secure a 40mph speed restriction on the stretch of road between the canal and railway bridges. Staverton's old Victorian school celebrated its centenary in 1980 with events in the playing-field, all pupils receiving a commemorative mug and specially minted Staverton School coin, and a local history exhibition in the schoolroom.

Geoff Woodman, Parish Clerk for the past nine years, died in 1981 after a short illness and the community mourned the loss of one of its most loyal and dedicated servants who had involved himself in the affairs of the parish for many years. Anthony Williams-Pugh from Bradford-on-Avon became the new clerk but remained in the post for only two years, being forced to resign because of continual health problems. Councillor Bob Beaven left the village to emigrate to Australia, Pete Lavis was elected Parish Council chairman later that year, and in 1983 Vivienne Wuckings took on the vacant role of Parish Clerk.

Increasing traffic volumes and the erosion of the village's bridges were constant concerns in the early 1980s and regular representations to the local authority to promote some effective solutions resulted in references being made to a possible village bypass

Staverton Reading Rooms 50th anniversary, 1970. Left to right, back row: *Brian Jacobs, Harry Beaven, Amelia Rogers, Bertie Blease, Tony Parr;* front: *Ruth Matthews.*

scheme. Over the next two years Ken Shepherd, Brian Raines and Mel Thomas joined the Council, planning permission was granted for more new housing on land at the bottom of School Lane, and the first village newsletter, on a single sheet of A4, was produced and distributed to every household in the parish. The village vicarage, sold in 1971, was put up for sale again in 1984 and bought by Ambrose and Carol Stickney with plans to convert it into a care home for the elderly. The only remaining village shop, run by Ernie and Jean Hawkins, finally closed up in the mid 1980s because severe competition from the new supermarkets in the town had made it impossible to continue as a going concern.

Staverton's relentless campaign for solutions to the village's traffic and road bridges problems came to a climax in 1985 when the local authority presented plans for a village diversion. The plan, costing over a million pounds, was to divert the B3105 from a new roundabout by the Square, re-route it across the fields behind the Old Bear, bridge the River Avon below the meadows, and then skirt around the east of Bradford Woods to link up with a junction at Forewoods Common. Immediately, some villagers were up in arms over the new scheme complaining that it would not solve all the village's traffic problems and an action group, headed by Harriet James, was set up to organise a series of protests and marches and to campaign for a complete village bypass. The Parish Council and the action group strongly opposed the diversion plan on the grounds that it would worsen the situation in the upper part of the village, increase the pressure on the already deteriorating canal and railway bridges, and create additional safety hazards for villagers and their children who would still have to negotiate a very busy section of the B3105 to access the school. Highways' response to Staverton's objections was to state that a complete bypass was out of the question because of

Staverton snooker team, 1930. Left to right, back row: *Bert Matthews, Len Wells, Bob Allison, Ken Fryer, Col Loud, Harold Scrine;* front: *Dick Scrine, Jack Osborne.*

147

Left: *The Reading Rooms 50th anniversary, 1970. Founder members Harry Beaven, Bertie Blease and Amelia Rogers were guests of honour.*

Right: *Mick Osborne with his prize catch, a pike weighing 20lbs 13ozs, and 42 inches long, caught in the River Avon on 21 September 1963.*

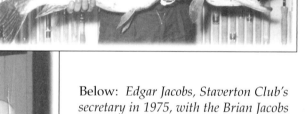

Below: *Edgar Jacobs, Staverton Club's secretary in 1975, with the Brian Jacobs Memorial Trophy.*

Above: *Staverton Club snooker team, 1956. Left to right: Mick Osborne, Bert Gay, Len Pictor.*

Left: *Staverton ladies' skittles team, 1950s. Left to right, back row: Betty Ludlow, Margaret Wickham, Pat Allison, Brenda Moore; front: Joyce Fielding, Olive Ludlow, Margaret Selman, Margaret Tucker.*

the cost and later the disputed plans were shelved to be re-examined at a later date. In 1986 the 900th anniversary of the Domesday Book was commemorated and Staverton, listed in the famous Norman manuscript, recognised its historical link by purchasing a special Domesday plaque and putting it on permanent display near the school entrance.

A massive new development at Nestlé's factory commenced in June 1987 and new access roads were constructed into the site which meant the demolition of half of the remaining Nasmilco cottages and the provision of a new factory car park on land adjacent to the C. & B. plant. Building work continued at the factory site through 1988 and 1989 and in early 1990 the brand new, state-of-the-art, hi-tech chilled desserts manufacturing plant, costing £25 million, started its first production run. The massive development at the factory site was one of a number of major changes in the late 1980s, the most visual being the demolition of the old 175-foot red-brick factory chimney, with its distinctive bulbous water tank, which had towered over the village for 75 years.

Further changes to the composition of the Parish Council came in 1987 with the retirement from office of Phylis Blease and Ken Knight who were replaced by Harriet James and Marion Whitton. Phylis Blease had been a Staverton councillor for many years, some of it as chairman, had represented the village on the District Council, been a churchwarden and school manager for a number of years and had been instrumental in starting up Staverton's WI group in 1959. Her unstinting devotion and commitment to serving the parish had been legendary and her great interest and past involvement in every aspect of village life had earned her the very highest esteem from generations of Staverton people.

A new housing development of 22 red-brick dwellings in a cul-de-sac off School Lane was completed in 1987 and a further four detached houses in School Lane Close were added the following year. In 1988 the Old Bear was given permission to convert its old skittle alley into a restaurant which on completion was named Samuel's after landlord Laurie Bird's grandfather. The following year Harriet James became the new Parish Clerk, Mel Thomas resigned, and two more residents, Elizabeth Bodell and Ambrose Stickney, owner of the Old Vicarage Care Home, joined the Parish Council. During 1987 the Smallbrook lands were sold off and in January 1988 plans were submitted by the purchasers, Erostin, for a massive canal-side development which would incorporate a marina and boat yard, 50-bed hotel with restaurant and bar, and over 600 new houses. The planned development would be accessed via a new road bridge over the canal from a roundabout on Hammond Way and this would require the removal and relocation of the 190-year-old Parson's bridge which would be rebuilt as an attractive entrance feature to the new marina basins. Public

Staverton's only pub, the Old Bear Inn, in 1975 before extensions were added to the front (above). *It was taken over by landlord Mike Lewin in 1999* (below).

meetings were held to present the plans and it was soon evident that villagers were totally opposed to so large a development and it was subsequently rejected by the Parish Council. Despite Staverton's objections, the local planners gave their approval to the scheme and the new bridges and access roads were completed by early 1990. Planning applications that followed for the first phase of housing on the marina development were rejected by West Wilts. Council forcing Erostin to lodge an appeal, and in 1991 the local authority's decision was overturned giving the developers the green light to go ahead. The first phase of housing on the Slipway, Marina Drive and Swan Drive was completed by 1992 and the new Staverton residents began moving in.

Christine Webster replaced Harriet James as Parish Clerk in 1990 and added the names of new councillors Ray Wickings and Lesley Warne to the minute-books in 1991. Control of village street lighting was transferred to the County Council and the first can banks were set up in Staverton Club car park using converted metal drums and magnets to separate the steel and aluminium cans. These were replaced with proper plastic recycling containers several years later and villagers were encouraged to use the facility via the Staverton newsletters. Plans for a new village school were presented in 1993, to be built on the existing school sports field, and staff, pupils and governors were delighted that, at long last, they would be able to vacate the old, cramped, damp and draughty Victorian building that had served the village's educational needs for over 100 years. Wallis Western commenced building the new school in 1995 and a piece of land at the bottom of School Lane was acquired from the marina site developers for a replacement school sports ground.

In the early 1990s the ongoing decline of the

British milk industry forced the Blake family to abandon their long-standing dairy farming business in the village and sell off their select herd of Friesian milking cows, rendering the Staverton farm lands and buildings virtually redundant. Michael Blake, who had taken over the running of the farm on his father John's retirement, decided to move into the equestrian business and converted many of the empty farm buildings into stabling and facilities for horses and owners for his new Staverton Farm Riding School. The business grew over the next few years, more and more horses appeared in the fields around the village and, in 1998, a new covered exercise arena was added to the riding school facilities which, by the turn of the century, were catering for over 40 horses and their owners. Another business changed hands in the early 1990s when Patrick Padfield took over the Old Bear Inn and Restaurant from Laurie Bird, who had made many internal and external modifications and improvements to the old pub, including the addition of front bay windows, an entrance porch, restaurant and enlarged car park.

Rodney Hart, from School Lane Close, replaced Michael Blake on the Parish Council in 1993, a new slide was installed in the children's play park, and growing concerns about dog fouling in the village resulted in a concerted 'clean up after your dog' campaign and the provision of dog bins around the village. A project to provide bus shelters came to fruition in 1994 after sufficient funds had been raised, aided by a generous grant from Nestlé, to purchase two and install them by the entrance to Elm Close and on the top road by New Terrace. Two important milestones in the village's history were reached in 1995 when a village committee was formed to plan celebration events for the 50th anniversary of VE Day and the centenary of the Parish Council, which was formed in 1895. A street party and dance was held on the old school's playground, many villagers donned costumes and uniforms from the war era, and everyone was presented with specially made VE Day

The River Avon in flood 1985.

souvenir mugs with a unique Staverton design on each. A cake commemorating the Parish Council's 100 years was cut by guest of honour Phylis Blease ably assisted by town crier Trevor Heeks who also acted as Master of Ceremonies for the day's events. Trevor, a resident of School Lane, was one of the most well known and colourful characters in the village and had become renowned across Britain for his town crier skills in proclaiming the good tidings at civic functions and social gatherings. He was appointed official Trowbridge town crier in 1986 after which he became quite a celebrity at Council ceremonies and civic occasions throughout the region. His fame also spread worldwide with his attendance at town crier competitions around the globe, winning the World Championship in 1989, the European Championship in 1992, and going on to become the British Open Champion in 1999. Besides his busy civic duties, Trevor has always made himself available to support village events and is also recognised locally for his acting talents after playing parts in the annual village pantomimes held at Staverton Club.

The Parish Council's composition changed again in 1995 with the election of Helen Cosslett and the addition of two of the new marina residents, Paul Jones and Mervyn Saunders. Staff and pupils moved into the new village primary school the following March, a Staverton neighbourhood-watch scheme was set up with ten area coordinators, and annual village clean ups, carried out by parish volunteers, commenced in April. Major changes came to the Nestlé factory in 1995 with the closure of the Culinary Plant and canning operation, causing 145 job losses, including some villagers who had worked at the factory for many years; this drastically reducing the workforce and leaving the site with just one manufacturing plant for the production of chilled desserts.

The marina hotel plan remained a sticking point and prevented further housing development on the site, now taken over by Beazers, who submitted amended plans in 1996 to replace the originally agreed hotel complex with a public house. Marina residents were strongly opposed to the new proposals, protests were lodged with West Wilts. planners and the developers, and local pressure eventually

Staverton Club men's skittles team, 1980s. Left to right: *Mick Lovell, Barry White, Andy Matthews, Mick Osborne, Ken Shepherd, Alan Osborne, Dave Whitton, Richard Mortimer.*

persuaded Wadworths, who were supporting the scheme, to withdraw the planning application. A fund-raising initiative was launched in 1996 to upgrade and re-equip the village children's play area and over the next couple of years, thanks to large donations from Cereal Partners, West Wilts. Council, the Parish Council and some residents, new play equipment was purchased and installed, safety surfacing was laid and a new fence erected along the railway boundary. Village recycling, aided by the addition of extra bins, had proved very successful and was so well supported by villagers that Staverton had become one of the top communities for recycling in the West Wilts. district.

The number of new dwellings being built in the village in the 1990s was added to in 1998 with the completion of Smallbrook Gardens, an exclusive close of nine detached houses constructed on the former gardens of Smallbrook House. Plans to convert Smallbrook House into a small hotel had not yet materialised and the fine old residence and former home of the Blease family was left empty, abandoned and slowly becoming derelict. Further large-scale development at the Nestlé factory started in October 1997 with the construction of a brand new breakfast cereals plant on the site of the recently vacated C. & B. unit. The new facility, under Cereal Partners UK, required the construction of a 50-metre-high process tower and, although residents living close to the factory were concerned about the impact it would have on their outlook, the building went ahead with the company promising to plant tall trees in front of the factory to screen the tall tower. The old Victorian school was purchased by the Emmaus Group in 1997 and reopened as a religion-based school initially using the adjoining mobile as a classroom. Alan Spiers replaced Paul Jones on the Parish Council which, in 1998, was studying proposals to over-come the marina hotel stalemate, the plans offering a motel and restaurant complex, doctors' surgery, shops and community facilities. After many discussions with the developers, planners and other interested parties, the Parish Council agreed to the proposals and looked forward to the long-standing delay of future development on the marina site being resolved.

A village pre-school, called Nestlings, was started up in 1998 catering for three- to five-year-olds and operating from a vacant classroom in the new village school. Staffed by three qualified pre-school teachers and parent helpers, Nestlings was immediately popular with local families and by 1999 had 33 young pupils on its books. The following year the preschool had to vacate its accommodation in the village school, which was needed to cope with a big rise in infant pupils numbers, and moved into a refurbished and modified Pratten building on the edge of the old school's playground. A village amateur dramatic group, called the Staverton Players, was formed in 1992 and staged their first

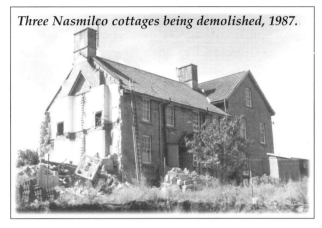

Three Nasmilco cottages being demolished, 1987.

pantomime, *Cinderella*, at Staverton Club in March the following year. Its annual productions, written, produced and directed by Sylvia Matthews, created an ideal platform for up-and-coming village thespians, and many village children, to display their acting talents, and the three performances staged each year were usually played to packed audiences. The club, now being run by chair Marion Whitton, secretary Malcolm Jacobs and treasurer Bernard Taylor, was hosting two snooker teams and three skittle teams in the 1990s but support for its many other social activities was beginning to wane and, despite the best efforts of the committee, the club was finding it difficult to attract more members. Bernard Taylor, the club's treasurer for over 50 years, sadly passed away in 1999 and, due to the sudden illness of secretary Malcolm Jacobs at the same time, the club was plunged into a crisis finding itself with no officers to look after its affairs. Marion and Dave Whitton, keen supporters of the club for many years, came to the rescue and kept it running until replacements could be elected. They subsequently took on the roles of secretary and treasurer, and Malcolm Jacobs, who had slowly recovered from a very serious illness, came back as chairman. A new committee was elected in 2001 and set about planning events and activities that would attract more villagers to the club. An annual summer skittle league for village teams was started up, the first winners being 'Mike +3' and 'Family Affair'. Regular quiz nights and family social events were organised, a crib team was formed and entered the Melksham league, and a fête was held on the club car park in the summer.

Traffic problems continued to worsen and concerns were expressed about the stability of Staverton's ancient river bridge which was frequently being damaged by heavy-goods vehicles trying to negotiate its narrow and bendy carriageway. Appeals were made to the Highways Authority to re-examine the village bypass plans but they declined and instead decided that the installation of traffic lights would solve the bridge problem by reducing the traffic flow to single file. Villagers opposed the lights scheme fearing that it would cause long traffic tailbacks, increase congestion and cause obstructions outside their properties but, despite their protestations, the traffic lights were installed on the bridge in January 1999.

Marina resident Geoff Platten joined the Council in 1999 and Lesley Warne, after a short absence, returned as a councillor to fill the vacancy left by the departure of Alan Spiers. One of the most emotive issues to confront the community in recent times was the Amber Foundation's proposal to build a Youth Support Centre on land near Ladydown. The rehabilitation centre for young drug offenders immediately received a hostile reception and a village action group, headed by councillor Geoff Platten, started a series of protests and a campaign to get the plans rejected. Several public meetings took place at which Amber directors were confronted by angry villagers who demanded that the plans be scrapped. Local businesses, neighbouring parishes, planning committee members, county and district councillors were all canvassed and presented with a strong case against the proposals which were finally rejected by West Wilts. planners, and Amber had no choice but to concede and withdraw their application. It had been an exercise in harnessing the power of public opinion against an ill-conceived plan and Staverton residents heaved a sigh of relief that, thanks to the efforts and determination of a group of concerned residents, an historic battle had been won.

With the Amber crisis resolved the Parish Council concentrated on the fast approaching millennium and considered ideas for an appropriate project to commemorate the beginning of the twenty-first century. One idea that generated a lot of local interest was the creation of a village tapestry with unique designs of Staverton features portraying the parish's history past and present. Volunteers from all sections and age groups around the community were recruited into a tapestry team and an action plan was formulated in early 1999 to get the project under way. A small design team of Angie Hulin, Gwen Davis, Helen Cass and Pete Lavis set about planning the format of the tapestry, purchased and distributed the required materials, and the project got under way in early May. The ten feet by four feet tapestry was made up of 36 individual foot-square panels, a larger centre panel with titles, contained over 600,000 individual stitches, and used hundreds of skanes of wool in 180 different colours. Over the next 12 months the tapestry team beavered away stitching the designs and by the end of April 2000 the 37 panels were ready to be stitched together. The completed tapestry was framed and officially unveiled in June at a special millennium event in the village school, where the tapestry now hangs on permanent display. It had been a tremendous community achievement, encompassing over 50 local people in its creation, and the colourful, informative and superbly crafted masterpiece was Staverton's contribution to the new millennium and a tribute to the skill, dedication and commitment of the many volunteers who were involved in producing the magnificent work of art that will be studied and admired by many future generations of Staverton residents. To coincide with the unveiling of the tapestry, a colour booklet was published explaining the project, how it all began, its technical details, a brief description of each design, and listed all the people who had been involved in making the tapestry and the many others who supported the project in a variety of different ways.

As Staverton moved into the twenty-first century other community projects were instigated by the Parish Council including the setting up of a village good-neighbour scheme in January 2000, coordinated by Julia Meeres with a team of 15 local volunteers. Marina resident Jenny Murray joined the Council in 2000 replacing Ray Wickings, parish vice-chair and church treasurer for many years, who moved away in July to live in his retirement home in North Devon. At the start of the new millennium the village made plans to provide a safer access to the canal towpath off the busy and dangerous canal road bridge, a bench and tourist information board on the side of the canal opposite the marina, the purchase of more apparatus for the children's play area and, the biggest community project ever, the provision of a village sports ground with amenities building and other sports facilities costing over £250,000.

Persimmon Homes took over the marina development land in 2000 and submitted new plans for the hotel site on which they proposed to build high-density housing, a community centre, shops, and a hard-surface recreation area. Further planning applications sought permission to build a link road from New Terrace to Marina Drive, again stimulating a great deal of local opposition, and several phases of house building, including 45 units of affordable housing on land to the south of the new marina road bridge. All the land that had once been part of Smallbrook Farm would eventually be filled with housing, more than trebling the size of the village and ultimately changing its long-established style and culture for ever.

Staverton, for many centuries a closely grouped cluster of old cottages, farms, a church, an alehouse, and a mill, had experienced very little outward growth for over 900 years and it was only in the latter half of the twentieth century that the village began to expand southward as new housing began to appear in the parish. This housing growth accelerated towards the end of the century and by the year 2000 Staverton had grown considerably in size and its population more than doubled. The early decades of the new millennium will bring further dramatic change, and Staverton's unique and idyllic rural way of life, enjoyed by villagers for a thousand years, will slowly disappear as the parish adapts to the tremendous changes and advances the technological age will bring in the twenty-first century.

Left: *Staverton's rural environment is captured in this picture of cows crossing the road in front of the Nestlé factory.*

Above: *Nestlé managers presenting a cheque for £3,000 to Staverton Parish Council towards their play area fund-raising appeal. Left to right: Peter Smith (Cereal Partners manager), Chris Webster (Parish Clerk), Cllr Ray Wickings, Pete Lavis (Parish Council Chair), Cllr Helen Cosslett, David Findlay (Nestlé factory manager), 1998.*

Above: *Staverton WI founder members celebrate their 30th anniversary. Left to right: Phylis Blease, Gladys Rose, Vera Malyn, Alice Purnell, Eileen Gamble.*

Above: *Staverton's VE Day celebrations, 1995. Phylis Blease about to cut the VE Day cake aided by town crier Trevor Heeks.*

Above: *Narrow boats in front of Staverton's marina development, 1990s.*

Right: *Staverton soccer team, 1985. Left to right, back row: Simon Mercer, Andy Gee, Eddie Fairclough, Paul Morgan, Stuart Parfitt, Stuart Mercer, Mark Gee, Rob McMillan, Paul Dyer, Pete Strawbridge (coach); front: Dave Morris, Adrian Blake, Mike Lavis, Martin Hall, Stacy Hawkins, Cliff Hughes (manager), Simon Spong.*

Left: *Annual village clean-up team, with Julie White, Jenny and Patrick Murray and young helpers, 2002.*

Above: *Staverton villagers pose for a millennium photograph in front of the new school.*

Right: *Staverton Player's pantomime* The Lost Sheep, 2002. *Left to right, standing: Diane Lavis, Jane Keen, Danika Ridgewell, Maria Matthews, Dave Whitton, Helen Morgan, Marion Whitton, Corrinne Swaine, Carly Matthews, Stephanie Jones, Katie Matthews; kneeling: Kirah Mortimer, Rhys Mortimer, Chelsey Swaine, Andy Matthews, Jacob Stainer, Steph Morris, Dave Jones, Mark Gee, James Escott, Jason Gee, Tracey Jones.*

Left: *Staverton's millennium tapestry and many of the team that created it. Left to right: Pete Lavis and Lily Escott, Diane Lavis, Sarah Escott, Angie Hulin, Gwen Davis, Lillian Heeks, Claire Magill, Steph Morris, Marian Matthews, Bobby Magill, Helen Cosslett, Janet Blake, Ruth Matthews, Helen Shepherd, Peggy Akerman, Joan Hunt, Roger White, Grace Stickley, Gillian Lucas, Carol Stickney, Lesley Warne, Chris Webster and Natasha, Betty Osborne, Joan Mallows, Mary Gredington; kneeling: James Escott and Rebecca Webster. Tapestry team members not in the picture: Betty Russell, Helen Cass, Jean White, Brenda Wakeford, Brenda Payne, Jane Wickings, Jacky Connell, Lily Bristow, Mary White, Marjorie Beard, Teresa Russell, Miriam Binto.*

CHAPTER TWELVE

THE BLEASE FAMILY OF SMALLBROOK HOUSE

One of the most influential Staverton families of the twentieth century were the Bleases of Smallbrook House, the grandest dwelling in the village with its adjoining farm and lands that lay between Lower Wyke Farm to the east and the canal at Ladydown to the south of the parish. The Blease family bought Smallbrook House just before the start of the First World War and eldest son, Thomas, a qualified solicitor, took over the dairy, pig and poultry farm which had previously been owned by village vet Thomas Bazeley. Julia, with sons Thomas and Bertie, and daughter Ethel, immediately took an active part in village life and, when war broke out in 1914, were prominent in organising many events for the war effort. Tom set up and managed a local depot to collect eggs for the war wounded. The family organised regular concerts, musical evenings and whist drives to raise funds for war charities. Ethel Blease played an active role in the local Red Cross detachment in Trowbridge eventually becoming its commandant. In 1922 she was awarded a medal for her VAD work and valuable service to the Red Cross during the war. The Blease family's acting and musical talents were used to good effect at the village concerts and such events held during the war years raising hundreds of pounds for Red Cross hospitals that treated the wounded, blind and disabled servicemen who had returned from the trenches.

Members of the family were prominent in the setting up and running of the Staverton Reading Rooms after the war and served on its committee for many years. This involvement continued between the wars with the Bleases taking part in the fêtes, flower shows and carnivals held in the village. Julia Blease was a dedicated supporter of St Paul's Church and not only gave considerable financial donations but also many of the furnishings and fittings that are used in the church today. She died in 1935 and her affection for the church lives on in the form of the Blease Fund, an investment she bequeathed to St Paul's in her will.

Thomas married Phylis Stone of Wyke Farm in 1932 and they later had a daughter, Julia, who still lives in Brookfield, the family property adjacent to the big house. Thomas died in 1948 at the age of 66 and Phylis dedicated the rest of her life to serving the community. Her prolific fund-raising work continued, she served the village as a school manager and churchwarden, was Staverton's representative on the District Council for many years and a Parish Councillor in the 1970s and '80s. She was also instrumental in starting up the Staverton WI Group in 1959 and became its first president. Like her mother-in-law, Julia, she was a dedicated worshipper and benefactor to St Paul's Church and on her death in 1996 the village mourned the passing of one of its most respected and community minded figures.

The prominence of the Blease family in the first half of the century was evident from the number of domestic servants they employed and one of these, Alice Purnell, remained in their service throughout her lifetime, in the latter years not only acting as their housekeeper but becoming a close friend and companion to the widowed Phylis.

During the Second World War, accommodation was found for evacuees and lodgers in Smallbrook, and Land Army girls helped run the farm. Julia's future husband, Barry Meeres, arrived at Smallbrook after the Second World War. He later took over the running of the farm and its egg business which he expanded by building poultry houses at the bottom of School Lane and additional units in Whaddon in 1968. Barry and Julia married in 1958, produced five children, and in 1968 took over Smallbrook House as their family home whilst Phylis moved to Brookfield, a modern chalet bungalow built in the grounds of the big house.

In the late 1980s the Meeres family vacated Smallbrook House, most of the children having already dispersed, the land was sold for development and Staverton witnessed the end of an era for one of the most prominent and influential village families of the twentieth century.

Above: *Phylis, Ethel, Julia and Tom Blease outside Smallbrook House.*

Above: *Smallbrook House.*

Below: *Julia Blease.*

Above: *Blease family outing to the countryside.*

Above: *Phylis Blease with a retirement gift from the Parish Council, 1987. Ken Knight (left) retired from the Parish Council at the same time.*

Above: *Tom and Phylis Blease on their tandem, 1930s.*

SOURCES & BIBLIOGRAPHY

Bradford-on-Avon Tithe Map 1841
Chalfield Garrison Accounts 1644–45
'Cotswold Archaeology Excavation Report',
    Staverton 2002
Duke of Rutland's Estate Map 1780
Kelly's Directories – Various
Old Bear Papers – WRO
Salisbury Diocese Bishop's Presentments &
    Visitations – Various

Staverton Tithe Maps 1802, 1812, 1836
Staverton Village Field Map 1845
Staverton Enclosure Awards 1815/17
Staverton Parish Census Returns 1801–1901
Staverton Parish Council Minutes 1895–2002
Staverton Club Committee Minutes 1919–2002
Staverton Village Newsletters
Staverton School Head's Annual Reports
Staverton School Newsletters
Staverton School Log Books 1850–1975
Staverton School Governors' Minutes – Various
Staverton School Managers' Minutes – Various
Staverton School PTA Minutes – Various
Staverton Mill Sale Notice 1813
Staverton Mill Sale Notice & Plans 1891
Staverton Mill Sale Notice & Plans 1897
Staverton Canal Wharf Papers – WRO
Staverton Vicarage Appeal Notice – 1860
Staverton Chapel Minutes & Accounts
St Paul's Church Registers – 1673–2002
St Paul's Church PCC Minutes 1920–2002
St Paul's Church Vestry Minutes 1797–1921
St Paul's Church Faculty Grants – Various
St Paul's Quinquennial Surveys 1991–2001
St Paul's Log Book & Terrier
St James' Church Vestry Minutes – Various

Trowbridge Manor Sale Notice 1785
Trowbridge Water Acts 1873 & 1878
Coins & Medals Magazine
Railway Magazine
Wiltshire Archaeological Society Magazines

Bath & W. Wilts Chronicle Reports – Various
Devizes Gazette Report 1824
Trowbridge Advertizer Report 1859
Wiltshire Times & News Reports – Various

West Wilts. Directories – Various
Wiltshire County Archives – Various
Wiltshire County Library, Trowbridge
Wiltshire County Records Office
Wiltshire Coroner's Bills 1752–96
Wiltshire Records Society Publications

Nestlé Staverton Factory Archives 1897–2002
Nestlé & Anglo-Swiss Roll of Honour 1914/19
Nestlé News Reports 1966–2002
Nestlé Factory Picture Library 1897–2002
Nestlé Factory Plans – Various
Nestlé Factory Railway Siding Plan 1916

Devizes Museum
Kennet & Avon Canal Trust Museum, Devizes
Trowbridge Museum
Late Alice Purnell Recollections
Late Mabel Beaven Recollections
Smallbrook Recollections – Julia Meeres
Wyke House Recollections – Roger Hammond

John Buckler Paintings 1806
Victoria County History of Wiltshire, Volumes 4 & 7
Bradford-on-Avon – Canon Jones
The Book of Trowbridge – K.H. Rogers
Warp and Weft – K.H. Rogers
Wiltshire and Somerset Woollen Mills – K.H. Rogers
Trowbridge and its Times – Goodrich
Buildings of England, Wiltshire – N. Pevsner
The Kennet and Avon Canal – K. Clew
The Woollen Industry of the South West – K. Ponting
An Unhappy Civil War – J. Wroughton
A Century of Nestlé at Staverton – Author
A History of St Paul's Church, Staverton – Author
The Story Behind the Staverton Millennium Tapestry –
    Author

SUBSCRIBERS

Jane and Frank Anderson, Holt, Wiltshire

Walter W. Ash, Holt, Wiltshire

Mr and Mrs S.G. Baldwin, Staverton, Wiltshire

R.C. Bazley, Dalby, Queensland, Australia

Bazley family, Toowoomba, Queensland, Australia

Mrs Mabel E. Beaven (née Vezey, Staverton), Trowbridge, Wiltshire

Mr Michael Blake,

Mr M. Blake, Staverton Farm, Staverton, Wiltshire

Barry Bodman, Hampton, Middlesex

Frank and Barbara Bodman, Holt, ex Staverton

R.E. Brown, Westwood, Wiltshire

Elsie R. Brown (née Buckland)

Peter Carr, Trowbridge, Wiltshire

Barbara and Malcolm Childs, Staverton Marina

John V. Clare, St Mary's Gardens, Hilperton Marsh, Wiltshire

The Cosslett family, Staverton, Wiltshire

Joan Coxon, Staverton, Wiltshire

Mr and Mrs E. Crucefix, Trowbridge, Wiltshire

B. and E. Curtis, Staverton, Wiltshire

Sally and Keith Daborn, Westbury, Wiltshire

Carol A. Dunford, Leicester

N.A. and S.J. Edwards, Staverton, Wiltshire

Emmaus School, Staverton, Wiltshire

Christine M. Escott, Staverton, Wiltshire

Sarah Jane Escott, Hilperton, Wiltshire

Jill Forsyth, Bridgnorth, Shropshire

Mrs D. Franks, Reading, Berkshire

Sylvie Fursdon, Staverton, Wiltshire

Eileen Gamble, Trowbridge, Wiltshire

Mr and Mrs H.T.W. Gay, Holt, Trowbridge, Wiltshire

Jane C. Gilbert, Hilperton Marsh, Wiltshire

Alfred Grimwood, Staverton, Wiltshire

Colin Groves, Hilperton, Wiltshire

Jean Groves (née Endru), Trowbridge, Wiltshire

Mrs Louisa Hallett, Staverton, Wiltshire

Chris and Carolyn Hamblett, Staverton, Wiltshire

R. Gordon Hammond Esq., late of Wyke House

The Hargreaves family

Debra A. Harmon (née Osborne), Florida, USA

Kay Harper, formerly of Hilperton Marsh, Wiltshire

Councillor Rodney Hart, 'The Swallows', School Lane Close, Staverton,

Mr Trevor P. Heeks, Staverton, Wiltshire

Rev. Richard Hicks, Brampton, Cumbria

Mike and Peggy Hoddinott, Staverton, Wiltshire

Pauline Hodgson, Hilperton, Trowbridge, Wiltshire

Georgina J. Hodgson, Trowbridge, Wiltshire

Peter J. Hodgson, Malmo, Sweden

Carolyn, David and Katy Holland, Staverton, Wiltshire

Ted and Marlene Hulbert (née Pearce)

Muriel N. Illman, Holt, Wiltshire

Mike and Jean Jeanes, Kidlington, Oxford

Tony Jones, formerly of Hilperton Marsh

Mrs L. Keats (née Beaven), Trowbridge, Wiltshire

Colin Knight, Southampton

Judy A. Lacey, Hilperton, Wiltshire

Grace Legg, Roden House, Hilperton, Wiltshire

Louise Lewis-Palmer, Hong Kong

Andrea Love (née Palmer), Coleford, Somerset

John Lovell, Hilperton, Wiltshire

Tom Ludlow, Staverton/Hilperton, Wiltshire

Betty M. Ludlow, Trowbridge, Wiltshire

Dr Rachel A. Macmillan, Aldbrough St John, North Yorkshire

Robert A. Macmillan, Trowbridge, Wiltshire

Jane S. Macmillan, Bradford-on-Avon, Wiltshire

Fiona C. Macmillan, Hilperton Marsh, Trowbridge, Wiltshire

Lorna Mallows, Staverton, Wiltshire

Vera Malyn, Staverton, Wiltshire

Stephen L. Matthews

Mrs M.J. Matthews, Staverton, Wiltshire

Marjorie W. Matthews, Whitley, Wiltshire

David F.G. Maunder

Shirley McGuckin, Ontario, Canada

Julia Meeres, Staverton, Wiltshire

Barry Meeres, Exmoor

Stuart Mercer, Hilperton, Wiltshire

Jennie and Bob Mizen, Holt, Wiltshire

Marion Moody, Holt, Wiltshire

Reg Moore, Coombe Bissett, Salisbury

J.D. Moore

Stephanie Ann Morris (née Lavis), Hilperton, Wiltshire

Marjorie Mortimer, Holt, Wiltshire

Graham A. Mortimer, Hilperton, Wiltshire

Maureen P. Mundy, Hilperton Marsh, Wiltshire

Former Nasmilco resident

Mr Bren Neal A.R.P.S., Enfield

Roger F. Newman, Blind Lane, Southwick, Wiltshire

Jill F. Noad (née Stevens), ex Staverton

B.M. Osborne, Trowbridge, Wiltshire

Michael J. Osborne, Staverton, Wiltshire

Judith and Anthony Palmer, High Wycombe, Buckinghamshire

Queenie Pearce, Staverton, Wiltshire

Monica and Chris Penny, Bradford-On-Avon

Rebecca Perratt (née Palmer), Yeovil, Somerset

Mrs Nancy Perry, formerly of Staverton, Wiltshire

Geoffrey M. Platten, Staverton, Wiltshire

J.R. Powell, Trowbridge, Wiltshire

Miss Lynne Bailey, India and Luke Pronick, The Square, Staverton, Wiltshire

Brian Pullen

Mr Kevin Pullen, Staverton, Wiltshire

Robert Victor Purnell, Bradford-On-Avon

K. and M. Purnell

John Radoczi, Hilperton, Wiltshire

Syd Ricketts, Melksham, Wiltshire

Sheila Sawyer, Hilperton, Wiltshire

Jacqueline Sharp, Staverton, Wiltshire

John Smith, Steeple Ashton, Wiltshire

David R. Smith, Melksham, Wiltshire

Mair N. Smith, Hilperton Marsh, Wiltshire

James R. Smith, Petersfield, Hampshire

James W. Spirit, Trowbridge, Wiltshire

John Stacey, Corsham, Wiltshire

Miss Mary Stevens, Trowbridge, Wiltshire

Peggy Sugden, Hilperton, Wiltshire

Rob and Liz Summerson, Hilperton Marsh

Jacky Sumpter (née Ransome), Hilperton, Wiltshire

Mr and Mrs J.M. Swaine, Staverton, Wiltshire

Kristyan Swinnerton, Hilperton, Wiltshire

Mary E. Tasker, Crediton, Devon

Mr Timbrell D.A., Shaw, Nr Melksham, Wiltshire

Mick and Sue Townsend, Calne, Wiltshire

Margaret L. Tucker, Devizes, Wiltshire

Jeffrey D. Tucker, Trowbridge, Wiltshire

G. and J. Turvey, Hilperton, Wiltshire

Julia Turner and John Volrath, Broombridge, Hilperton, Wiltshire

John F.W. Walling, Newton Abbot, Devon

Mrs G. Waylen

Donald C. Weston, Melksham, Wiltshire

Pam I. Wetheral, Stampford, Lincolnshire

Roger and Mary White, Staverton, Wiltshire

Dick Whittington, Hilperton Marsh, Wiltshire

David and Marian Whitton

Ray Wickings, Appledore, Devon

Ann J. Wilmot (née Stevens), ex Staverton

Jim and Marion Witney, Staverton, Wiltshire

Titles from the Series

The Book of Addiscombe • Various
The Book of Addiscombe, Vol. II • Various
The Book of Bampton • Caroline Seward
The Book of Barnstaple • Avril Stone
Book of Bickington • Stuart Hands
Blandford Forum: A Millennium Portrait • Various
The Book of Bridestowe • R. Cann
The Book of Brixham • Frank Pearce
The Book of Buckland Monachorum & Yelverton • Hemery
The Book of Carshalton • Stella Wilks
The Parish Book of Cerne Abbas • Vale & Vale
The Book of Chagford • Ian Rice
The Book of Chittlehamholt with
Warkleigh & Satterleigh • Richard Lethbridge
The Book of Chittlehampton • Various
The Book of Colney Heath • Bryan Lilley
The Book of Constantine • Moore & Trethowan
The Book of Cornwood & Lutton • Various
The Book of Creech St Michael • June Small
The Book of Cullompton • Various
The Book of Dawlish • Frank Pearce
The Book of Dulverton, Brushford,
Bury & Exebridge • Various
The Book of Dunster • Hilary Binding
The Ellacombe Book • Sydney R. Langmead
The Book of Exmouth • W.H. Pascoe
The Book of Grampound with Creed • Bane & Oliver
The Book of Hayling Island & Langstone • Rogers
The Book of Helston • Jenkin with Carter
The Book of Hemyock • Clist & Dracott
The Book of Hethersett • Various
The Book of High Bickington • Avril Stone
The Book of Ilsington • Dick Wills
The Book of Lamerton • Ann Cole & Friends
Lanner, A Cornish Mining Parish • Scharron Schwartz &
Roger Parker
The Book of Leigh & Bransford • Various
The Book of Litcham with Lexham & Mileham • Various
The Book of Loddiswell • Various
The Book of Lulworth • Rodney Legg
The Book of Lustleigh • Joe Crowdy
The Book of Manaton • Various
The Book of Markyate • Richard Hogg
The Book of Mawnan • Various
The Book of Meavy • Pauline Hemery
The Book of Minehead with Alcombe • Binding & Stevens
The Book of Morchard Bishop • Jeff Kingaby
The Book of Newdigate • John Callcut
The Book of Northlew with Ashbury • Various
The Book of North Newton • Robins & Robins
The Book of North Tawton • Various
The Book of Okehampton • Radford & Radford
The Book of Paignton • Frank Pearce
The Book of Penge, Anerley & Crystal Palace • Various
The Book of Peter Tavy with Cudlipptown • Various
The Book of Pimperne • Jean Coull
The Book of Plymtree • Tony Eames
The Book of Porlock • Denis Corner
Postbridge – The Heart of Dartmoor • Reg Bellamy
The Book of Priddy • Various
The Book of Rattery • Various
The Book of Silverton • Various

The Book of South Molton • Various
The Book of South Stoke • Various
South Tawton & South Zeal with Sticklepath • Radfords
The Book of Sparkwell with Hemerdon & Lee Mill • Pam James
The Book of Staverton • Pete Lavis
The Book of Stithians • Various
The Book of Studland • Rodney Legg
The Book of Swanage • Rodney Legg
The Book of Torbay • Frank Pearce
Uncle Tom Cobley & All: Widecombe-in-the-Moor • Stephen
Woods
The Book of Watchet • Compiled by David Banks
The Book of West Huntspill • Various
Widecombe-in-the-Moor • Stephen Woods
The Book of Williton • Michael Williams
Woodbury: The Twentieth Century Revisited • Roger Stokes
The Book of Woolmer Green • Various

Forthcoming

The Book of Bakewell • Various
The Book of Barnstaple, Vol. II • Avril Stone
The Book of Brampford • Various
The Book of Breage & Gurmoe • Stephen Polglase
The Book of the Bedwyns • Various
The Book of Bideford • Peter Christie
The Book of Bridport • Rodney Legg
The Book of Buckfastleigh • Sandra Coleman
The Book of Carharrack • Various
The Book of Castleton • Geoff Hill
The Book of Edale • Gordon Miller
The Book of Kingskerswell • Various
The Book of Lostwithiel • Barbara Frasier
The Book of Lydford • Barbara Weeks
The Book of Lyme Regis • Rodney Legg
The Book of Nether Stowey • Various
The Book of Nynehead • Various
The Book of Princetown • Dr Gardner-Thorpe
The Book of St Day • Various
The Book of Sampford Courtenay
with Honeychurch • Stephanie Pouya
The Book of Sculthorpe • Garry Windeler
The Book of Sherborne • Rodney Legg
The Book of Southbourne • Rodney Legg
The Book of Tavistock • Gerry Woodcock
The Book of Thorley • Various
The Book of Tiverton • Mike Sampson
The Book of West Lavington • Various
The Book of Witheridge • Various
The Book of Withycombe • Chris Boyles

For details of any of the above titles or if you are interested in writing your own history, please contact: Commissioning Editor Community Histories, Halsgrove House, Lower Moor Way, Tiverton Business Park, Tiverton, Devon EX16 6SS, England; email: naomic@halsgrove.com

In order to include as many historic photographs as possible in this volume, a printed index is not included. However, the Community History Series is indexed by Genuki. For further information and indexes to volumes in the series, please visit: http://www.cs.ncl.uk/genuki/DEV/indexingproject.html